MOCKINGBIRD THEATER

THE
MANCHURIAN
JOURNALIST

LAWRENCE WRIGHT, THE CIA, AND THE
CORRUPTION OF AMERICAN JOURNALISM

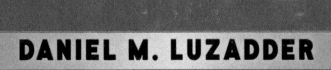

DANIEL M. LUZADDER

THE MANCHURIAN JOURNALIST: LAWRENCE WRIGHT, THE CIA, AND THE COR-
RUPTION OF AMERICAN JOURNALISM
COPYRIGHT © 2023/2024 DANIEL M. LUZADDER

Published by:
Trine Day LLC
PO Box 577
Walterville, OR 97489
1-800-556-2012
www.TrineDay.com
TrineDay@icloud.com

Library of Congress Control Number: 2024934161

Luzadder, Daniel M.
–1st ed.
p. cm.

Epub (ISBN-13) 978-1-63424-455-8
Trade Paperback (ISBN-13) 978-1-63424-454-1
1. POLITICAL SCIENCE Intelligence & Journalism. 2. Church of Scientology International. 3. Journalism History 20th century. 4. Mass media and public
opinion. 5. Lawrence Wright(1947-). I. Luzadder, Daniel. II. Title

FIRST EDITION
10 9 8 7 6 5 4 3 2 1

Printed in the USA
Distribution to the Trade by:
Independent Publishers Group (IPG)
814 North Franklin Street
Chicago, Illinois 60610
312.337.0747
www.ipgbook.com

Publisher's Foreword

Whither shall I go from thy spirit?
or whither shall I flee from thy presence?
If I ascend up into heaven, thou art there:
if I make my bed in hell, behold, thou art there.
If I take the wings of the morning,
and dwell in the uttermost parts of the sea;
Even there shall thy hand lead me,
and thy right hand shall hold me.
If I say, Surely the darkness shall cover me;
even the night shall be light about me.
Yea, the darkness hideth not from thee;
but the night shineth as the day:
the darkness and the light are both alike to thee.
– Psalm 139:7-12, KJV

CHAIRMAN SPECTER: *Well, we prize ourself very, very highly of being a nation of laws, and laws that cannot be violated even by the President. We have precedent for that with the Supreme Court having said so. The President himself is another citizen when it comes to this–*
MR. KOPPEL: *With all due respect, sir, we also have precedent for the intelligence agencies of the United States routinely violating laws and simply assuming that they won't be held to account. All too frequently, I am afraid, they are quite right.*
CHAIRMAN SPECTER: *Well, I think that is because they are not detected. It is not because they are not held to account; they are not detected. The hard part is to find out about it. The toughest thing to do is to find the facts. Find the facts, then there is less problem of agreeing on what the appropriate policy is if we can find the facts. But finding the facts is very, very hard, and that is a matter of congressional oversight. And we do too little of it.*
–CIA's Use of Journalists and Clergy in Intelligence Operations, Hearing before the Select Committee on Intelligence, July 16, 1996

“They're called sway pieces." This was at the end of a talk that my ex-spook father initiated. He had started the conversation years earlier, when he had asked me what I thought of the Vietnam war. I gave him a snarky teen-age answer: "You have a sack of hand-grenades, throw them at the rice paddies and win it for the good guys wearing the white hats." I had been raised on John Wayne and WWII. My father and all of my uncles had been in *that* war.

It was 1969, the day before my nineteenth birthday. I was married, had a six-month old daughter, owned a record store and was helping to put on Grateful Dead shows. I was having fun! I had come to the family home to celebrate with cake and ice cream.

My father had a friend visiting, a professor from Vanderbilt Dr. D.F. Fleming, and took me into a room with Dr. Fleming and proceeded to tell me about secret societies and drug-running, then his twenty-year intelligence career – *which had never been mentioned*. After informing me of his activities and positions held, my father and the professor proceeded to tell me that "they" were playing out a "lose scenario" in Vietnam. I did not comprehend, and seeing my mute blank stares, Dad began to tell me about psychological warfare and propaganda. I was still thinking about things they had said earlier.

"They're called sway pieces…" Realizing that I had no idea of what he was talking about … that was the end of the "talk."

Daniel Luzadder has done a tremendous job of helping all of us to understand those "sway pieces" my father spoke of. THE MANCHURIAN JOURNALIST is a tour de force of investigative journalism. Showing how forces "from the shadows" unduly influence our national discourse and common good. Dan has performed a great service for our country, a ten-year journey uncovering deceit, duplicity and disinformation slumbering onto our world's stage: taking the unaware for a ride, and laying bare the guardrails of our freedoms. Leaving us to the vagaries of secrecy and raw power instead of the rule of law whereby persons, institutions, and entities are accountable to laws that are: Publicly promulgated. Equally enforced.

Whither shall we go...

> *The most effective way to destroy people is to deny and obliterate their own understanding of their history.*
>
> – George Orwell

Onward to the Utmost of Futures,
Peace,
Kris Millegan
Publisher
TrineDay
4/8/24

"To all the journalists, in all the newsrooms, who have ever had a story they could not tell...."

- Mike Dooley,
Henry's Cosmopolitan Bar
December 23, 1983

CONTENTS

Photographs and Illustrations

- Lawrence Wright

- Alex Gibney

- Robert G. Storey
  - U.S. Civil Rights Commission with Kennedy
  - Nuremberg Trials

- John McCloy
  - With Truman

- American University in Cairo

- Karl Hoblitzelle

- Shepard Stone

- Helen Venn
  - With Michael Levy
  - With Richard Bernstein

- Cass Canfield

- Author
  - With Norman Starkey, executor and trustee of the L. Ron Hubbard estate
  - With David Miscavige, ecclesiastical leader of the Scientology religion

- Church Committee CIA Hearing '72 / '99

CAST OF CHARACTERS

Thomas W. Braden – *WWII OSS recruit who became operations director for CIA media propaganda programs, specific cultural cold war recruiting and media influence campaigns; former newspaper publisher and later columnist; CNN Cross Fire co-host; author of* Eight is Enough; *defender of use of journalists for intelligence.*

H. R. "Bum" Bright – *Friend, associate of Donald Wright, close associate of Karl Hoblitzelle, Robert G. Storey and others, director, major shareholder, CIA-linked Republic National Bank of Dallas; owner of the Dallas Cowboys, and of the East Dallas Trucking Company where Lawrence Wright wrote that he worked a summer job in college.*

William Broyles, Jr. – *Former military intelligence officer who was named by* Texas Monthly *Founder Michael Levy as the magazine's first editor; hired Lawrence Wright, founder of the Rice University Publishing Procedures Course with Helen Venn and Levy; screenwriter for* Cast Away, Apollo 13, Flags of Our Fathers, *and other films.*

Charles Cabell – *Air Force Intelligence officer who served in World War II with friend and associate Robert G. Storey; CIA deputy director fired by President Kennedy over the Bay of Pigs invasion of Cuba, brother of Dallas Mayor Earle Cabell, close friend of Charles Porter Storey, son of Robert G. Storey.*

Earle Cabell – *Mayor of Dallas when JFK was murdered; close associate of Robert Storey, Karl Hoblitzelle, and major players of the Texas political venues, brother of Deputy Director of the CIA Charles Cabell.*

Cass Canfield – *Titan of American publishing, head of Harper and Brothers (Harper-Row), recruiter of publishers, editors, writers to the CIA cultural cold war networks; mentor and publisher for Rosalind Wright, Lawrence Wright's sister; a director of CIA front Farfield Foundation.*

Mamadou Chinyelu – *African American author, poet and civil rights activist who raised questions about Wright's intelligence connections following the World Trade Center attacks coordinated by Osama bin Laden.*

Len Colodny – *Author and entrepreneur who first exposed* Washington Post *reporter Bob Woodward's Office of Naval Intelligence ties and role as a White House briefer for Alexander Haig, prior to Woodward's hiring as a reporter.*

Allen Dulles – *Director of the CIA, fired by President Kennedy over the Bay of Pigs fiasco, served on the Warren Commission investigating the assassination; spymaster and close friend of Robert Storey, John McCloy, and the major representatives of the private intelligence network for which the CIA served at times as a private army.*

William (Wild Bill) Donovan – *World War II intelligence officer and OSS leader, who inveighed against a document-based approach to prosecution of Nazi war criminals, advocating for human witnesses; a central figure in the development of the CIA.*

Jack Evans – *Dallas political figure, employed by Lawrence Wright's father at Lakewood Bank & Trust with close connections to Republic National Bank; later became mayor of Dallas, participant in Dallas Council on World Affairs, and the Dallas Citizens Council with other local power brokers.*

Jim Garrison – *New Orleans prosecutor who brought the only criminal case connected to the JFK assassination; author of a book first serialized in* Freedom *magazine, the investigative and in-house religious journal of the Church of Scientology.*

Frye Galliard – *Writer and author, friend of Lawrence Wright's wife Roberta Wright and former editor for* Race Relations Reporter; *endorsed Wright for his first magazine job there.*

Reinhart Gehlen – *Nazi spymaster under Hitler, with Otto Skorzeny, war crimes suspect recruited to American intelligence operations after WWII to obtain Germany's eastern bloc spy network, influential in rogue intelligence operations.*

Robert Gemberling – *Senior resident FBI agent in charge of the Dallas field office when Kennedy was murdered; long-term supervisor of FBI Kennedy assassination-related matters; hired by Donald Wright at Lakewood Bank and Trust as a loan officer after retirement from FBI.*

Alex Gibney – *Documentary film maker, partner with Lawrence Wright in film productions, son of journalist-editor-intelligence operative Frank Gibney.*

Frank Gibney – *Father of Alex Gibney, closely tied to the media-intelligence networks through Henry Luce, C. D. Jackson, other close associates of the American intelligence cartel, recruiter of Gloria Steinem to cultural cold war roles for the CIA.*

Paul Haggis – *Hollywood director and screenwriter, former Scientologist who turned highly visible critic of the Church, subject and source for Wright's initial stories about the Church in The New Yorker.*

Paul Hellmuth – *Close associate of Richard and Helen Venn, attorney and director of CIA front organizations in the funding of CIA operations, influential director of the Boston Museum of Fine Arts.*

Karl Hoblitzelle – *Multi-millionaire Texas theatre developer, chairman emeritus of CIA-linked Republic National Bank of Dallas, oil and gas multimillionaire; his Hoblitzelle Foundation was a front for CIA cultural cold war activities that included propaganda.*

L. Ron Hubbard – *Author, philosopher, founder of the Scientology religion.*

C. D. Jackson – *Director of the office of Psychological Warfare, influential journalist and editor tied to the Time-Life publishing empire.*

Leon Jaworski – *Close associate of Robert G. Storey, trustee of CIA front-related foundations, Nuremberg trial prosecution team.*

Michael Levy – *Founder of* Texas Monthly *magazine who – along with* Texas Monthly's *first editor, William Broyles Jr. and Helen Venn – founded the Rice University Publishing Procedures Course, modeled after the Radcliffe Publishing Procedures Course.*

James "Jim" Lynch – *Former* Chicago Sun-Times *editor who worked for* Freedom *magazine as an investigative reporter.*

Robert Lowell – *Poet and American literary figure, who was part of the CIA's cultural cold war programs and whose travel outside the country was funded through intelligence-related programs.*

Henry Luce – *Owner of the Time-Life publishing empire, associate of Allen Dulles and major political leaders, witting provider of CIA assistance through publishing outlets, and member of the establishment publishing elite.*

John McCloy – *Chairman of the Establishment; New York attorney, Amherst and Harvard Law ('21) with intelligence interests dating to World War I; co-architect of Cold War intelligence strategy, advisor to presidents, one of the founders of the private intelligence cooperative that used the CIA like a private army and deep state resource for international and domestic propaganda; High Commissioner for the Occupation of Germany; Chairman or leader of the: World Bank (International Bank for Reconstruction and Development), Chase Manhattan Bank, Ford Foundation, Rockefeller Foundation, Council on Foreign Relations; overseer of Japanese internment* in WWII; war crimes prosecution influencer and advocate of "black bag" intelligence techniques.

John McCloy, Jr. – *Son of John McCloy, long-term trustee of the American University in Cairo.*

Charles McGrath – New Yorker *and* New York Times *literary critic and reviewer who provided positive reviews for Wright's book on Scientology while in violation of* NY Times *ethic guidelines.*

Lowell Mellette – *With Nelson Poynter, director of the board of censors of Hollywood films in the Roosevelt administration in leadup to World War II.*

Judith Miller – New York Times *reporter caught up in reporting on unsubstantiated allegations of weapons of mass destruction during Iraq war; former co-worker with Lawrence Wright at* The Progressive *magazine.*

David Miscavige – *Chairman of the Board of Religious Technology Center and the ecclesiastical leader of the Scientology religion.*

Steve Nickeson – *Former managing editor of* Race Relations Reporter *who hired Lawrence Wright for his first magazine job.*

Daniel Okrent – *First "public editor" at the* New York Times, *editor-at-large for* Time *magazine, and managing editor of* Life *magazine; an editor and writer at major U. S. publishing houses and for major national magazines; Pulitzer finalist in history (2007), author of six books, screenwriter; alumni of* Texas Monthly – *and an original trustee with Helen Venn, Michael Levy and William Broyles Jr. of the Rice University Publishing Procedures Course.*

Oleg Penkovsky – *Russian military officer who was alleged double agent for the U.S. and supposed author of* The Penkovsky Papers, *which was unveiled as a CIA publication primary crafted by Frank Gibney.*

Nelson Poynter – *Newspaper publisher and prominent American journalist, founder of the Poynter Institute, a think-tank on journalism, also prominent in the CIA-media relationships.*

L. Fletcher Prouty – *Former U.S. Air Force Colonel and liaison between the CIA and the Joint Chiefs of Staff in the 1960s. Later spoke out and authored a book against illegal intelligence activities on the part of the U.S. government; one of the sources for Oliver Stone's film, JFK; his book was serialized first in* Freedom *magazine.*

Mark "Marty" Rathbun – *Major source for Lawrence Wright's book* Going Clear, *who divorced himself from the Scientology apostates to criticize Wright's characterizations of the Church.*

Janet Reitman – Rolling Stone *staff writer and war correspondent, close friend of Lawrence Wright and author of* Inside Scientology.

Leah Remini – *Former sitcom actress and Scientologist who left the religion and became an anti-Scientology apostate.*

David Remnick – *Editor of* The New Yorker, *who has praised and supported Wright's investigative reporting.*

Mike Rinder – *Anti-Scientology apostate who was excommunicated from the Church for misconduct.*

Charlotte Robinson – *Former assistant to Helen Venn who was active in working with journalists, publishers for speaking engagements with Radcliffe Publishing Procedures Course.*

Jack Ruby – *Assassin of assassination suspect Lee Harvey Oswald, subject of anecdote by Lawrence Wright's concerning a family member; was visited in Dallas County Jail by Robert Storey and Supreme Court Justice Earl Warren.*

Peter Dale Scott – *Former Canadian diplomat, author of books on "deep state" politics, the Kennedy assassination and terrorism.*

Norman Starkey – *Executor and trustee of the L. Ron Hubbard estate, an informal historian of the Scientology religion and close friend and associate of L. Ron Hubbard.*

Gloria Steinem – *Influential writer, author and feminist who was a witting participant on behalf of the CIA's cultural cold war activities at European youth festivals and cultural events.*

Margaret Stone MacDonald – *Daughter of Shepard Stone, classmate with Lawrence Wright in the 1969 Radcliffe Publishing Procedures Course.*

Shepard Stone – *Press representative for John McCloy during the German Occupation and Ford Foundation liaison to CIA front groups and cultural cold war propaganda programs.*

Charles Storey – *Son of Robert G. Storey, former U.S. Air Force intelligence officer, close friend of Charles Cabell, CIA deputy director, close friend of Lawrence Wright's father, Donald Wright.*

Robert G. Storey – *Nuremberg War Crimes trial executive prosecutor, advisor to and confidant of presidents, member of the U.S. Civil Rights Commission, Chairman, Board of Foreign Scholarships (Fulbright) U.S. State Department, head of the American Bar Association, developer of international legal systems, author of much of the South Korean legal codes; major influence and architect in* *development of private clandestine American intelligence networks in coopera-tion with the CIA throughout all corners of American culture. Founder of Lake-wood State Bank (Lakewood Bank and Trust) and chair of its board; director, CIA-linked Republic National Bank of Dallas, close associate of Karl Hoblitzelle with whom he was co-founder of the Southwestern Legal Foundation; dean of the Southern Methodist University Law School; hired Donald Wright, Lawrence Wright's father, as president of the bank he owned and appointed him a fiduciary of the investment committee for CIA-linked Southwestern Legal Foundation.*

Christopher Thoron – *CIA operative who offered Lawrence Wright an al-legedly short-noticed scholarship to American University in Cairo and later served as president of the CIA-Cold War linked university.*

Helen "Doylie" Venn – *Director for more than 20 years of the Radcliffe Pub-lishing Procedures Course – a tool for recruiting into American and foreign pub-lishing for the purpose of developing intelligence-related relationships; liaison between U.S. State Department and foreign book programs, including Franklin Books, a CIA cultural cold war propaganda program; reference for Wright for his AUC-Ford Foundation-supported graduate program.*

Hugh Whatley Stevens Venn – *Father of Richard "'Diggory" Venn, British intelligence officer and member of British aristocracy.*

Richard "Diggory" Venn – *Husband of Helen Venn, journalist, public rela-tions consultant with close associations witihin intelligence networks, worked with the Boston Museum of Art, assisted in recruiting individuals for intelligence purposes.*

Tamsin Venn – *Daughter of Helen and Richard Venn, goddaughter of Frank Gibney, who is the father of Alex Gibney.*

Louis Jolyon West – *CIA-funded psychiatrist and UCLA psychiatric research-er in LSD experiments on human and animal subjects (famously killing an ele-phant in the process) who interviewed Jack Ruby in the Dallas jail, and evaluat-ed him in reports that became part of the Warren Commission record.*

Arthur Wright – *Fraternity brother of Lawrence Wright at Tulane University who wrote a letter for Wright supporting his conscientious objector application to the Dallas Draft Board; later became closely affiliated with the Southwestern Legal Foundation, founded by CIA front-organization funders Karl Hoblitzelle, and Robert Storey.*

Don Wright – *Lawrence Wright's cousin, to whom he attributed a story about Jack Ruby.*

John Donald Wright – *Close business and social confederate of Robert Storey, World War II military combat experience and service in the Korean War, author of two books on banking, service on the investment committee of Southwestern Legal Foundation, which served as a conduit for CIA-related domestic intelligence; President of Lakewood Bank and Trust, of which Storey was founder and chairman, and which had the earmarks of a CIA "NOC" – nonofficial cover – location.*

Lawrence Wright – *Author of non-fiction and fiction books on subjects from religion to terrorism, psychology and psychiatry, crime, science and politics; playwright, screenwriter, documentarian; staff writer for* The New Yorker *and* Rolling Stone, *winner of a Pulitzer Prize.*

Rosalind Wright – *Author, writer, friend of poet Emily Bishop, within the literary circle of Bishop and poet Robert Lowell, who was closely connected to the CIA's cultural cold war programs of exportation of western culture; her literary career was encouraged and mentored by New York publishing titan Cass Canfield.*

Prologue

An Invitation to Investigate

In the spring of 2011, Lawrence Wright – one of America's best-known journalists and the winner of a 2007 Pulitzer Prize for his post-9/11 book investigating Al Qaeda – penned a story in *The New Yorker* magazine about the Church of Scientology.

I did not see the story at the time, nor would I have been particularly interested in Lawrence Wright's take on Scientology even if I had noticed it. I was busy with freelance writing of my own, working independently in the wake of a long career primarily as an investigative reporter and columnist for daily newspapers.

In the wake of an investigation into the Columbine High School massacre, and a series of stories that followed, I left daily newspapers for a New York magazine that covered the Internet, and whose editors were happy to have me work from home in Colorado. My two youngest children were still in grade school. I investigated telecommunications companies and white-collar crime, traveling the country until the fallout from 9/11 drove the magazine under in 2002. I scrambled to find freelance work after that, selling stories to a wide range of outlets, from technology and environmental magazines to wire services, local mags and the *New York Times*. I traveled for the *Times* business page and worked as a correspondent for *The New York Daily News*, covering the Kobe Bryant rape allegations in Colorado, helping break a major development in the story, and later bird-dogged Yankee star Alex Rodriquez for *The News* when he had surgery in Vail. I hustled up story work wherever I could, supplemented with late-night editing assignments for a private financial wire service in London, and occasional word-smithing for a New York or L.A. communications firm.

The writing and investigative work had led to exposés on national political and judicial corruption, drug trafficking, human rights abuses in state and federal prisons, national political payoffs and police corruption. I later developed sources deep within the hierarchies of Chicago's organized crime syndicate and afterward within the American intelligence community. My last major investigative stories for daily newspapers gave a detailed account of the "inside" of the police investigation into the Columbine High School murders. Getting "inside" was always the thing I was after. I liked the adrenaline rush, the methodical investigative work, aided by intuition and imagination, following the thread to unravel the mystery. All my heroes had been detectives.

So, in early 2011, as Lawrence Wright was hitting the newsstands with his *New Yorker* piece on Scientology, something was stirring unseen in my own future, a taste of the past; I was grateful for a productive post-newspaper freelance career sufficient to keep bills paid, even if, in truth, I still missed investigative reporting. It was too expensive to do on a freelance basis, too complex and uncertain for freelance outlets with tight story budgets to even attempt. Even for the *New York Times*, where I had sometimes paid part of my own travel costs to have the opportunity to publish, there was no budget for freelance investigative work, or at least none coming my way. I kept my interest in investigation alive with FBI FOIA requests on my own time, exploring records to clarify what I had learned from a mentor who had helped me explore the badly distorted history of the Chicago mob.

But some months after Wright's story appeared, on a particularly sunny October morning in Colorado, the day after the first major snow that year, while Wright was quietly turning his *New Yorker* piece on film director and ex-Scientologist Paul Haggis into a book, I found myself at breakfast in a busy pancake restaurant on the east side of Denver, meeting with a well-known private detective, Rick Johnson.

Rick had been a prosecutor's investigator when I was working for the venerable and now deceased *Rocky Mountain News*, and I had gotten to know him then as a go-to source who knew the local terrain. In addition to his vigorous PI practice, he was operating a small school for novice private investigators and he and I had been talking about encouraging pro-bono public interest investigations by PIs who wanted to sharpen their public records skills. We were meeting that morning to explore the idea when we were joined unexpectedly by a suburban reporter for the *Denver Post*, Garrison Wells, another of Rick's contacts.

Amid the din of that noisy pancake restaurant that morning, Garrison told me that in his own search for freelance assignments he had come across a small but interesting magazine in Florida that was trying to reestablish itself and was looking for professional journalists to help with that. He said that the magazine had at one time amassed a distinguished history of hard-core investigative reporting, in some cases internationally,

mostly in the arena of human rights, political freedoms, religious tolerance, mental health abuses and government misconduct.

The magazine was called *Freedom* and he'd already written a couple of
stories for them, good rates, paid on acceptance, but nothing published yet.
He mentioned that the magazine's editor had asked him if he was familiar
with anyone with extensive investigative experience and he wondered if I'd
be interested in talking with them. The caveat, he said, was that the magazine was owned by a religious organization – the Church of Scientology.

At the time, I couldn't have recited the difference between Scientology
and Christian Science, or described much of anything about either religion. I was a casual Episcopalian, a teenage refugee of the American evangelical tribes. While a religious organization didn't seem like the place to
mount hardcore journalism, I knew religious groups had sponsored numerous magazines, some doing credible and important work particularly
in the arenas of social justice and reconciliation, even as others simply
propagandized and proselytized. Having grown up around religious publishing, I was nominally wary of anything that sounded like faith-based
motivation. But the suggestion of some real investigative work, however
unlikely that might be, had its attraction. It had been a long time.

Our friendly discussion would prompt a very unexpected turn in my
own path – and lead me to an investigative project into the heart of two
things I knew nothing about: The Church of Scientology, and a powerful
secret behind Lawrence Wright's own stellar career in journalism.

The first, an inquiry into the media coverage of the Church amid our
changing journalistic landscape, would shed light on the fault in our journalistic stars. The second, an attempt to first make sense of Lawrence
Wright's investigation into the Church, would lead to something of larger
consequence – the discovery of his involvement in a powerful and clandestine network of public influence and propaganda by the U.S. intelligence community – under the auspices of private allies of the CIA – dating to the Cold War and into the Age of Terror. Lawrence Wright's direct
associations in that network – never before revealed by or about one of
America's most influential journalists – would also uncover yet another
shadowy chapter in our mass media's unholy relationship with the Central Intelligence Agency.

Wells had spoken with Ben Shaw, editor of *Freedom* magazine's Florida
edition, and Shaw called to gauge my interest in some freelance reporting.
He wanted to send me a packet of information about the Church as background and then talk about some possible stories. When the package ar-

rived by FedEx a couple of days later there were folders of facts one might pick up in a Church sanctuary; background on the Church's founder, L. Ron Hubbard, a CD that described the Church's international expansion and mission work, some background on *Freedom*, and a few copies of the magazine published two decades before.

I looked it over and, curious, began to look for background on the organization behind the magazine. I was surprised at the depth of controversy I stumbled across. I could see why mainstream reporters might appear to be bucking a trend with even-handed reporting about the Church. The majority of stories seemed tinged with a vague antagonism and suspicion, and often outright hostility. It wasn't just the notorious Hollywood and national tabloids that broad-handedly criticized this "Hollywood religion." Mainstream publications had taken their shots, here, and elsewhere in the world, going back to the late 1950s, really, on and off again with various intensity through the years that followed.

A set of "exposés" published in Florida in 2009 were beyond accusatory and seemed bent on raising suspicion about the "legitimacy" of Scientology as a religion, suggesting something vaguely sinister inside: an accidental death, characterized by the paper as mysterious, amid unsubstantiated allegations of mistreatment within its clergy.[1] The headwaters for the reporting came out of Florida, near where the Church's spiritual headquarters are located; and, from New York, where a campaign of negative reporting had been initiated by a controversial editor at the once-proud *Village Voice*, someone who would later turn his anti-Scientology campaign into a business; and, from Los Angeles, where Hollywood tabloids and celebrity culture magazines oft spoke ill of the Church.

What *was* the story here?

As Shaw and I began to talk, the conversation came quickly to the past coverage of the Church and the exposés from the *St Petersburg Times*.

The paper's coverage of the Church, Shaw told me flatly, was biased. Not this reporter or that, but the paper itself, he said. As a result, the Scientology beat had become a plum for any cooperative reporter who "saw things their way." The history of that alleged bias went back a long time, back to the mid-1970s, he said, and directly involved a prominent American journalist, Nelson Poynter, whose name is still borne proudly by the think-tank he created, the Poynter Institute – one of the nation's most heavily-promoted voices in institutional journalism.

I certainly *had* heard of the newspaper and the Institute and knew that top J-school grads for decades had bid for jobs in St Petersburg, often, as with other well-respected regional papers like the *Times-Picayune* in New Orleans, as a springboard to major papers. Nelson Poynter was a proud alumnus of Indiana University where I'd once taught classes in reporting and writing as an adjunct professor. Poynter and his success were legends at IU's vaunted journalism school.

The multi-Pulitzer-winning *St. Petersburg Times* itself was more than well-known throughout the American journalistic community. The Institute, which took over ownership of the paper after Poynter died, had become a major ally of corporate media giants like Knight Ridder, Scripps Howard, and Gannett, the massive newspaper and television chains that helped fund the Institute and that were already transforming the journalistic landscape in other ways. Their acquisition sprees in the 1980s-90s, buying out venerable and profitable local newspapers to expand their national media empires, had changed the world of journalism dramatically.

The Florida-based Poynter Institute helped guide public perspectives on journalism, ethics, and responsibility in those years – and for these giants of journalism it offered profitability theories and advocacy for their approach to the business. Later, as I dug deeper into the coverage of Scientology by the *St. Pete Times* and others, I would see some not-so-vaunted activities, allegations of questionable financial maneuvering that allowed the *Times*, a for-profit company, to be operated by the Poynter Institute – a non-profit entity – in seeming contravention of non-profit rules.[2] I noticed little to no scrutiny of that relationship from the Institute's many allies in the public press – nor from Columbia University's Pulitzer Prize Committee, where the *Times* was and is a frequent applicant and winner.

Shaw asked me a question. If the *St. Pete Times* was the *ideal* of what journalism was supposed to be, why wouldn't it report on the Church fairly and in a balanced way? Why wouldn't it afford the Church an opportunity to respond, and fairly report that response? He could show me evidence that the Church had tried to cooperate with the paper to improve the coverage, including scheduling an interview with the Church's chairman, David Miscavige, only to see the paper cancel the interview, even though the series was about Miscavige.[3]

Why, he wanted to know, would the paper's editors take that attitude? Wasn't it a journalist's obligation to get both sides of a story and report in a balanced way? Was that something I could look into and write about? Perhaps a series of stories that could be part of a relaunch of *Freedom* magazine?

It was an interesting idea, if fraught with problems. I had formed opinions about the world of media by being immersed in it – and sometimes battered by it – over decades of work. I knew some of its flaws well and some of its systemic faults generally. Investigate my own industry, examine one of its iconic institutions – the *St. Pete Times*? And on behalf of an organization – religious or not – that the paper had virtually condemned as an artifice and religious scheme? It was either a fool's errand – or yet another opportunity to "go inside" into a tribal arena, a socio-journalistic investigation into this vast controversy. And, into what was true.

Shaw said he would provide copies of the *Times* stories, some packets of information on the Church's response and perspectives, documentation proving assertions about what the *Times* had gotten wrong, and some other background that they'd pieced together about those who were doing stories about them.

A torrent would follow. It was to be the first lesson in a lengthy education that would eventually take me around the world.

Some of that information, Shaw said, came from respected journalists who disagreed with what he called "attacks" on the Church and the biased coverage the Church had received. Among them was John Sugg, a former *Miami Herald* editor, and Jim Lynch, a former editor of the *Chicago Sun Times*. Sources within the *St. Petersburg Times*, Shaw said, had told them that there was quiet dissent within the newsroom staff on how the Church was covered, but that dissent was firmly suppressed.

Why, he wanted to know, did the paper persist when it had been pointed out to them that certain facts, which they continued to publish, were not true. Their stories were driven by excommunicated apostates who had an axe to grind against the Church. And now, he said, Lawrence Wright had written a piece in *The New Yorker* that gave more high-profile credence to these apostates who had turned against their former fellow Scientologists. He said it seemed part of a larger picture that bore looking into.

Whatever was going on there, whatever was being said to whom by whom and about what, didn't seem, at first blush, all that hard to sort out. Hadn't anything at all interesting about the Church of Scientology already been long settled? I had heard of L. Ron Hubbard, the Church's founder, but I couldn't have then described anything much about his history. I knew only that he had been a science fiction writer and that he had established a religion. My sense was that this was a story with a mysterious line running through it, so I began looking more deeply at what was being said – and who was saying it. What had been written, and who was writing it. What did the legal landscape look like, the lawsuits and depositions and the yield from those. What was the history of the controversy over the Church and where did it come from?

I spent weeks looking behind headlines, asking questions of Shaw, being offered records to support certain arguments, and eventually meeting with reporters in Florida who had questioned the coverage of the Church and the motivations behind it. When I looked behind the headlines, weighed the ample tabloid and opportunistic reporting, considered the Hollywood hype, I found something far more interesting than even the scathing *St. Petersburg Times* stories from 2009, or Lawrence Wright's swipe at the Church in *The New Yorker* two years later. You could find it decades ago, within records of investigations into the Church by Interpol, notes from Internal Revenue Service criminal investigators, from the FBI and CIA, government intelligence organizations from Europe to Australia, challenges mounted no doubt on the heels of press-driven warnings about the "mysterious" religion of Scientology.

Even more difficult to explain, where did the idea come from – an idea fed liberally and promoted heavily in the writings of Lawrence Wright – that the Church of Scientology was somehow "dangerous?" Dangerous to whom? And why? That compelling question in itself would pull me in. I had had experience with "dangerous" organizations, and those investigating them. The Church had been a target of government agencies, private investigations, propaganda campaigns. How dangerous could a religion be – especially one that advocated for peace and religious tolerance, and spent millions sending volunteers into disaster zones around the world?

It hadn't taken long in those first inquiries to get to the critical reviews of the Church and its leadership. To a casual reader, the *St. Pete Times* stories looked plausible; they were reported mostly in a typical, if aggressive fashion. And, one couldn't help noticing, its original stories on the Church in the 1970s were obviously deemed important by the American journalistic community. The stories had won a Pulitzer Prize.[4]

But over time, and looking more deeply – especially with access to records and documents that the Church had collected on the issues over years – I found the stories increasingly less plausible, even deeply flawed. When I went back to the original *Times* stories – in the beginning, when Scientology landed almost literally from aboard ship on the Gulf Coast beaches of Clearwater in the mid-1970s – I pulled apart the "exposé" by the *Times* of the Church "secretly" buying land in the St. Pete-Clearwater area under the names of other entities.

The paper had characterized this as a plot to hide a secretive organization's mysterious agendas. There was arguably an "attitude" within the accounts, a note of alarm, and, I noticed, no mention of the fact that business organizations avoiding escalating real estate prices in development communities routinely used such techniques. In fact, the *Times'* non-profit owner, the Poynter Institute, would itself be involved in secretive local land transactions some years later, a matter ignored by the *Times* – much as the Institute would ignore questions about the *Times'* "special" coverage of the Church.[5]

Those *St. Pete Times* stories read like warnings against an invasion by a "non-Christian" religion. They were hyperbolic, broadly critical stories that raised ominous questions about the organization and encouraged local residents to express suspicions. Other than property records, the stories were light on facts. Decades later, the Church's spiritual home in Clearwater is well-established; it draws tens of thousands of visitors to the community every year and has proven to be a good neighbor. By most accounts it contributes time and service to the community, as it has demonstrated in a similar fashion in cities around the world.

The *Times*, even in these days of decline for daily papers, still carries an authority within the journalism community, and it would become clear later that the pattern of its reporting had an obvious influence on Lawrence Wright when he decided that Scientology was a suitable subject for his inquiries. There would prove to be other prominent influences as well.

After some four years of digging into his story, seeking clues to questions about such journalistic legacies, about media honesty and performance, and even to Lawrence Wright's grand motives in writing about the Church of Scientology, I discovered an even more curious relationship in this media milieu: the unseen hand of the American intelligence community within the nation's "independent" press.

As I deepened my probe into the handling of the Church coverage by the *St. Pete Times* into the coverage at large, small details shed light on this enigma and were found in unexpected places: declassified CIA and FBI documents, Justice Department records, dusty academic writings, bankruptcy court pleadings, non-profit filings, documents from lawsuits and appellate proceedings. The more I looked the more I found that was interesting and story-worthy.

In the end I wrote a 12,000-word package about the *Times* that included some analysis of questionable dealings. They involved the for-profit paper's ownership by the non-profit Poynter Institute, curious dealings that raised legal questions over a take-over attempt of a Washington-based reporting service, including accusations of break-ins and stolen data, the Poynter Institute's own politically-charged real estate deals – and a litany of problems in its long-term coverage of the Church. Relationships that editors of the *Times* had enjoyed with Nelson Poynter had made it clear that his views, even those that perpetuated a paternalistic approach to the Tampa-St Pete-Clearwater region, were going to be represented far into the paper's future through his successors. One of those views was Poynter's perspective on Scientology and its presence on the Gulf Coast, which had deeply annoyed the region's most powerful citizen. Poynter was not a William Randolph Hearst, perhaps, but he had made an indelible mark on journalism. When it came to using the press like a bludgeon, some would suggest, that mark became a stain.

For what it was worth, the package, I assumed, was a beginning and end to a short-lived if interesting project, and I was happy to put my name on it. I was no stranger to disputes with newspaper management. But what did surprise me was that the editors at the *St. Petersburg Times* had no interest in talking to me about the coverage. But, my brief foray into *Freedom*'s revival – the stories were never published – became instead a starting point toward a much larger inquiry, one that carried me places I never expected to go.

* * *

Lawrence Wright, like Nelson Poynter, has made a mark on journalism and a more indelible mark upon the minds of American and foreign readers on matters of social, cultural and political importance, here and internationally. He is roundly and widely praised, promoted and protected by peers in the mainstream press, even described as an often "prescient" journalist by those he has worked for, and by those who say his work seems to capture cultural currents at the very crest of the wave.[6] And, of course, he is lauded by fellow media luminaries with whom he has worked, broken bread and been called friend.

Yet none of those fellow journalists, I would conclude, know who Lawrence Wright really is, where he really came from, and who helped him get where he is today. Or, if they do know, they are compliant friends contributing to an atmosphere otherwise antithetic to independent, democracy-supporting journalism. No one – until now – has ever attempted publicly to unravel the mystery of Lawrence Wright's influential position as an American writer and journalist. But what will follow here is fact, well-documented.

Ironically, Wright's "prescience" as a journalist might actually be borne out by the very investigation I conducted into this secret history. He seems to have predicted with a certain aspect and awareness early on the advent of an investigation directed at himself, the kind he had carried out about others.

He said so in a book he published about religious leaders, called *Saints and Sinners,* as he was describing his own persistent attempts to probe the mind of Will Campbell, a man considered an icon in the milieu of religious and social activism.

Wright wrote:

> I would not want someone like me going through my life with the same remorseless curiosity, holding me to account for everything I have said or done, noting with a cold eye all my habits and flaws. It would not be just the inadequacy of my life, but the emptiness of the observer's that would appall me – that he would be so flexible and unresistant as to be able to pour himself into my mold. That had always been my greatest talent as a reporter, and my biggest failing as a human being. I could be anybody.[7]

I stumbled across those words early in my investigation as I read, with the same remorseless curiosity that he had described, everything major and minor that Wright had written, tracking his life and career and his claims.

I doubted then that Wright was ever truly daunted by such concerns. But as I dug deeper those words would take on a new meaning. Wright seemed to have something to hide. He was not the independent journalist he claimed to be. He had not been truthful about his past. And, more than not being truthful, there appeared to be secrets that could alter what he had worked so long to build – his reputation.

Within what was true, was a larger truth. One that was important to a far larger world than that of Scientology, or even Wright as an individual. It was a glimpse into a world that revolves around what we believe is true, and what is not, and how that determination has been the subject of extreme, even primary importance to powerful individuals – including not only those within the many-tentacled Central Intelligence Agency, but also its so-called "deep state" compatriots.

LAWRENCE WRIGHT AND JOURNALISM'S HIDDEN LEGACY

All we know of our cultural life and national history – all that we understand or imagine about our place within it, all that colors our concept of our daily world and complicated social economies, all that we believe about who and what we are as modern human beings, inside and outside of our cultural tribes – is described, informed, and at times created by America's media.

Our "daily journalism" – which here refers to news accounts and to stories long in development, from magazines, documentaries, and books – offers up the record of our daily lives. It also characterizes and offers meaning to our unfolding story, both as we are living it and as we reflect upon it, creating history's permanent record. In doing so, the books which compose our most credible and powerful records of the past became of particular interest to those who would influence public opinion both in the service of a particular political and social ideology and for the preservation of a powerful elite.

It is no casual observation that this daily journalism portrays our beliefs and value systems and assumes leadership on what to accept as true, what to reject, what to consider credible and what should arouse suspicions or inspire doubt. The news and information it imparts issues to us a shield of knowledge to cope with threats, warnings, and cautions. It offers directions on who can be trusted and who cannot. Between hard covers, it takes on an authority and credibility found nowhere else. And this is something that Lawrence Wright – who never went to journalism school – apparently learned early in his career.[8]

This is media that has learned the importance of audience, based on social economics and financial returns. To draw audience, it conspires to entertain as well as inform us, developing along the way many of the truisms with which we live. In its reportage it creates a basis on which we as individuals, families, groups, political parties, and special interests make both mundane and life-changing decisions. It has the power to teach values, good and bad. And while this daily journalism, wearing the cloak of democracy's watchdog, claims to serve a high ideal – comforting the afflicted and afflicting the comfortable – its principal record shows that most often it protects the powerful, and only notices the powerless when they are in the streets.

We permit this conflict. We treat it as normal and because it is institutional, we have come to expect it to be this way. The fabric of the media is the collection of ideas and information and the packaging of them to be sold. It is what led to newspapers with something called "second-coming" type for shocking headlines on shocking stories. It was what led to the inverted pyramid, newspaper journalism's no-nonsense format for conveying the top of the news in the fastest time. It was also the foundation on which sensationalism – yellow journalism – was first built.

Much of what we understand about this system has been long recognized, debated, evaluated, praised, and degraded. As with any institutional structure that contributes to a functional society, the bad comes with the good. With no vehicle to support the news, and with no competition to keep journalists honest – even if that system sometimes, or even often, fails – there would be no meaningful reporting at all.

But the media empire as it has developed has also created a powerful tool for inequity and unseen influences, for shaping public ideas, for making certain perspectives acceptable and others unacceptable, and most importantly, for creating a platform that is malleable and susceptible to manipulation when it strives to appear otherwise.

The evidence of this, of course, is everywhere. It is in the lack of coverage about police brutality that allowed the killing of George Floyd to become the image of unexpunged racism among American police.

The evidence is not only in the media's failures to tell us the truth about other important issues – the environment, poverty, racism in general, discrimination, religious intolerance – but in the industry's failure to tell us about itself, about who and "what" controls media decisions that so affect every American life. There are powerful questions about powerful institutions that arise over what role journalists have taken in shaping our perspective on history, and to what purpose. Where does a journalist's loyalty lie? With his institution? With the truth? With something else?

The revolutionary idea that the public press would speak consistently to and defend the rights of commoners – particularly in a nation first ruled by religious authorities, then by nobility and oligarchies, and finally by democratic ideas – was derived from Socratic values and the wisdom of the commonweal. The American traditions of journalism give witness to its philosophical attachment to democratic ideas and to the protection of those ideas by being truth's standard-bearer. By holding a mirror to society, exposing its faults and foibles, allowing it to see itself clearly, the press would serve those aims. But the mission of protecting a certain democracy, a certain cultural elite, would eventually serve to distort both the aims, and the mirror image.

What we don't see in the back alleys amid the shadows of this journalistic empire is evidence that sometimes distortions are no accident. There are interests and forces unseen that have the ability to influence directly this empire itself. One of those forces, perhaps the most powerful, has been the American intelligence network, which has often allowed agents to pose as foreign journalists for covert processes, or has convinced domestic journalists to serve as sources for intelligence.[9]

But there is much more to that story. Just as America could imagine in its Cold War fears the development of a fictionally inspired "Manchurian Candidate" – a brainwashed individual who would do anything he was told – we can imagine the power and influence of a domestic "Manchurian journalist," whose loyalty is not to the truth, but to a particular perspective and those who serve it. And the investigation chronicled within these pages, focused on a single example of a powerful American journalist with what appears as undisclosed secret connections and secret loyalties, explores those ideas.

The power of the press to affect and provoke outcomes has long been recognized by the nation's elected and unelected leadership. Under successive political administrations – beginning with Franklin Roosevelt and the advent of World War II, through the ensuing Cold War and into the War on Terror – the American intelligence community, an interlocking network that far exceeds the authorized domain of the Central Intelligence Agency's official activities – has come to a symbiotic relationship with private domestic interests, representing enterprises and individuals.

Consequently, one of the most powerful, yet nearly invisible, institutions influencing the debate about American journalism would involve that intelligence community – whose threads are woven much deeper into the fabric of American life than most people imagine. Many Americans can imagine an invisible surveillance network that protects them from terror and foreign influences and that, at the same time, robs them of their democratic rights to both privacy and transparency. But that intelligence community has done much more than that. It has robbed us often of an independent press.

Many of the powerful players involved have been written about, in biographies, in historical accounts, and even in connection with the intelligence network. Media infiltration by the CIA has been documented now and again for decades.[10] But the programmatic recruitment of journalists through a clandestine network – the same one through which American journalist Lawrence Wright participated on his path to be what he became – has never been individually detailed, until now.

Like all institutions, the media have forgivable faults, deserve a certain tolerance for their failures in certain arenas. Reporters, editors and publishers get facts wrong, and when they admit and correct them, they bring integrity to the process. A media elite that tolerates social ills in the name of profits is still subject to public scrutiny and entitled to earn public censure, even if long in coming. Newspapers once derived advertising revenue from slave auctions, from their support for segregation, for their tolerance of racial hatred, protection of a white status quo and promotion of religious bigotry, by rejecting "outsiders" and "undesirables." Yellow journalism destroyed lives and changed political outcomes.

Even into the 1980s, in the once Klan-ravaged Indiana, the state's largest newspaper still carried a front-page squib on the weather with a homey saying from "Joe Crow," whose image of a blackbird in a jockey-like vest needed only to substitute "Jim" for "Joe" to be fully appreciated for its subtle suggestions.[11] Those are attitudes alive within a "comfortable" media that refuses to hold itself accountable.

But this is not the story of that media or its failures. Whatever its faults, and whatever its strengths among those within that media environment – and there are many who have tried and still try to uphold journalistic ideals – this is instead the story of a systemic and purposeful coloration of the world we think we know as Americans, employing clandestine and classified efforts and programs to influence perspectives of the American public with the direct help of journalistic "assets."[12]

Those journalists who have played a witting and secret role in cooperating with an intelligence community for the purpose of influencing public opinion are neither independent nor credible. Instead, they assist in the maintenance of a porous and secret relationship between powerful private business interests – banks, foundations, legal systems, born of direct ties to the CIA. This network has operated largely in the shadows, inside and outside of our borders. It's reach today remains undescribed.

That, at its heart, is what this story is about. And the existence of this public-private network, which has been in flower since the days of World War II, is revealed by its perfect example: a journalist whose loyalties and perspectives appeared to be influenced by his direct and undisclosed connection to that intelligence network – and whose loyalty appears to have proven its value in the Age of Terror.

In 1999, Frances Stonor Saunders, a British filmmaker and author, made a film, followed by an insightful and well-researched book on the Central Intelligence Agency's Cold War propaganda efforts. She shone a light upon its friends in the power elite and their extensive efforts to recruit writers, poets, artists, actors, performers to promote Western cultural values, democracy, anti-communism – and to share intelligence through the U.S. State Department and the CIA – domestically and internationally.[13]

To disguise that this American spy network was directing those cultural efforts to propagandize its own people, private foundations and front organizations were used to shield these self-described patriots from accusations that their independence was compromised. Those institutions included the Ford Foundation, the Rockefeller Foundation, and numerous others, including one from Dallas, Texas, that plays a significant role in this story: The Hoblitzelle Foundation.

Saunders detailed the witting and unwitting involvement of writers, journalists, artists, and cultural celebrities in what she termed the Cultural Cold War. She particularly noted the existence of the Franklin Books program, which has on occasion come under scrutiny by academics for its hand-in-hand cooperation with CIA leaders and the intelligence community.[14] Its funding through foundations that were CIA fronts supported the Cold War anti-communist effort with propaganda programs – like the Congress for Cultural Freedom (CCF) – that not only projected Western cultural and political ideas behind the Iron Curtain and in third-world nations, but also inward, to the American home-front.

The CCF was tied directly to programs in which Lawrence Wright participated, funded by foundations his father's circle of friends had created, or where they enjoyed particular influence, and which were central to this creation of a "deep state" of influence. Their influence privately, and through CIA strategies, would spread throughout America's publishing, news, and entertainment media.

15

Because of revelations in *Ramparts* magazine in 1967 we have long known of intelligence programs developed to infiltrate and influence cultural, and counter-culture organizations; *Ramparts* exposed the CIA's manipulation of the National Student Association, showing that top executives and other members were on the CIA payroll, as witting participants in espionage and propaganda, funded and controlled. We learned from Sen. Frank Church's committee hearings in 1975 of intelligence abuses including the highly controversial practice of allowing intelligence agents to use journalistic credentials as cover, sometimes arranged for them by prominent publishers, including *Time-Life*, the *New York Times*, the *Washington Post*, the *Louisville Courier Journal*, and many more.[15]

As was also eventually revealed, through declassified documents, testimony of participants, and journalistic investigations, the CIA paid existing journalists for intelligence, co-opted the institutional reach of newspapers and magazines, and worked closely with prominent journalists, literary figures, and producers of film, in their quest for influence over public perceptions of foreign and domestic affairs.

The CIA's well-publicized *Operation Mockingbird* program explored and exploited many such options, and developed many avenues for its relationships with journalists. Some of those were detailed by famed investigative reporter Carl Bernstein – who suggested some 400 mostly-unidentified reporters were paid for their cooperation by the CIA.[16]

Yet, as I plunged deeper into the story, I would see how Bernstein neglected to mention the intelligence relationship of one journalist he knew particularly well – Bob Woodward – his partner in the Watergate exposés that, according to journalistic legend, brought down a sitting president. Woodward's own intelligence connections, never addressed by the mainstream press but never convincingly refuted, were the subject of a detailed, factually-supported examination by authors Len Colodny and Robert Gettlin more than 30 years ago.[17]

The elite publishing and media industries in American have maintained more than a handshake relationship with the U.S. intelligence community – as has been demonstrated time and again, and as we will see here. Sometimes – as in the case with publishers like Time-Life's Henry Luce and his adjutant in the Luce empire, C.D. Jackson – there has existed an unseen ability to convey credibility on whom they choose. That network of influence also surrounded Lawrence Wright.

The American media has managed to marry the creative arts and the art of the creative to the production of ideas; it assumes a pose of legitimacy in which, the institution contends, it provides an independent format for writers and artists and other creators to reflect on who and what we are, in ways we can accept as true. Yet, the media does just as much to limit ideas and control them, as a gatekeeper to what is acceptable, or permissible, and it has viewed such decisions through a cold capitalist eye by way of controlling the larger narrative, to limit it, to shape it, to insure conformity. More than that, it winnows the writers and creators whose voices and creativity will be heard and seen.

Over the course of it all there has existed a moral dichotomy between profitable efficiency and the power of the written word to feed a human hunger for knowledge. The private commercial network involved in reporting "news," which became known as the Fourth Estate, would rise to its position of influence over culture, religion, education, political, and social relations in the U.S. as a representative of the egalitarian dimension of democratic ideals. Its own history is replete with examples of the Fourth Estate fulfilling its democratic responsibilities.

But closer examination finds aspects of that work wanting, from the halcyon days of yellow journalism's creation of the Spanish-American war to reporting evidence of weapons of mass destruction in Iraq by the *New York Times*, when there was no such evidence.

Or, say, the reporting on the hideout of Osama Bin Laden in Tora Bora – deftly described by major media as Al Qaeda's hidden high-tech nerve center, which became a target for billion-dollar U.S. bombings, when the caves there were only hiding scattered light weapons, and not Osama bin Laden.[18] There are many examples of such "accepted" media truth that bear no semblance to truth at all, yet becomes endlessly repeated – and acted upon.

Still, in our increasingly fractured media world the Fourth Estate has managed to tell its own story in such a way that it holds onto at least some shred of integrity, clinging to the perception that its mission as democracy's watchdog champions the rights and interests of the Third Estate – the common people.

Yet, it has quietly hidden the story of its unseen influence, a useful tale too seldom told of how the powerful American press has been used not to serve the common people but to manipulate them. At times it has been a willing and witting partner in that deception.

The ideals of a free popular press unfettered from government, and beyond the power of special private interests, predate the country. They are perpetuated by the vision of solitary scribes and later printers who graduated from the careful calligraphy of hand-bound books to hand-set type and hand-cranked presses that then owed their proliferation to cheap rag paper and to the hawkers of "news." Information, ideas, and perspectives were created and distributed by those who plied the cobbled and dirt streets of our emerging cities and towns.

The trouble was, like any tool of power, it attracted those for whom power is an end in itself. And not all of those who saw it as such were committed to the virtues of the Fourth Estate, or democracy. The power of the press to sway public opinion was a potent political tool as well. Though American schools do little to teach the full history of the media, the excesses of their past – sensationalized journalism, censorship on behalf of political and ideological interests, a tolerance for corruption, racism, bigotry and repression – are no secrets in the American cultural landscape now.

The power of the press is not so much the ability to level the playing fields of common interest, but to shape and control ideas for the protection of those who control that media. And that story, within the milieu of American journalism, is the one least known to those most affected by it. That is the story that an investigation of the American writer Lawrence Wright has revealed. And this is that story.

CHAPTER ONE

THE COVER STORY

The lives of America's notable writers, and particularly the influences upon their work, have long been the currency of cultural discussion and examination, and there are good reasons for that. As E.B. White, one of Lawrence Wright's more revered predecessors at *The New Yorker* magazine, once observed: "Writers do not merely reflect and interpret life, they inform and shape life."

White, in an interview with George Plimpton in 1969, was talking about his own social responsibility as a writer, because "going into print," as he put it, was serious business. "A writer has the duty," White said, "to be good, not lousy; true not false; lively, not dull; accurate, not full of error."[19]

Graded by that simple criterion, Lawrence Wright – oft described as among America's most prominent, praised, and influential writers – has done his duty only half of the time. He is a good and lively writer, but his work appears to have been both false and full of error. What the American public and the world beyond knows and believes about Lawrence Wright and his work is a carefully crafted story that he himself has created, with the extensive help of others whom he has kept carefully cloaked within a web of secrecy.

These secret influences in his life set him on his path toward journalism, and helped him reach his position of prominence and trust as one of the country's most literate and unassailable *investigative* journalists – one who was able to pierce the veils of the terrorists Al Qaeda. But Lawrence Wright has never breathed a word of the existence of those who helped make him who he is today, nor of their deep connections to the American intelligence network, and its interest in influencing public opinion.

Since the moment Wright first refused to speak with me about his work, one Sunday night in late 2014, in a little Texas blues bar in Austin where I asked for his autograph and introduced myself, I have come to understand that secrecy shrouds his public life. And I came to believe there was a reason for that: Lawrence Wright participated in programs used to "groom" journalists and those in the literary cultures as "assets" of the cultural Cold War – programs developed by other "assets" of the CIA, to whom he had close ties. And he appeared to have disguised that history with a cover story.

***

As I began to explore Lawrence Wright's body of work, I found it odd that he had written his autobiography before his rather extraordinary journey as a journalist had begun. The book had launched him into the world of literary non-fiction – the so-called "new journalism" – in which the observant writer is injected into the story by those observations.

Wright's literary memoir began as an essay about growing up in Dallas at the time of the Kennedy assassination. It was published 20 years after the murder, in November, 1983, in a magazine piece in *Texas Monthly*. The highly-literate cultural magazine published in Austin had attracted top journalists and Wright won a job there as a staff writer in 1980. He turned the essay into a book that was published in 1987 by Alfred Knopf as *In the New World: Growing up with America from the Sixties to the Eighties*. Wright was 39 years old, a time when most journalists are deep into their career, but a long way from memoir.

The book detailed Wright's observations on Dallas, where his family had moved from Oklahoma and Kansas to settle in 1960, and on culture and politics of the era. On the cover is the now-famous Texas School Book Depository Building and Dealey Plaza, and his opening lines in both essay and book talk of the Dallas of post-November 1963, after Kennedy was killed there, and muse on the attitude of the country toward Dallas after that. The original essay was headlined, *"Why do They Hate us so Much?"*[20]

But Wright was really describing his own life and experience from the 1960s through 1984, as he worked toward his journalistic goals. Later – after peeling back layers of detail and exploring the plausibility of his story – I would look at the end-date of that timeline and be struck by its Orwellian implication.

It would take me more than four years, tens of thousands of miles of travel, archival research into untold stories and relationships in cities across the country, thousands of hours of pouring through library documents, FBI files, books, de-classified intelligence documents, congressional records, trial records, historical events and academic records, before I began to understand what must have been in Wright's mind a cleverly "coded" first paragraph in his "New World."

He opened with a gentle Mayberry-like description of his family's arrival in Dallas: his father driving their station wagon into the city, Wright reflecting on his recollections from the backseat on the cityscape – then new to him – his adolescent gaze falling on the tallest hotel west of the Mississippi, an edifice for Mobil Oil, and on the Republic National Bank building, which he describes as "the largest bank in the Southwest."

In light of my research, I would wonder whether his observation was just a matter of irony, or foreshadowing for a special readership, since the Republic National Bank in Dallas – deeply and mostly secretly connected to the American intelligence network, an operative in its Cold War missions – would be at the heart of Wright's world to come.

* * *

John Donald Wright, Lawrence Wright's father, took a job in Dallas in 1960 as the new president of a little store-front bank, housed in a '50s-era strip mall in East Dallas. Don Wright, as he was known, had left home early, graduated from an Oklahoma teacher's college in the mid-1930s, worked his way through law school, and was admitted to the Oklahoma bar in 1939. He practiced law in Oklahoma City until the war broke out and then enlisted, fought on the battlefields of Europe and later served in Korea, leaving active service with a bronze star. He continued to serve in the Oklahoma National Guard, rising in rank to major.[21]

But when he returned home after WWII, he mysteriously gave up the practice of law for a career in banking, moving through minor executive positions at a series of small banks that, I would notice later, were owned or managed by former military officers and personnel, some with the Oklahoma National Guard. As I dug deeper, I could see the importance of the military to Donald Wright, and I would learn that he had hired a large number of ex-military men as loan officers at Lakewood Bank & Trust, where he had assumed the role of president the year of his arrival in Dallas.[22]

Wright's father's patriotism would become a point of contention between them, or so Wright claims in his memoir, when, after graduating from Tulane University in 1969, Wright applied for status as a conscientious objector to avoid being drafted to fight in the Vietnam War.

Wright describes his father in his memoir as "typical" of the men who came to Dallas after WWII to build their lives, "…people who came out of nowhere with nothing," he wrote, "who came to Dallas because Dallas would give them a chance."

But I would find his father was hardly typical, nor were the men around him. Nor did he come to Dallas for the opportunities the city offered, but as a result of his military connections, which involved some of the most powerful and influential private individuals within the American intelligence community.

Wright's world as he described it was one of modest but comfortable circumstances in a conservative, very religious, and very white environment. The coming-of-age story, as he told it, was also a journey of conscience that caused him to write another successful essay – so eloquent that it convinced a panel of tough, no-nonsense Dallas Draft Board members to exempt him from military service on the basis of conscientious objection.

As Wright detailed his own journey to becoming a journalist, revolving around his curiosity over the human condition, he made it clear he was interested in a world wider than the one he'd grown up in. His unfolding personal story would indeed become a roadmap that, as I followed it, would weave its way out of the territory of memoir – and into the realm of fiction.

* * *

In the New World was written in a casual but intimate literary style, "... almost like a novel," the *New York Times* opined[23] in a review. It followed the contours of the new journalism, which had emerged decades earlier out of the creative work of post-war novelists like Joseph Heller and Kurt Vonnegut, and journalists, describing their own new worlds through literary non-fiction, like Tom Wolfe, Joan Didion, Gay Talese, Norman Mailer, Gloria Steinem, Hunter Thompson and many others. Through the '60s into the '80s, they drew many admirers, imitators, and followers.

Vivid, lively, and provocative, Wright's account of coming of age in the Sixties in Dallas, and the story of his quest to find himself as a writer, was embraced at the time and praised roundly in major national reviews like the *Times*. Fifty years after the Kennedy assassination, in a look-back edition, *Texas Monthly* magazine praised Wright's essay and his book as among the best things written about Dallas – and the attention the city had received in the wake of Kennedy's assassination.

By all appearances, it was a tour de force by a new and upcoming voice in American letters, sufficient to catapult a talented writer from the great swamps of literary hopefuls to the bright lights of New York journalism. Soon after the book was published, that is exactly what happened. Wright moved into big time journalism, leaving behind *Texas Monthly* for a job with *Rolling Stone*, a coveted position for writers with ambitions and a place where a long list of literary lights from Wolfe to Thompson had published.

Five years later, in 1992, Tina Brown, editor at *The New Yorker*, would put Wright to work as a contributing editor there, a pinnacle for American magazine writers. David Remnick, Brown's successor, would go on to promote Wright's work over the years, and particularly his magazine stories on origins of the September 11 terror attacks, which provided the foundation for Wright's 2007 Pulitzer Prize-winning book on Al Qaeda – *The Looming Tower.*

It was a late but sudden and meteoric rise for a journalist, who, by his own admission never took a class in journalism and was – I gathered from videos of appearances he'd made at journalism schools and elsewhere – proud of that fact.

Wright's break-through memoir in 1987 and his transformation into a national magazine writer – working on the cusp of emerging American culture, and now with the kind of access to individuals and institutions afforded writers of *The New Yorker* – had to have been heady stuff for a writer who started his career after graduate school working for a small non-profit magazine affiliated with Vanderbilt University in Nashville, Tennessee.

Wright had joined the well-respected but obscure little semi-monthly, *Race Relations Reporter*, shortly after graduate studies at the American University in Cairo, where he'd served his mandatory two-year conscientious objector community service requirement by teaching English. The magazine covered integration, segregation, and other civil rights issues in the U.S. It had long been funded by the Ford Foundation, and documents obtained through Freedom of Information revealed that it was also on the radar of the Federal Bureau of Investigation, as part of J. Edgar Hoover's infamous CoIntelPro domestic surveillance programs. Part of the reason for that, it seemed, was *Race Relations Reporter's* board of directors member Dr. Carlton Goodlett, civil rights activist, publisher of a Black newspaper in San Francisco, the *Sun Reporter*, president of the San Francisco NAACP – and a friend of American radical and Black Panther Party member Angela Davis.[24]

Steve Nickeson was the managing editor of *Race Relations Reporter* under the well-respected Vanderbilt professor and journalist, Jim Leeson. Nickeson hired Wright. I had tracked Nickeson down on a New Mexico reservation where he was working with native Americans. He remembered Wright as "arrogant" for a novice journalist, and that he was fired "for racism."

Wright would address that issue himself with a somewhat different characterization in his memoir. Though he was fired from the job, he found work nonetheless with a related east coast publication, *Southern School News*, which, like *Race Relations Reporter*, was also a non-profit that had been supported primarily by the Ford Foundation, and which was also on the FBI's CoIntelPro watchlist.

From 1972, when he finished graduate school at the American University in Cairo, until 1980 when he was working for *Texas Monthly*, Wright supported himself and his wife through small publications primarily subsidized by foundation support. From *Southern School News*, Wright would go on to *The Progressive*, the liberal-left magazine that attracted up and coming writers at the time and was also supported by charitable grants and subject to persistent attention by the FBI. Wright worked there with Judith Miller, who would go on to a high-profile and controversial career with the *New York Times*.[25]

As he developed his freelance writing career, Wright also wrote his first book – a small tome about a non-profit foundation-supported program for inner-city children from the boroughs of Manhattan who were sent by New York's Fresh Air Fund to spend summers at Amish farms.

Foundations, it would seem, were to play an important part in Wright's development as a journalist and writer. And while his first major magazine freelance piece – for *Look* magazine, about American astronauts on the Apollo moon missions – had no apparent foundation support – the magazine editors and owners had a history with foundation directors and officers who, I noticed, were also deeply linked to the American intelligence community.[26]

* * *

These were tidbits that surfaced early in my inquiries into Wright's background, and would surface again and again as I pressed further. Over time, these disparate facts would not seem so disparate, but instead common denominators. Foundation support during Wright's education and employment history and links to organizations that attracted government surveillance would lead me to deeper questions and deeper inquiries.

But that was far down the road as this rare piece of investigative reporting began – one in which one reporter was investigating another. There were to be many twists and turns along the way, that included several direct – if unproductive – conversations with Lawrence Wright in Austin, Texas and in New York.

In the beginning, there was very little beyond what Wright had written about himself, and the subjects of his stories, that compelled my interest in him. I didn't become engaged in this inquiry until examining closely his book on Scientology, *Going Clear*, and then working backwards in time. My inquiry into the history of news coverage of Scientology led me to an in-depth analysis of Wright's examination of the Church, and the choices Wright made in his reporting raised red flags for me.[27]

As I compared what Wright had written in *Going Clear* to his source references and his footnotes, examined his claims of more than 200 interviews with Scientologists, I found fewer than a handful were active. His characterizations of the Church's history, were marred, at worst, by fundamental errors and, at the least, by conclusions drawn from unreliable information, assumptions, and unsubstantiated accusations – including numerous cases where allegations against the Church had by then been adjudicated and proven wrong.

Beyond that – as the Church itself in online postings repeatedly complained – he used sources who clearly had an axe to grind. They were primary sources. Markedly missing from Wright's story on Scientology were sources among the non-celebrity, real-world practitioners of the faith. The Church had offered Wright access – under certain conditions – to Church executives and prominent members, and he in fact spoke to several – including actress Anne Archer and her son Tommy Davis, then a spokesperson for the Church. As it became clear that Wright's approach was going to be negative, those cooperative sources dried up. And Wright, to the detriment of his book and magazine story, was not able to get beyond that. He had to rely on the work of others. Which he did, regardless of the reliability of those sources.

* * *

It would take many unproductive forays into things I didn't understand before I began to recognize what was missing from Wright's accounts of his own life. What was missing would prove more important to Wright's career than what he had revealed. As my investigation developed, I would be not a socio-journalist exploring Wright's past, but an archaeo-journalist, because the clues to Wright's career were buried deeply in the clandestine history of the Cold War, the creation of the nation's post-war intelligence apparatus, and the culture of elite individuals who shaped it.

It was not until those clues were recognized that I began to suspect that Wright's memoir could be a cover story for an intelligence asset of the CIA, and the work of pulling apart that story began.

***

In mid-winter in 2015, I was working for a private, New York and London-based financial wire service that provided intelligence to the municipal bond world. Its editor, Paul Greaves, a smart, gregarious, and engaging journalist, a good and careful writer, also taught part-time at Columbia University's journalism school. We had developed a strong relationship as I helped him tune his newsroom and improve his reporters' news-gathering skills to make the intelligence for bond buyers and sellers more reliable. I built an electronic newsroom and shepherded early morning reporters based from Budapest eastward, filing stories as the sun made its way across the Western hemisphere. It could be high-paced and I enjoyed the work and the occasional trips to New York.

I had been at that job nearly two years, and before signing on had, in the two years previous, conducted some general inquiries into Wright's book about the Church of Scientology. But when the documentary film of the same name by Alex Gibney was about to be released, I began to take a closer look. I had looked into the book's handling, and issues around it. I saw that a friend of Wright's, who was a former colleague at *The New Yorker*, and was then working for the *New York Times* as an editor of the book review section, had done one of several *Times* reviews – all fawningly positive – on *Going Clear*.

But when I saw that the *Times* reviewer had stayed at Wright's home in Austin in January 2013 while preparing for his combined profile and book review, I called the writer, Charles McGrath, to ask him about what appeared to be a conflict of interest – and about some obvious flaws in Wright's reporting that McGrath had not mentioned. McGrath's son, I noted, was also a writer at *The New Yorker* and a good friend of Wright's. I wrote a piece about it for the media & ethics column in *Freedom* magazine, which was mailed to *The New York Times*. There was no swift outreach from an ombudsman or editor over the apparent breech of its ethics policy on independent reviews. Nor any other kind of response. *Freedom*, I would learn, was routinely ignored by the mainstream press – something that had not always been true.[28]

* * *

In late 2014, when I first began seriously to examine Lawrence Wright's journalism, purely with the thought of determining how accurate and truthful that work had been in his Scientology book, I did what any investigative reporter would do: I contacted him. I saw that Wright's campy blues band, The Who Do, was playing a pre-Christmas show at the One-2-One bar, a little tavern nestled in an aging Austin strip mall. Wright plays keyboards in the band, which is made up of mostly journeymen journalists and writers. I caught a flight to Austin and went looking for a bookstore. Several members of the band had written books, I'd noticed, and I bought copies of them all. After the band had finished for the night, I approached band members and asked them to sign their books. They seemed flattered, were friendly. I asked one if he thought Wright would mind signing his book, and he assured me he wouldn't.

Wright was packing up his keyboard, still on the small stage at the back of the bar, and I eased up to the edge below and asked if he would sign a copy of *Going Clear*. He was cordial, smiling.

"Sure," he said in his light-Texas twang, "How would you like me to make it out?"

I told him my name and he stopped, looked up, and smiled again. He scribbled out a note.

He wrote my name and spelled it correctly, then added: *"You know the story."*

At that moment, his comment was a bit of hyperbole, but it would prove true. I asked him that night to sit down and talk with me. But he declined.[29]

Three weeks later, at the Sundance Film Festival in Utah, Home Box Office unveiled the documentary that Alex Gibney had made from Wright's book on the Church. Wright had worked with Gibney before, on a film on Wright's investigations of Al Qaeda and terrorism that led to his book *Looming Tower*. They called the film, *My Trip to Al Qaeda*.

The following March I flew to New York for a *Times Talk* in Manhattan, joining the audience as Wright and Haggis talked about Wright's book and the film. I listened to him describe the Church in terms that sounded very unlike the people I would come to know inside, and who opened up their records and documents and introduced me to people on three continents who talked about their history. I charted their arguments on public

"distortions" about the Church – from the media, international governments, international law enforcement, the FBI, the IRS, the CIA, and
foreign intelligence organizations to find a story different from Wright's
version.[30]

I had, by that time, come to wonder what it was that made Wright so
interested in the Church – and yet, though he had billed his book as an
"in-depth investigation" aimed at understanding Scientology, his sourcing
was shallow, heavily dependent on prior published work, the effort tepid,
and, I had to agree with the Church, the balance non-existent. From looking at his reliance on sources that included previous authors, and sometimes *Wikipedia*, it seemed he'd put in far less effort – and gotten much
more attention – than others, including a close friend from *Rolling Stone*
who had written a book about the Church two years earlier.

Wright, Gibney, Haggis, and yet another ex-communicated member of
the Church, Mike Rinder, fielded questions about the book that night and
showed excerpts from the impending public release of the HBO documentary that Gibney and Wright had crafted. But I wondered about what
I did not see.

Conspicuously absent from that event was a principal source for
Wright's book, Mark Rathbun, an apostate and former Church executive
who had gotten caught up in misconduct allegations and been excommunicated. Rathbun wasn't invited to the event, and it seemed obvious why
not. After Wright's book appeared, nearly two years earlier, Rathbun had
written a critical review on an anti-Scientology website he'd created. He
accused Wright of distorting factual information he had given him about
the Church's famous controversies with the Internal Revenue Service
over its tax status – and in which Rathbun had played a peripheral and
functionary role.[31]

As a few patrons lined up for questions, I did, too. When I came to the
mic, I asked Wright from the aisle in the nearly-full auditorium, "How did
you verify that what your sources were telling you about the Church was
true?"

Wright, in his button-down manner, smiled affably and gave a prepared answer. He knew by then that I was a freelance writer, trying to
write about his book and the Church, and that I had refused to adopt the
popular anti-Scientology media line he'd championed. Later, through social media, he told others in published statements, on his website, and on
a *Joe Rogan Experience* podcast – falsely, and he knew it was false – that I

was not a reporter but a private investigator hired by the Church to "stalk" him.[32]

As I walked out of the event that night in New York, several people approached me. My question was a good one, they said. He hadn't answered it. A few minutes later I found Wright at a table on a mezzanine above the second floor, signing books, and stood in line, said hello, and told him again I'd like to talk with him. He told me then, and in subsequent emails, that HBO would now have to approve any interview.

We would see each other twice more, both times in Austin, once at the Paramount Theatre's showing of Gibney's documentary. He and I discussed again an interview with him, and he and Gibney hit upon a bargaining point. If I would intermediate an interview for them, on film, with Scientology leader David Miscavige, Wright would agree to an interview with me.

I told him I would see what I could do, but I knew that it would not happen. The Church had tried to respond to fact-checking questions from *the New Yorker* when Wright was originally preparing to write about the Church in 2011. I had seen copies of letters their attorneys had written to HBO and others about egregious errors and falsehoods that Gibney's film supported. That the responses were ignored, they said, and that Wright had persisted with false accounts in his book, had broken any sort of trust that an interview with the religion's leader, David Miscavige would be handled any differently. They responded with no uncertainty in a letter that I would hand to Wright. He read only far enough to see the answer was no.

I tried one last time to speak with him at a showing of Gibney's documentary at the Violet Crown Theatre in downtown Austin that he attended without an entourage. It was a local crowd, hometown people, some of whom Wright knew personally. I had spoken to him briefly immediately before the event, and asked him if I would get an opportunity to ask him a question. He told me cordially that he'd save the last for me.

He introduced the film, slipped out for a drink while it played, and came back for questions. Near the end he was asked whether he was ever worried that the Church might retaliate against him for what he'd written. The film had portrayed events that – according to an academic reviewer I spoke with later – made the Church sound more like a "terrorist" organization than a religious "cult," as the Hollywood media was fond of describing it. I had noted Wright's comments elsewhere that his wife expressed concern for his safety over his exposé on the Church.[33]

"Well, in fact there is someone here from the Church, tonight," he said in answer, pointing at me in the third row. People turned in their seats to look toward me, warily I thought. Though I wasn't a Scientologist, I felt a palpable sense, for the first time, of the air of intolerance that I knew so many of them had experienced for decades in quest of respect for the right to their religious belief.

And yet I found myself, in a sense, denying them.

"I'm not a Scientologist," I said immediately. It was the same thing I had said to Wright in New York when he asked. And to the *L.A. Times* when Wright – falsely – accused a reporter working with me at *Freedom* of hang-up calls in Wright's L.A. hotel room.[34] I told him then I was an Episcopalian, and I might have said the same thing again. I told them I was a journalist, like Wright, and I turned and asked that last question.

I saw him outside afterward, by the elevator in the adjacent parking garage and we had, finally, a frank discussion, the scene lit by the reflection of neon and street lights glowing along the downtown boulevard below. I expressed some of my initial concerns about his book, questions about its accuracy, and some of the work that he'd done before. I also intimated then, and later outlined in a better-informed email, that I had questions about his conscientious objector status and his father's relationship with political figures in Dallas. And, about the memoir he had written – a story that had stuck loosely to the truth, just close enough, I would come to believe later, to disguise an entirely different story behind Wright's journalistic journey.

He was about to turn to go, but he stopped.

"Why are you doing this?" he asked.

For a moment I considered what a rare situation this must have been for him. Another journalist, an investigative reporter, who wasn't part of "the club," asking challenging questions, raising doubts, suggesting not only errors, but an agenda. I doubt it had ever happened to him before.

"Why did you write what you wrote about the Church?" I responded. "Things we both know are not true? Even your source Marty Rathbun now says they're not true."

"Who's going to publish what you write?" he asked. "The Church?"

"I don't know," I said. "Maybe that depends on what I find."

CHAPTER TWO

MOTIVES AND OPPORTUNITIES

Long before I concluded that an investigation into Lawrence Wright was likely to yield anything of interest, I had agreed to come to Los Angeles for a meeting with executives of the Church's Sea Organization, who had become involved in responding to the Wright saga. We met in the old *Freedom* magazine offices, in a corner of the 12th floor of the historic Guaranty Building looking out over Hollywood Boulevard.

We stayed late into the night around a conference table on that first evening, discussing Wright's *New Yorker* story and his then-forthcoming book, which, in conjunction with Gibney's film would eventually amount to one of the highest-profile attacks on the Church in decades. With it had come a media publicity campaign mounted by Wright and his publisher, and later by other media firms, including Home Box Office, for which Wright traveled the country with Gibney touting his "investigation" of the Church. He decried Scientology's alleged illegitimacy as a religion pointedly suggesting that the Church was a "terrorist" organization to be feared and should be denied its hard-won legal recognitions around the world as a non-profit religious organization.[35]

We talked about the history of the media treatment the Church had received and about the history of attacks on the religion that had occurred over decades on four continents. From state intelligence agencies in a dozen countries, to Interpol, to the FBI, IRS and CIA, the Church witnessed an incredible degree of scrutiny. I had already seen and read stories, and I listened now and commented.

I found they believed, with an almost stoic expectation of success, that they could find justice in that world, a belief that a free and honest press would recognize the media prejudice built up against them and acknowledge all the *evidence* of past injustice, and intolerance. That was something they certainly did believe in – evidence. And they were good at finding it.

Later, as the Church's corporate secretary carted boxes and boxes of files into an office on Sunset Boulevard, and as I worked inside over many months, evidence to document answers to any and all of my questions about the Church was made available. There were long conversations with members who had been involved since the '70s. One had shared an apartment at one time with Paul Haggis. Another told me a chilling story about a physical attack she had endured one night by another of the departed, and now highly-visible, apostates.

I would, from some six months after Wright first published his magazine story until the publication of his book on the Church, and into 2015 with the release of Gibney's film of *Going Clear*, gradually gather information both from and about the Church, exploring its history as I worked on unrelated freelance assignments. I combed through the negative stories that emanated from the apostate critics in the U.S. and dug into the long history of organized, political opposition to the Church around the world. I studied the events particularly in the UK, in Ireland and Australia, in Germany and Hungary, Russia, Spain and Africa. I would later visit some of those existing congregations.

I was interested to see that despite major court rulings that overturned laws designed to discriminate against Scientologists, members had still been denied jobs, their children denied access to schools, their possession of the literature of the Church classified as a crime.[36] In the 1960s homes had been raided in parts of Australia, religious materials seized. There were physical attacks against Scientologists. While much had changed, active and widespread discrimination persisted. In St. Petersburg, the Russian port city, one Church official among a group of Scientologists jailed in 2017 for practicing their religion, was finally released from prison in 2023, a victim of the government's apparent strategy to discourage the faith, despite European Court of Human Rights decisions against Russian religious oppression.[37]

As a picture of the past emerged, I began to wonder and wanted to understand what could have seemed so "dangerous" about this organization and these individuals that governments and their investigators banned the very ideas behind Scientology. What ideas did Lawrence Wright – a man who said he'd sought interviews with terrorists, including Osama bin Laden, only to muse in print about stabbing them to death with a butter knife – find so dangerous that he would feel compelled to warn the world. Wright's inflammatory accusations had infused the public consciousness with exactly those ideas about Scientology, with no similar forum provided for the Church's side of the story.

In almost all the existing literature about the Church, including Wright's, there were many accusations that seemed hard to believe and, if true, would be outrageous enough to explain why the IRS and FBI, and even Interpol, might assign agents and conduct international inquiries.

I read about what Wright had called in his book "Operation Snow White" – referring to a policy that L. Ron Hubbard called "Snow White" and came in response to misinformation and disinformation driving such things as rumors that the Church's ship, *The Apollo*, was a CIA "spy operation." But records show that Hubbard designed the program to use "all legal means" – and only legal means – to discover and correct false information in government files worldwide, as the Church has publicly detailed.

Wright's version is far more inflammatory because the context and certain details are left out. The previously-reported facts of the arrest and conviction of Hubbard's wife, Mary Sue, and ten other members of the Guardian's Office – for illegally "infiltrating" government agencies – are crafted to sound like a broad conspiracy within the Church as a whole.

But members of the Guardian's Office, known inside as "the GO," had become in the 1960s and thereafter autonomous and independent of other Church leadership and Church functions not related to its "security," – the GO's auspice – entirely under the direction of Hubbard's wife.

Members of the unit had indeed "infiltrated" government agencies, though the members were simply hired through normal government employment channels, it turned out. They did secretly copy – not steal – documents about the Church being kept by the IRS and the Justice Department. But the "intelligence" operation was also the GO's direct response to illegal tactics by investigators of the IRS Criminal Investigations Division which, court records and other documents now show, had burglarized Church property and attempted to bribe potential witnesses, in violation of the law. Those activities were eventually exposed, though little of those details of the IRS's conflict with the Church made it into Wright's descriptions, and almost nothing about the government's own misconduct was ever widely noted in the public press.

Church members responsible for obtaining the government documents served jail terms of under a year. And the special unit of the Church known as the Guardian's Office was disbanded and its tactics disavowed by Church leadership. Yet, despite the Church's rejections of those kinds of activities and reforms – specifically designed to prevent a repetition of those events, executives note – the popular press repeatedly cites "Snow White" to raise questions about Church operations and make it appear such illegal practices were and might remain common within.[38]

I would learn eventually that that intelligence operation itself had been a threat to the Church's survival, and that David Miscavige – the man who had been named by Hubbard himself to take over its leadership – had been responsible for ending the Guardian's Office and its excess, also eventually navigating an end to the IRS' antagonism toward the Church.

As Wright detailed what had been previously reported about it – most of those accounts at odds with the Church's internal documents and re-cords – Wright described Snow White as "the largest domestic intelli-gence operation in U.S. history."

But it was far from that, by any stretch of his imagination. Had Wright researched the record himself, he might have discovered his error. What I drew from his description was the irony of his observation.

In fact, the largest domestic intelligence operation in the U.S. was the one in which a man named Robert Storey – Wright's father's mentor and boss, along with other powerful figures in a largely undisclosed chapter of American political history – had helped create. Theirs was indeed a mas-sive domestic network involving the witting and unwitting participation of journalists, academics, student leaders, legal and banking community leaders, and government investigatory agencies, ultimately in close coop-eration with the CIA.

It was the same operation in which I believe that Lawrence Wright be-came an intimate, willing and secret participant, a role that could have adversely affected his ability to rise to national influence as a journalist, and may well have, had he ever publicly disclosed those associations.[39]

Instead, he kept them secret.

* * *

Within that deep dive into the history of accusations about the Church, there was plenty of room along the way to wonder what was true, what could be true, and what had simply been fabricated into fact from rumor and innuendo. Certain stories had bothered me because they suggested outrageous, unethical, even criminal conduct. One of those that circulat-ed widely – and was repeated by Wright – concerned rumors that a dog belonging to a judge who was presiding at the time in a major civil suit against the Church, had been found drowned in the judge's swimming pool, ostensibly by someone from the Church.

Over time similar claims would be made by other people in unrelated situations, with patterns like urban myths. But the story about the judge's dog – which was elderly and likely fell into the pool and could not get out

– contained a far more important element that illustrated how inflammatory and fact-free accusations became frequent and pejorative propaganda tools against the Church.

In the case of the judge and the civil suit, the important detail that
receives no mention is this: The alleged "mysterious" drowning of the
judge's dog, and the judge's own concerns that it might have been done
purposely by a Church "operative" to intimidate the court, had, in fact,
and the record shows, been leaked during the trial to the jurors who found
against the Church in the court case. That, in itself, seemed to create a
caricature of justice. Yet, Wright didn't mention the leak. [40]

Wright's even more outrageous accusation – without detail or any supporting evidence, nor apparently any effort to find any – was his recitation
of a tale alleging that Church staff had coerced a member into participating in a California bank robbery in order to pay off a debt to the Church.
He bolstered credibility of that story by saying he interviewed the anonymous source with his attorney, but failed to mention the attorney, Graham
Berry, had been suspended by the California courts and fired from his
law firm over misconduct related to litigation against the Church. [41] Such
breathless accusations ascribed ill will to an organization that seemed to
preach something quite different – peace, anti-war, anti-abuse, personal
freedom. It didn't add up.

* * *

My first few meetings with Wright – my visit to his band's show in Austin and our subsequent discussions in person – had also included some
emails and an exchange of handwritten letters. At the time I had not started pulling apart the fabric of the story Wright had told about himself, nor
had I any reason to believe it might be a "cover story" for someone who
had come to his place at the pinnacle of American journalism by means
other than those he'd described.

I had started with an examination of his work, first in *Going Clear* and
subsequently over time in most all of his other writings. He'd written consistently and repeatedly about religion and religious matters. Some interesting magazine essays he'd written on televangelists and devil worshipers,
scholars of religious belief, atheists and the aesthetics of witchcraft were
collected into the book *Saints and Sinners*. He'd written about ghetto children summering in Amish homes under the auspice of New York-based
foundation The Fresh Air Fund, and since Amish culture was something
familiar to me – I'd once spent six months working with a crew of Amish

carpenters – I read that with interest. He wrote about false memory syndrome and later, as my investigation proceeded, I would marvel at how the sources he turned to as experts on recovered memory and hypnosis would have their own links, and a shared interest, with the CIA in operations focused on religion and belief. I wondered at Wright's own pointed interest there.

I found criticisms of Wright's recovered memory narratives, and I found other small criticisms here and there of his magazine work.[42] But any journalist with a reportorial record as long as his would draw some criticism. His was surprisingly limited. I found only one "serious" correction published, and he seemed to weather it all under a raincoat of strong reputation, like armor against doubters or critics. Despite minor complaints or unsettled comments I heard about in my own interviews and emails with subjects and sources of Wright's, I found little in print to mar the street-cred Wright had spent years building, both with his work and his associations. One former professor of his who'd done Wright the kindness of a reference to graduate school in Egypt complained he'd been embarrassed by him later in a biting and factually lean piece in a Tulane University alumni magazine.

I had asked the Church for access to their analysis of *Going Clear,* done by staff immediately after the book was published. They had assembled small teams of clergy to break down by parts what Wright had written about the Church, and to compare it with source material, checking for accuracy, attribution, journalistic integrity, and, at my suggestion, potential plagiarism. In dozens of instances, they found Wright had abridged the process of absorbing the essence of his source material by instead repeating direct phrases from other books, articles, and even the internet's notoriously unreliable Wikipedia, sometimes verbatim, often with no attribution at all.

There were strong arguments to call it plagiarism, and a university journalism professor in Washington State I talked with called it so outright. Even where it didn't meet the strictest of tests on plagiarism, from the perspective of investigative reporting it reflected sloppy handling of material.[43] Yet, Wright had employed two researchers for his work and had managed to publish his expanded story of apostate accusations against the Church in just over a year, quickly emerging as an "authority" on Scientology.[44]

The film of the same name by Alex Gibney followed soon after Wright's book. It debuted at the Sundance Film Festival, where friends of the Church saw the narrative power of Hollywood-like film turned against them, watching from the audience and reporting in afterward by cellphone about what they had seen. Gibney had refused to discuss with the Church what his documentary reported before its release, despite repeated requests by Church officials.

For all the circus atmosphere that surrounded the subsequent media campaigns for Wright's book and film, and the efforts by both Wright and Gibney to contact government officials, past and present, on their own, to urge investigations and prompt reportable reactions in the press, there would, in the end, be no official government reaction to Wright's work at all. The book and documentary's only "success," the Church would argue, was to stir hatred and intolerance toward its members. And sadly, as time would tell, that whipsaw of intolerance would contribute to one young Australian Scientologist losing his life, and to the endangerment of others.

* * *

By reading and cross-checking references in *Going Clear* I realized that Wright had filtered his unnumbered footnotes – explanations of disputed facts, the Church's own arguments, or matters affecting source credibility – in a peculiar way. In some cases where the Church had plausibly refuted parts of his story, he included their disclaimers not in his narrative, but in the agate-like reference material at the back. It's not unusual to use that device to bolster credibility, but a curious way to handle "balance" in a story. To even get a sense of the Church's perspective on some of Wright's more outrageous accusations required the reader to break the narrative and flip back and forth to the notes, something I knew few readers would bother with. It seemed deliberate.

Moreover, as I pored through the reference notes and the source citations, I could see he had leaned most heavily on two others who had written critically of the Church and its founder: Russell Miller, a British journalist and biographer, and Jon Atack, a former Scientologist who wrote *A Piece of Blue Sky* and had helped in distributing Church materials to outsiders. The Church disputed factual errors in Miller's biography of L. Ron Hubbard, *Bare-Faced Messiah*, characterized as being based, as was Atack's book, on papers, diaries, and other writings he had stolen from the Church's founder.

Both books had been recognized in print by other writers, including critics of the Church, as deeply biased. Yet press coverage and reviews upon their publication readily accepted and even argued for their factual underpinnings, adopting the perspective of the narrators with little question of their accuracy, motives, or even the authors' illegal access to diaries and personal writing of Hubbard. Both works, as I read them, reeked with salacious gossip. But in the popular press, no criticisms of those books gained any traction. And Wright clearly accepted them at face value.

New Era Publications, the European publisher for L. Ron Hubbard's works, brought suit in the 1980s to challenge Miller's use of stolen and unpublished material, but in an appealed ruling the higher court refused to overturn a lower court's decision to deny the Church's right to stop publication and distribution of the book.[45]

I would later spend a little time with the lead attorney on that appeal as we shared rides across L.A. with Isaias, a young man who had grown up on the violent gang-ruled streets of East L.A., found the religion, began to value education, and had become a manager at the Celebrity Center, known within as The Manor. He was independently studying the history of American law. As Isaias drove, he compared notes with attorney Michael Hertzberg on the power of the federal courts under rulings in *Marbury v. Madison*. I noticed that many of those working "within Scientology" shared an intense curiosity about the world, its cultures, its spirituality and intellectual life, a high contrast to a picture often painted of Scientologists as uninformed, distanced from the world at large, closeted.

In Sydney one afternoon, in a green-room at the opening of a massive new Church there, I would meet and talk with Dr. David Bennett, Australia's former Queen's Counsel and Solicitor General, who had won a major legal victory for the Church down under, a case that challenged the laws written against them, establishing the right of Scientologists there to practice their religion as they saw fit, with no state-sanctioned interference.

The case became a cornerstone in the Church's successful arguments for its existential rights elsewhere, first in the courts of Great Britain and later around the world, long before it resolved its 40-year dispute with the U.S. Internal Revenue Service in 1993. Those events would nearly level the playing field in the English-speaking world on the right of Scientologists to own their religious freedom.[46]

But Wright never mentioned these cases. And the field wasn't really level. At least not in the press, since hardly a word at all was mentioned of those events in stories about the Church or in their reviews of Miller's and Atack's *biographical* attacks. The deep bias both writers exhibited, even publicly acknowledged, cut nothing from Wright's hard reliance on both, nor from that of his close friend and former colleague at *Rolling Stone,* Janet Reitman, in her story for the magazine on the Church in 2006.[47]

Five years later – just as Wright was breaking his *New Yorker* magazine story – Reitman was going to press with her own book on Scientology, long in development. The two friends would end up marketing their books at the same time, but Reitman's book would get far less attention, and far less marketing support. Given the depth of their friendship, I found the timing of their work unusual, and worth exploring.

*****

Those events, concerns, questions and explorations in the narrow venue of Wright's assessments of the Church would continue for months afterward, but as I finally began to broaden the investigation and to explore what Wright had written about his own life, my focus would change. There was much more to Lawrence Wright than his writings about the Church or religion. His growing influence in political and cultural circles was almost mythical – a young man, whose self-described modest beginnings in life and the cultural prejudices and perspectives within – had led him to the top of American journalism on the strength of his literate skills in non-fiction narrative, in the "new journalism." I knew how hard that path could be; even in my admiration for Wright's skills as a writer, something nagged at me. Great writers rise to the top by skill but also by seizing opportunities, good decisions, well-connected literary agents, respected publishers. But not by motive – at least not as I understood the world of the narrative arts as these inquiries began. I had grown up believing in the power of the written word to transform, and believing that merit, intelligent insight, and well-crafted writing could carry anyone to the top. But Wright's success, it came to seem later, could be attributed to something in addition to his talent. Or luck.

CHAPTER THREE

A LITTLE BANK IN TEXAS

During the course of the investigative journey that began by exploring what Wright had to say about himself, I collected notes and files, records of document requests, and leads. At the beginning, I expected to find nothing startling about Wright, other than how well, or poorly, he'd practiced his craft.

The notes and files accumulated into an avalanche of small clues in the investigation and they filled up thumb drives. Disparate pieces of an elaborate picture did emerge, but parts were dark or hard to see. *In the New World*, Wright's youthful memoir – a tapestry held together by chronology and the perspective and experience of its author – the clues in the narrative were everywhere. But, like individual threads in any tapestry, obscure. On first reading, I found the substance of the memoir thin. A narrative about growing up in the '60s, cultural observation, a personal view, held together by an unremarkable personal history, seemed a little lightweight. But reviewers from the *New York Times* on down had praised its insights and literary style. I marveled at Wright's ability to attract that kind of attention.

Unraveling threads would in time require combing out significant historic events – the national conscience at the start of the Cold War, the response of America's powerful elite to the emerging world power the country was assuming, and the people involved in events signaling preparation for America's intelligence needs. Individuals and events began to stand out, but clarity could proceed only by understanding the complex web of influences from which Lawrence Wright had sprung.

With the help of L.A.-based journalist and researcher Joe Taglieri, and by following leads that came from casting wide nets, my attention turned to a somewhat obscure book about the September 11 terrorist attacks, written by Mamadou Chinyelu. A Black civil rights activist who explored racism and social conscience as a teacher, advocate, writer, poet and friend of poets, he had changed his name from Eugene McCall as he began traveling within circles of art that led to academic and literary undertakings.

He wrote narratives on the world as he saw it, from the streets of Harlem and Brooklyn, New York. While most of those narratives addressed race discrimination and its limitations on democracy, one focused on questions that lingered after the 9/11 terror attacks in New York. What didn't the public know about the attacks, he was asking, and who, beyond the attackers, might have been complicit? Curiously, Lawrence Wright – years before Wright wrote and published his famed account of terrorism in *Looming Tower* – became part of Chinyelu's focus, raising issues of press propaganda and the "conditioning" of the American public over threats of terrorism tied to religious extremism.

In his book *Motive, Means and Opportunity: Probable Cause for Indicting George W. Bush, his Sponsors and Aides for the Attack of September 11, 2001* – now out of print – Chinyelu explored unexplained matters surrounding 9/11, including potential involvement of Saudi Arabia. The book was published by Mustard Seed Press, a small publisher with roots in Brooklyn and South Carolina, but which had *disappeared* into the ether in the years since the book was published in 2006. My efforts to satisfy my curiosity about the publisher, and other matters pertaining to Chinyelu, proved elusive.

What interested me was that Chinyelu devoted an entire chapter to Lawrence Wright, stemming from his examination of *The Siege*, a movie released in November 1998 for which Wright had written the screenplay – or at least provided the idea and impetus for it. I didn't see Chinyelu's specific concerns referenced anywhere else, except for a couple of mentions that surfaced on chat boards exploring 9/11 theories. There had been open public controversy raised by anti-defamation organizations that the film was racist, filled with anti-Arab and anti-Muslim rhetoric. That wasn't Chinyelu's motive for what he had written, though. He was bothered by the similarities between the film and the attack – similarities that even Wright himself would note later in his own film with Alex Gibney.[48] I was curious to know more about what had prompted Chinyelu's questions about Wright.

Unfortunately, I found him too late.

He had died of Hodgkin's disease in a Baltimore hospital in 2009, and despite repeated efforts to reach out to members of his family and friends, no one responded. I wanted to know more about him as well as his project. Perhaps he had talked with others about the questions he'd raised about Wright. I was interested in what unpublished research he might have done, but that eluded me also.

His chapter on Wright raised unanswered questions, but the book itself had keyed on the issue of "propaganda" over the 9/11 attacks – the salting of public opinion with stories and information leaked and planted in the popular media, ostensibly by elements of the intelligence community – to shape opinions on the threat of terrorism. Engendering fear, prompting public reaction, using the press for such purposes, was hardly unfamiliar territory to the CIA's Cold War strategies. Chinyelu postulated that *The Siege* itself could well have been a piece of orchestrated propaganda, preparing the American public for the idea of terrorist attacks on home soil.

Chinyelu had read Wright's memoir as he pondered these questions, and he picked apart some pieces of the story where Wright had talked about himself. He questioned the "swiftness" with which Wright had obtained his conscientious objector status in 1969 to avoid the Vietnam War. He based conclusions on the assumption, of course, of the timeline that Wright himself had described for his decisions. That timetable itself would later seem problematic to me as more pieces of Wright's "cover story" came to light.

Chinyelu was also suspicious of Wright's less-public affiliations, like his membership on the Council on Foreign Relations, an organization with direct ties to creators of the American intelligence community.[49] Most particularly he was disturbed by Wright's conclusion in his memoir that Lee Harvey Oswald acted alone in the Kennedy assassination.[50] It was part of Wright's fundamental world-view from growing up in Dallas, but seemed to offend Chinyelu's sense that Wright's perspective was too much in lock-step with the propaganda exercises by the American intelligence network he had outlined elsewhere.

The Council on Foreign Relations, despite its deep and widely-recognized ties to the CIA and to private organizations involved in intelligence work, has long been a point of controversy for journalists. But many prominent American journalists have membership there because of the exposure to sources and information that membership might bring. Membership provided no evidence that Wright's relationship with the intelligence community was different from what any other journalist might experience.

But Chinyelu complained in the context of Wright's disingenuous description of a commonplace, middleclass upbringing. Chinyelu pointed to obvious privilege in Wright's life, couched in terms of the commonplace, serving to disguise a more elite environment. He noted that Wright's father was president of a Dallas bank, that he had been active in civic affairs and was well-connected; he implied that Wright's father could well have influenced the Dallas Draft Board in his son's favor, though he cited no evidence to support that.

His guesswork, however, would prove uncanny.

Over time, and after thousands of hours of research, I would come to consider how close to the mark Chinyelu had come in his suppositions about Wright and Wright's seeming *prescient* knowledge aforehand of the realities of a homeland terrorist attack – including his curious ability to describe in *The Siege* a ubiquitous terrorist mastermind resembling Osama bin Laden – when relatively few people, outside government and private intelligence networks, knew much of Al Qaeda or of the true potency of Bin Laden's prophecy about retaliation against "infidels."

Chinyelu's implications were practically sacrilege considering Wright's much-honored and lauded career in big-league journalism, where he'd been repeatedly embraced and characterized by the American mainstream press as one of its best and brightest. Bob Schieffer, on the CBS Sunday news program *Face the Nation*, introduced Wright, shortly after *Looming Tower* was published, as the "most knowledgeable Western man on Al Qaeda."

Chinyelu's concerns about the ability of the CIA and its private cooperatives to influence public opinion through movies and co-opted journalists were expressed before Wright's *Looming Tower.* What, I wondered, might he have thought about an interview like Schieffer's – in light of the fact that the famed broadcaster is a personal friend of Wright's, and an occasional sit-in musician with Wright's homespun Texas band – something not disclosed to his audience.

While Chinyelu's concerns had generated little interest, I took them to heart. They were at least a starting point. What he was asking, as he closed his obscure chapter in his obscure book on the cultural media's subtle 9/11 propaganda, was for someone to answer his questions: What was Wright's role and intent in bringing *The Siege* and its Hollywood star power to bear on a political question, one that was then alive and is alive still within debates over what former diplomat, author and professor Peter Dale Scott has tagged "deep politics," the so-called "Deep State."[51]

That question, in the mid-and-late 1990s, as Wright was fully coming into his own as a writer for *The New Yorker,* was a pressing one for the public-private intelligence partnerships that had long operated at elite political and social levels, and had become integrated into the very heart of the CIA intelligence networks in the wake of World War II. Its private

parts included banks, law firms, legal organizations, charitable foundations, academia, and powerful individuals who were involved with those
institutions. They were as important and as clandestine as the network's
public part, the legal creation known as the CIA, governed, in theory, by
the rule of law. But those within this circle of influence were the informal
directors-at-large for the agency's foreign and domestic Cold War battle
against communism.

The questions Chinyelu raised were also about the shift in focus of the
intelligence apparatus from the Cold War to the War on Terror, where
its best weapon was its reach into the American media to influence public opinion, to control the story, and draw public support. Was Lawrence
Wright, Chinyelu wondered in print, an example of this influence? Was he
an independent journalist, a brilliant and persuasive observer and writer
of and about his times? Or, as with hundreds of journalists during the
Cold War, did he have secret allegiances hidden in the place where things
are often best hidden – in plain sight – cloaked in a cover story?[52]

I decided to see if I could answer some of those questions. To do so
would require a meticulous dissection of the stories that Wright had
told about himself. The first question to answer seemed obvious. How
did Wright manage to get his conscientious objector status approved by
the Dallas Draft Board, one of the toughest draft boards in the country?
By 1969, it had sent thousands of young men off to the draft and to the
jungles of Vietnam. How had Wright managed not only to win his C.O.
status on the strength of an essay, as he had said, but also to turn the legal
requirement for C.O. community service into a graduate degree at a university in Egypt that just happened to be a focal point of CIA spy work.

The search for answers would take me to the doorstep of a little storefront bank in Dallas where Wright's father, John Donald Wright, had become president in 1960. Looking back, my investigation would lead from
that little bank in Texas to some of the most powerful men in America
– the very creators of the CIA and the unseen public-private partnership
with the agency and other intelligence systems. They had also created a
sometimes-noticed but little-understood propaganda network operated
by that intelligence community, which had developed deep ties to major
components of America's media empires.

* * *

Lakewood Bank and Trust, Wright's father's bank, was itself a mystery.
If Wright had not made it a touch-point of his memoir, it would likely

have slipped into history as nothing more than it appeared to be – a storefront bank in a small strip mall on Gaston Street in East Dallas. There was nothing remarkable about its physical presence, and in fact it was remarkable only in its modesties. Don Wright, as he was known to friends and family, arrived to take over as president of what had earlier been known as Lakewood State Bank. But that seeming good fortune would come with invisible undercurrents running into the Cold War.

I needed to know something more about the bank and what Don Wright's professional life had been like. Who were his friends, what were his associations? Wright wrote that his father saw his position at the small bank as a way of being active in local civic affairs, and developing the East Dallas suburb and the city itself. He had in fact also become a member of the elite and powerful Dallas Citizens Council, a group of wealthy and influential businessmen that had its origins among bankers who, in the 1930s, had been members of Dallas' Ku Klux Klan. The organization's founder had been a Klan member, but the Klan's presence, if not the racism behind it, had subsided long before Wright's father – who was not a wealthy man – joined that oligarchical organization of major bankers, lawyers, and community leaders.

But, many of them, like Don Wright, were military men at heart who were restless with civilian life. Don Wright had come to banking as a second career after first earning a law degree in Oklahoma and practicing with a firm there before World War II.[53] Before Korea, he had worked in a regional federal regulatory job, then in vice-president positions with a string of small banks in Oklahoma, Kansas, and Texas, all owned or closely associated with families of military officers. Some were involved with the Oklahoma National Guard where Don Wright remained active after his service in the Korean War.

I would learn more about the bank in a meeting in Dallas with two former bank officers, Al Goode, who had been a senior vice president, and Larry Foster, a former director at Lakewood Bank. Both knew Don Wright well in the mid and late 1960s, respected and liked him, and were very familiar with the growth and evolution of the bank. Both were there in the days that Lawrence Wright became a conscientious objector and recalled their surprise. But they told me that the news of that event spread quietly through the bank, and wasn't talked about much openly, given Don Wright's own military background.

"No one really wanted to bring it up around him, I think," Foster said. "It was known, but not mentioned. I think people were just cautious."

More importantly, they noted two things that would assist in my research. Don Wright had hired far more loan officers than the small bank required – most of whom were former military officers. As I studied that issue, I came to the conclusion that the bank operated as non-official cover for intelligence activities – something that had been done in many places around the country through cooperative businesses owned by former military officers.

They also told me that directors of Republic National Bank, the largest in Dallas, would often meet with the directors of Lakewood bank at a small facility in East Dallas. The ties between the two banks were close, they said. It wasn't until later I would come to see the significance of that.[54]

Those details would come piece by piece over time as the probe gathered momentum. Joe Taglieri, who had unique skills in talking on the phone with librarians and keepers of documents to find obscure material, finally traveled to Dallas. We had discovered that Texas banking records were not easy to find, particularly for a small bank that had been sold more than a decade earlier and gone through three name changes. Eventually we found the original charter that carried the name of Lakewood Bank's founder. At the time, the name meant little to me. But it was to become the key to Lawrence Wright's untold story.

As Joe probed for records, I launched a series of discussions with a writer out of South Florida whom I had come to know through a former writer and editor with the *Miami Herald* and *Tampa Tribune*, John Sugg, who later co-owned a string of alternative newspapers in the South.

Sugg had watched for years the coverage of the Church of Scientology, had been an early critic and skeptic of that coverage, and had become well-acquainted with Ben Shaw, a spokesperson at the Church's spiritual headquarters in Clearwater. Sugg would later become editor at *Freedom* magazine. During a conversation one day he told me about Hank Albarelli, a skilled writer and investigator who had published with Sugg's alternative weeklies. Hank had developed a keen interest in the Central Intelligence Agency and particularly some of its more outrageous programs, like the infamous MK-Ultra where mind control experiments using LSD and other drugs were carried out by the CIA in its quiet war on communism.

Hank had been a labor organizer in the U.S. and in South Africa, and worked background investigations for federal appointees for the Carter administration. Both experiences, he told me later, sharpened his interest in the intelligence community. He spent two decades developing sources and uncovering documents to unravel clandestine programs. I was not surprised to find that he too was a skeptic of the coverage of Scientology.

Albarelli was best known for a book he'd written about Frank Olsen, a CIA researcher and bacteriologist whose death from a 10-story fall out a Manhattan hotel window in 1953 had been linked to his unwitting intoxication on LSD, apparently by CIA operatives. The book's publication launched Hank into several successful investigations of CIA misconduct, and he and I opened lengthy discussions on Wright and the concerns that Chinyelu had enumerated. Hank expressed doubt about Wright's story of how he evaded the Vietnam War. He knew conscientious objectors, and their stories were different from Wright's. Most had some religious standing, yet had to fight for approval. I would find the same to be true in conversations with successful and unsuccessful C.O. applicants across the country that we tracked down, including those who, like Wright, had found English teaching positions at American University in Cairo as part of their non-military public service requirement. It seemed to be almost like a club there – one described to me by a former professor at the university in Egypt as a "draft dodger's haven."[55]

Albarelli – who would succumb to a stroke as he was finishing his recently published book on the Kennedy assassination, *A Coup in Dallas* – had signed on to assist with some investigative work under *Freedom's* auspices. We discussed broadening the project to look more deeply into Wright's Pulitzer-winning work on *Looming Tower,* including a planned but never executed trip to the Middle East to track down individuals who'd questioned some of Wright's representations of the War on Terror.[56]

Albarelli, like Chinyelu, found Wright's blanket assertion in his memoir that Lee Harvey Oswald had acted alone in the Kennedy assassination, a curious conclusion for someone who painted himself as a refugee from military thinking, and patriotism. Hank had long delved into assassination matters related to the intelligence community and what he had learned about it while researching CIA drug experiments had raised his awareness of the agency's ruthless excesses. It had led him to dig deeply into whether the CIA was complicit in what millions of Americans now believe – a majority in fact – was a conspiracy to kill Kennedy. We'd talked a dozen times about that and the wide-ranging intelligence community connections that had existed in Dallas since World War II. By the time Joe Taglieri found the documents we were looking for from Lakewood Bank, we were deep into discussions about the mystery and intrigue that surrounded those elements.

I was working in my fourth-floor office in the Colorado mountains one afternoon, looking through copies of documents that Joe had obtained on the bank, when Hank called from South Florida. It was a phone call that would deeply impact the investigation. I told Hank we'd finally gotten Lakewood bank records and found the name of the man who had recruited Don Wright to take charge of his little storefront bank.

"It is someone named Robert Storey," I told Hank.

There was a long pause on the other end.

"You said Storey?" Robert Storey? He founded that bank?"

"Yes, Robert Storey. Robert G. Storey."

Another pause.

"You're kidding me," he said, and laughed. "Come on..."

"No – why? Who the hell is Robert Storey?" I asked.

"He was a heavy-weight in intelligence," Hank said. "He's all over the assassination conspiracies. He ran the so-called *Little Warren Commission* in Texas. He was a major player. A friend of Allen Dulles, deep into the agency's activities. He visited Jack Ruby in jail with Chief Justice Earl Warren."[57]

And, suddenly, a light went on.

* * *

That night, late, from my little office, deep in darkness, the house asleep below, a single light was shining from the top floor windows all night, my wireless modem flickered furiously as I raced through what I could find online about Robert Storey. Within a few hours, even though records were initially thin, I discovered that being a member of the "so-called Little Warren Commission" was just a starting point. Storey had been much more than that; he was a force in international affairs for decades. While he seldom made the news, often flying below the radar, he was a Cold Warrior in a well-tailored suit with an extremely powerful group of friends. [58]

The most interesting of those early discoveries was Storey's role as chief executive trial prosecutor in the Nuremberg War Trials. He'd been dean of the Southern Methodist University Law School, a principal in the operations of Republic National Bank of Dallas, president of the American Bar Association, and of the International Bar Association. He was on the committee of elite executives formed to reorganize the executive branch of the federal government under Harry Truman. He'd been long associated with presidents before Truman, from Hoover to Roosevelt, and later was influential during Kennedy's administration. He'd been chairman of the U.S. State Department's Board of Foreign Scholarships, which distributed Fulbright and other scholarships geared toward international relations – and used as an intelligence recruiting tool. He'd crafted original legal codes for South Korea in the wake of the Korean War. And he indeed claimed CIA director Allen Dulles among his friends – and in fact had been influential in Dulles being picked as the first director of the CIA. I would find through Freedom of Information small bits of evidence documenting all that – including a memo to Storey and his wife that Dulles had sent from Washington one Christmas holiday, thanking them for a crate of Texas grapefruit.

Robert G. Storey had been among only a handful of men in powerful elite positions with both the U.S federal government and within powerful private national and international interests that included bankers, lawyers and principals of philanthropic foundations, who together encouraged, informed and helped design the original CIA. They had also set it upon its course toward the many-tentacled relationships used to fight the Cold War around the world – including assassinations, creation of political disruptions, civil unrest, secret military interventions and coups in Latin America and the Middle East.

Storey had had a window-seat on that history, and the stories of his perspectives and exploits would unfold around Wright's own dining room table. Individuals who were deeply associated with Storey's little bank in Lakewood were unique in the roles they played within the city, and within the American intelligence community. Officers and directors, vice presidents and loan officers, many or most of them not only veterans of the war, but involved in military intelligence units, and others who were deep into the politics of Dallas, worked, in one way or another, for Robert Storey, or were within his powerful circle of influence.

Storey's son, Charles Storey, himself a veteran like his father of intelligence operations, had become a close personal friend of Wright's father, and closely involved in the Dallas banking and legal communities. Charles Storey was also a close friend of another prominent figure in Cold War intelligence, Col. Charles Cabell, brother of Earle Cabell, who was mayor of Dallas when Kennedy was killed there. Charles Cabell was a top official of the CIA and a central figure in the Cuban Bay of Pigs fiasco, fired in 1962 along with CIA director Dulles as Kennedy dismantled the CIA leadership just over a year before his assassination. After his firing, Cabell became a major critic of the president, traveling the circuit to speak at right-leaning, anti-communist civic organizations, particularly in Texas, to express his concerns.

Piecing together obscure documents from the archives of American history itself, obtained through the Freedom of Information Act (FOIA), congressional records and information from a researcher hired in Egypt to explore the archives of American University in Cairo, I found that there were major details missing from Wright's memoir. Wright's father's most prominent – and never publicly described work – was helping Robert Storey and Storey's close associate, Karl Hoblitzelle, bring important visitors from foreign countries to U.S. academic institutions through scholarships from the Southwestern Legal Foundation, including for the law school at Southern Methodist University in Dallas where Storey had been dean during the 1950s. Among them was Edward Ortega, an uncle of Daniel Ortega, the rebel leader of the Sandinistas who would become president of Nicaragua.[59]

Individuals were targeted for their specific value to the CIA and the intelligence community through their homeland associations and social connections, individuals whose friendship and loyalty were subsumed into the intelligence community with academic fellowships and private foundation funding.

From an obscure newspaper story published in Topeka, Kansas, in the mid-1970s listing brief biographies of speakers at a local banking event – which included Wright's father – I noticed that Donald Wright had served on the investment committee of the Southwestern Legal Foundation. Later I would learn of Karl Hoblitzelle's and Storey's direct participation in funding of an elaborate, secret program to infiltrate and influence American and foreign publishing interests – also supported by the Ford Foundation and other foundations that had been exposed in the 1960s and '70s as front organizations formed to secretly finance CIA foreign and domestic activities.[60] Parts of a puzzle, pieces of a picture, were slowly emerging. I began to realize that it was deep in the history of the Cold War that I would find the key to understanding Lawrence Wright's rise to prominence.[61]

* * *

In the video I found of Wright's visit to a University of Texas journalism class, he talked about eschewing journalism education and his own unique method for note-taking and organizing complex stories.[62]

He used a legal pad with margin notes and organized his stories on 3x5 index cards. I had read about that technique elsewhere; I realized it was in a novel by the writer of British spy-thrillers, John le Carré, who had described a similar technique by an intelligence operative in one of his fact-informed novels.[63]

I would later wonder if maybe those who were teaching him the skills of a reporter and writer were coming from a place where the agenda wasn't about reporting the truth and protecting democracy, but about power and control of the press.

The power, it seemed, could be traced to the intrigue that surrounded his father's little storefront bank in Texas. But to understand all that would require a different kind of investigative reporting – a major undertaking – delving into the deeper history of the intelligence community. As I followed that path, it would lead me to one of America's most powerful historical figures: A man named John McCloy whom the *New York Times* would describe in his obituary in 1989 as the "Chairman of the Establishment."[64]

It would also lead me to a woman who was much more obscure in history but a powerful influence in that "establishment" and in the intelligence strategy of the Cold War. Her name was Helen Venn, and she ran a little summer course at Radcliffe College in Boston called the Radcliffe Publishing Procedures Course, known to insiders as a "mini-master's degree" in publishing.

Wright had attended immediately after graduating from Tulane University in the late spring of 1969, and Venn would become another important figure in his life, bringing to bear her own deep connections to American intelligence through which she had become a secret *operative* in the literary realms of our culture.

Venn was just one of those powerful influences in his career that Wright failed to mention, and there would be good reason for that. She was part of the American Cold War propaganda project that Wright would become heir to – a cultural cold War project funded and designed under the auspices of the Congress for Cultural Freedom and its CIA bedfellows, and which would have a long and nearly invisible reach into the world of American journalism and the publication of politically-important books around the world.

For all intents and purposes, Helen Venn was an American intelligence operative whose work went on among publishers and cultural figures around the world, and most frequently at elegant literary gatherings in

Manhattan. Some of the programs Venn was involved in were funded in part by Wright's father's friends and close associates in Dallas: Robert Storey and Karl Hoblitzelle.

CHAPTER FOUR

THE ROAD TO RADCLIFFE

E arly in Lawrence Wright's memoir he depicts a scene that was apparently the conclusion of ongoing, uncomfortable battles with his father over Wright's lack of patriotism. During his last days as an undergraduate at Tulane University in New Orleans, Wright recalls that questions were rising about his own potential military service and recounts his feelings and confusions about the Vietnam War.[65]

In mid-May of 1969, Wright's father and mother had come to Tulane for his graduation, and the evening before, at dinner with his parents and his future wife, he describes another angry fight with his father, so bitter that he "contemplated" slitting his father's throat with a steak knife. The battle of words ended with his father's invitation to either "love or leave" America.

Wright's four-year college draft deferment would end within days, and with the Vietnam war raging and anti-war protests filling the streets, he knew he was about to be reclassified as 1-A, eligible for call-up at any time. His orphaned cousin Don, his father's namesake who lived with his family for more than a year, had already served in Vietnam, been injured in a helicopter crash, and discharged. Wright had signed up for Reserve Officers Candidate School at Tulane during his freshman year, even as military recruiting and campus programs were being picketed and ROTC buildings burned during student protests. But he'd abandoned ROTC, not over protests, but because he was too clumsy for close-order drills.

Later, wrestling with his conscience and his father's anger, he'd tried to enlist in the Marines before graduation to become a combat medic – a way, he wrote, to avoid a moral decision over killing another human being in war. But like the heavyweight boxer Mohammad Ali, he'd failed to step forward to be inducted. Instead, he would follow Ali's lead and declare himself a conscientious objector. Ali would be stripped of his heavyweight title, arrested, and threatened with prison. Wright would drive off to Boston and craft an essay to his local draft board, asking to be excused from military service over his objection to war.

Wright packed up his 1955 MG-TF, a British-made cherry-red road-ster convertible, and headed east toward Massachusetts, driving across country with the top down on his way to Radcliffe College, 1,500 miles away. He said he was taking diet pills to stay awake, and as I imagined the scene, he seemed in a hurry. His only summer plan, he had noted, other than waiting for his draft reclassification notice, and his likely induction, was to attend the Radcliffe Publishing course, located at Harvard in the heart of Cambridge.[66]

His description brought back a memory from my own youth, a fantasy more or less of someday driving exactly that kind of British roadster. As a first-semester sophomore in high school, still too young to drive, attend-ing my first integrated school, I would make a three mile walk home every afternoon to save bus fare. On the way, I passed by a foreign car show-room – the only one within a hundred miles – where inside was an MG-TD, cherry red, racy, a bench-seater with raised fenders and brown leather interior.[67] At least once a week I would wander inside, dawdle and look it over and one day a salesman invited me to sit in it. I imagined becoming a part of its elegance, top open, one hand on the wood-grained steering wheel, the other on the rounded wooden shift knob with the MG logo inset. It was nearly exactly the car Wright was describing.

By the time Wright made that trip I was the teenaged editor of a small weekly newspaper, and about to step into the gritty world of night-cops on a morning daily, an environment far different from the all-white and Christian evangelical upbringing I, like Wright, had endured. Though Wright would himself be fired from a job later for racist attitudes, he had criticized his own father for his casual racism, as prevalent in Dallas then as it was anywhere else in the country. It was present within my own fam-ily. I could understand that.

But unlike Wright's father, my own had a more tolerant heart. He was a Texaco man who liked an honest person, the only qualification by which he seemed to evaluate. He hired and trained mechanics regardless of creed or color, in a 1950s Klan town with no patience for such attitudes. I would only hear those stories when I became a young reporter, and I heard them on the street.

* * *

Any investigation has milestones, and this one had many along the way. Among the more significant was the discovery of the impact that Radcliffe Publishing Procedures Course, founded just after World War II and expanded through the 1950s, would have on American publishing.[68] It became a recruiting tool for the publishing empire through its deep ties to anti-communist counterintelligence programs, and functioned with unseen hands as an instrument of the Cultural Cold War's propaganda campaigns – something never reported until now.

It's true nature, and its place near the heart of the nation's public-private psychological warfare strategies, was revealed by combing through decades of records, piecing together bits of history, and unraveling connections, personal and political, through hundreds of leads and many dead ends. And, finally, by placing Lawrence Wright directly within its axis.

As I read of Wright's journey northeast from Dallas to Harvard Square, his narrative passed milestones along the way as well, mostly of conscience. He reflected on his anxiety over the dichotomy between his father's view of America and his own disgust with it, and over his objections to Vietnam. It was a convenient way of telling the story, and I admired the ebb and flow of a journey used to stream subconscious thought. But as I pulled it apart, and as certain records would later show, his sequences and timelines were out of order. A good detective, I told myself, would ask what was missing in a timeline, how gaps were explained. And I began to study what logistics would have allowed.

Wright said he arrived early on a summer morning and wandered Harvard Square until dawn on his first day, thrilled to be there, apprehensive about his reclassification as draft eligible. As time elapsed, he describes receiving his notice from the Dallas draft board that he'd been reclassified 1-A, and wrote that he made his decision to apply for conscientious objector status that night.

Yet, his fraternity brother at Tulane's Delta Tau Delta, Arthur Wright, (also from Dallas but no relation to Lawrence) told L.A. Rivera in a series of telephone interviews that he'd written a letter to the draft board in support for Wright's C.O. application, prior to Wright's graduation. But Wright wrote that it was after graduation and his arrival in Boston, that he decided to write his persuasive essay, outlining his "Christian existentialist" perspective. Again, the narrative timeline seemed askew.[69]

Wright wrote that to his surprise he received a swift reply from the draft board, approving his C.O. status, a letter he received by mail while he was at Radcliffe – a temporary address. He was compressing detail for the sake of the narrative no doubt, since that reclassification notice would have been sent to his permanent home address in Dallas. Did he also compress time? The clock was running. He had only two weeks, he noted, to find an alternative service job.

Wright said he took a bus from Boston to the United Nations in New York to look for something that would meet Selective Service requirements – and also take him out of the country. It seemed a plausible story. But I kept wondering why he'd taken the bus and left his little MG in Boston.

By happy accident, he reported, his half-day search in an unfamiliar city at the massively busy United Nations produced within hours an English language teaching position and admission to a university graduate studies program – with a fellowship sponsored by the Ford Foundation – half-way around the world.

This seeming fait accompli came, astoundingly, he wrote, from simply walking cold into the New York office of the American University in Cairo, which was, he said, printed first on a list of American "service organizations" overseas that someone had kindly given him at the United Nations – after informing him there were no appropriate alternative service jobs available there.[70]

Even more fortunate, he would discover at the American University in Cairo office in New York – a three-minute walk from the U.N. – that the school was so desperate to find teachers for its well-salaried English Language Institute program for the upcoming semester – only days away – that it also offered immediate admission to its graduate program in linguistics – under full scholarship. It was as if Wright had magically materialized at exactly the right moment. He was ushered into a meeting with the executive director of the New York office, Christopher Thoron, who granted Wright a Ford Foundation-sponsored scholarship on the spot for the asking, and who, just months later – according to archived minutes of university trustee meetings – would take over as president of the university.[71]

With the semester in Cairo about to start, Thoron appealed to Wright to catch a flight from New York to Egypt yet that same day, Wright wrote. Instead, he rushed back to Boston – on the bus – to say a hurried goodbye to his future wife, Roberta, who had joined him in Boston. He gathered his clothes, and the next day caught a flight to Egypt, calling his parents from Kennedy Airport to say goodbye. It sounded frenetic. Almost dizzying. Indeed, by his account, he landed in Cairo by the next day, in daylight, prepared to teach his first class a few days later.[72]

The scenario seemed ever more fantastic after I called the TWA Museum in New York and spoke to a helpful historian who herself had flown and been familiar with direct flights from New York to Cairo in 1969, and told me she could not recall a time when you could get a direct flight to Cairo from New York two days in a row. Most flights went through Paris, she said. And as I studied the situation, I came to realize as well that Egypt, in its growing cooperation with the Soviet Union, had had no diplomatic relations with the U.S. at the time, and hadn't had since 1967 when it had expelled American citizens for a time; there was no U.S. Embassy there in 1969, no visa application process. Records would show that the American University in Cairo had actually become the de' facto U.S. Embassy in Cairo. Diplomatic relations would not be restored with Egypt until 1973.

So, Wright had apparently taken a huge risk that the Dallas draft board would – as it had with his contentious objector application – approve as a matter of course his overseas teaching position as a public service alternative, and that this combination teaching and graduate study job would qualify for alternative service. He had done so without first contacting the Dallas draft board. It certainly seemed like an unusual kind of self-confidence. It would seem even more the case when difficult to find records showed that Wright was one of only ten individuals born in 1947 approved by the Dallas board as conscientious objectors. Of those we could find, all had some religious affiliation. Wright's good fortune seemed too fortunate to be true, but not the only unusual thing about it. AUC's own records would show that reporting requirements about his alternative service status between the university and the draft board would be oddly absent – a fact apparently ignored by the same draft board that sent some young men to their deaths.[73]

* * *

As a reporter I had come, over time, to an almost spiritual reverence for the frequency of coincidence, the good fortune that comes from being in the right place at the right time, and the recognition that irony frequently plays a part in our lives. But as I tried to imagine a scenario that worked so well for Wright, the story defied reason. He took, he said, an early bus from Boston, at least a two-hour ride. If he made a 30-minute walk from the Port Authority Terminal on 42nd Street to the East River, or even a 20-minute cab ride in 1969 traffic, it was likely tough to get to the U.N. offices across Manhattan much before noon. And then what? A walk to the reception desk to inquire who he might talk with about alternative service jobs for conscientious objectors – in particular jobs out of the country he'd been invited by his father to leave, for lack of national ardor?

Maybe, I thought, he'd been given guidance about where to go at the U.N. And indeed, I would find later, that Helen Venn was no stranger there. She had in fact once been honored by the United Nations for contributions to international relations. She would also show up as one of Wright's references on his hurried application to American University in Cairo, and the Ford Foundation scholarship program – all dated after he started graduate work at AUC.

I would also find that despite the unrest in Egypt over its relationship with the Soviet Union following the Six-Day War with Israel in 1967, there had been plenty of applications for teachers and graduate school positions at the university in the year Wright was hired. Many of its graduate assistant teachers had been recruited through the U.S. State Department, as former professor at AUC, Joseph Palmer, would tell me.

More than once I wondered what Wright's whirlwind trip to the Middle East meant for his little MG-TD. Maybe Roberta had driven it from Boston to her parent's home in Alabama. Maybe someone had picked it up for the rest of the ride to Dallas. Wright didn't say.

* * *

Why had Wright picked this obscure little Radcliffe summer course? Most of its graduates were women and I wondered what had attracted him there during the Summer of Love. He'd been an English major at Tulane, had an English class in his last semester of school. Maybe he'd stumbled upon a brochure.

But he hadn't mentioned that to his last college English professor, who'd already distinguished himself in his own literary offerings for periodicals and who was not much older than Wright when the professor began teaching literature at Tulane in 1968.

Wherever Wright heard about the six-week summer course at Radcliffe he must have been planning participation for some time. The course, I would learn, recruited most of its students itself – even using publishing houses and their agents to visit prospective journalism and English programs to search for promising candidates. [74]

Helen Venn, an assistant director of the RPPC upon its inception and director from the early 1950s until 1980, would herself travel to interview students, records showed. Wright made his enrollment sound like a whim, but in fact the program turned away two thirds of its applicants, and they made applications a full year in advance. It was a tough program to get into. But Wright had no problem enrolling.

Many people have heard of the Radcliffe Publishing Course's more notable public profile – its famous list of the "Top 100 books in English" – a reading list still handed out to high school and college students in English classes. But few people, even within the publishing world, and most particularly the world of the media elite, can tell you much about the course itself. It would in the 1990s be absorbed into Columbia University's journalism program. I could find few people who could speak to its true historical importance. I would find those clues quietly buried within accessible public records, and government files related to the cultural cold war.

At first blush, the summer course appeared an appropriate fit for someone who, like Wright, had ambition to become a writer. He'd described those goals during a meeting he'd written about with author Walker Percy, a southern writer who lived on Lake Pontchartrain when Wright was at Tulane, and who, like Wright, had both an interest in philosophy – and a bright red MG convertible.

I would quickly discover the Radcliffe Publishing Procedures Course wasn't really for writers, or even those who wanted to be writers. Nothing in the curriculum sustained that ambition or notion – other than exposing students each year to famous American authors. The course had been designed for those who would publish writers, for those who would pick a writer's work as viable, recommend and promote it as appropriate, and enable the mechanisms of publishing to make those works available to the reading public at large, by distribution and promotion.[75]

This "mini-master's degree" in the world of American publishing claimed something that would be the envy of any academic venture: a better than 95% placement rate for its graduates, many if not most among the elite empires of book and magazine publishing, literary agencies, and academic presses across the country.[76]

Wright's attendance in the class would not get him a ticket to represent writers at a top publishing operation. He was among the small percentage in his class of '69 who didn't get a placement – at least not in publishing. But it would help get his ticket punched into a different sort of English program – the English Language Institute (ELI), which had planted its roots in the sandy soil of the Middle East in the 1950s, at the American University in Cairo, under the auspices of the Ford Foundation, the U.S. State Department – and the CIA.

As an instrument of Cold War intelligence, the ELI became a flower of outreach for the CIA and its broader privately-based American intelligence community. The university president when Wright was there, Christopher Thoron, had a prior history as a CIA operative, and the university itself was much more than an ally in an unsettled landscape of international spies working the Middle East. [77]

The university was heavily funded after World War II by the U.S. State Department through its USAID program – United States Aid for International Development – which had become a front around the world for the CIA's intelligence gathering and counterintelligence operations. The board of trustees of AUC, this formerly Presbyterian-based English-language college in Cairo, would come to reflect the diverse interests represented there – from American and Middle East oil and gas companies, [78] to banking interests and publishing interests. AUC, at the veritable heart of this oil-rich region of the world, had become an American intelligence outpost and the wider intelligence community's platform for making friends and encouraging friendships with the West. It also developed the largest English-language book publishing press in the Middle East. [79]

The Ford Foundation's financial support for the university, and the facilitation of student and faculty exchanges through the U.S. State Department's Board of Foreign Scholarships, would share earmarks with programs around the world to help recruit potential intelligence assets among foreign students and academic nationals across politically sensitive regions. The CIA conducted training programs for operations officers at AUC, as an obscure report by a CIA Inspector General from the early 1970s would reveal. [80] The English Language Institute, in which Wright participated directly, would be used to export Western culture and reap intelligence assets throughout the Middle East, one of the more successful of the clandestine Cold War tools.

I would not connect those dots until I came to understand the role of the USAID and also of entities like the Board of Foreign Scholarships – for which Robert Storey, Wright's father's mentor and confidante, had been chairman, and of which Bernice Chronkhite, dean of Radcliffe College, was a member. So was Edward Booher, chairman of McGraw Hill publishers, a close associate of Helen Venn, and active in the cultural Cold War propaganda programs. The support of AUC from the Ford Foundation had come with the endorsement and encouragement of John Mc-Cloy, who had presided over the Ford Foundation's fortunes for years. And all of it was aligned cheek by jowl with the Central Intelligence Agency and its networks of friends.

***

Writers may not necessarily have been the targets of Radcliffe Publishing's long-time practitioner, course director, promoter, manager, and organizer, Helen "Doylie" Venn,[81] but she was on a first name basis with some of the most prominent writers, and publishers, on the world's cultural waterfront. Helen Venn had many close friends among those throughout the literary community, as well as among powerful publishing figures, friendships developed in part through grand soirees she held for them all at the Waldorf Astoria and the Algonquin Hotel in Manhattan, where she introduced writers to publishers and publishers to writers.

In the year Wright attended, Kurt Vonnegut came to speak to Venn's class; Wright mentioned in his memoir that class members had bumped into novelist John Updike at a theatre on Cape Cod. That was likely not entirely coincidence, since, as correspondence from the course archives would demonstrate, Helen Venn and her husband Richard "Diggory" Venn were close friends of Updike's. They had a cottage near his on Cape Cod.

I had found within the publishing course archives a letter Charlotte Robinson had written to Frank Gibney, Alex Gibney's father, fifty-seven years earlier. She was inquiring if Gibney could bring Gloria Steinem to speak at the 1963 course. Robinson had been the young wife at the time of historian and pastor H. Paul Santmire, who helped me find her in Cambridge. She'd graciously agreed to meet me off Harvard Square to talk.

Robinson worked in Venn's office for a time after graduating from Radcliffe and one afternoon at lunch in Cambridge in early 2020, she described for me Venn's world. Venn was, she said, a skilled host at bringing together the literati and iconic creators of America's cultural milieu with individuals who had an interest in them. What she also offered was her help in ushering the unwitting into the "intelligence" community of the nation's cultural war with communism, a cold warrior herself.

"She was very petite," Robinson told me, "and that gave her a certain air of frailty. But she was as hard as steel."

Some of those she helped develop became witting assets of the Cold War. It was a heady time to have such connections, and to be deep into the intelligence intrigue. But Helen Venn's ties went deeper than the record itself would show. Robinson was not oblivious to that intrigue, she said, noting Gloria Steinem's history with Frank Gibney, and pointing me toward Venn's husband's association with the Boston Museum of Fine Arts, another touchpoint of the cultural Cold War warriors.

I would learn that Venn held publishing seminars in Brazil, Turkey, Egypt, Europe, and other parts of the world. She brought foreign publishers to the United States for private seminars and training, most of which was paid for with grants from foundations, some of whom were fronting to hide the role the CIA was playing in that drama. She was a coordinator for the Franklin Books programs around the world – one of the agency's most prolific clandestine propaganda tools. She was liaison between the State Department and the books program.

Helen "Doyle" – her maiden name – grew up along the southern Oregon coast, granddaughter of a successful dairy farmer; records showed that she attended law school and was living in San Francisco before the start of World War II, when she met Richard Hugh "Diggory" Venn, four years after he became a naturalized U.S. citizen. He moved to America from the U.K. in 1934 to attend a private school in Asheville, North Carolina, and decided to stay. By 23 he was a reporter for the *San Francisco Chronicle*. Helen worked for the League of Nations there, and later for the prominent J. Walter Thompson public relations firm, and Conde Nast.[82]

I tracked records of her marriage in 1942 to Richard "Diggory" Venn – a nickname he'd picked up in school from the Thomas Hardy novel *Return of the Native* – in a ceremony in Reno, Nevada, and found that two months afterward he'd enlisted in the U.S. Army and became involved in intelligence and communications.

Intelligence seemed a natural choice. His father, Hugh Whatley Stevens Venn of Saltwood, England, I discovered, was a highly-decorated and well-connected lieutenant colonel in the British Intelligence Corps in World War I, and again in the second world war.

In searching their history together, I located a ship's manifest from January 1947 when the couple sailed from South Hampton to New York Harbor aboard the British ocean liner *Queen Elizabeth*. They traveled with their nine-month-old son, Christopher, and listed their address in London as 29 Eggleston Square. The address was just off Buckingham Palace Boulevard, and as I searched for other occupants of the row house along Eggleston Square in the year 1947, I found an interesting connection. When they'd left London for America just after Christmas, their neighbor at 33 Eggleston Square was British Prime Minister Winston Churchill.

Lawrence Wright never mentioned Helen Venn's name in his memoir or noted that she became a reference for his sudden, unexpected application to teach English in Egypt. He didn't mention that she had been an impetus to his fortunate tenure at the American University in Cairo as a conscientious objector, where he was instantly hired by American CIA operative Christopher Thoron. Thoron's own ties to the mysterious intelligence network led back to Robert Storey, and Storey's friends and associates around the world, and to Storey's banks in Texas, and to the international legal community in which he was involved. How could that much coincidence attach to anything? Those relationships all pointed to destinations for Wright that followed directly from his road to Radcliffe.

As I would come to see, there were ample signposts along the road to point to why Lawrence Wright's memoir was in parts as false as some of his accounts about the Church of Scientology.

* * *

One of those who illustrated the impact of the worlds of writing and publishing on their culture and society – and who served the interests of this unspoken and oft-denied intelligence-journalism combine – was Frank Gibney, to whom Venn and her husband were so close that he became godfather to their daughter, Tamsin. I had found letters in the Radcliffe archives from Gibney to Helen describing their social gatherings and friendship.

But the godfather relationship was something that Tamsin Venn would tell me herself, after I repeatedly sought an opportunity to talk with her about her globe-hopping mother and her mother's role as coordinator under the U.S. State Department's USAID programs for propaganda outreach to friendly publishers at home and abroad.[83]

That outreach also utilized a mechanism through the State Department's Board of Foreign Scholarships, for which Robert Storey, as board chairman, had been active in developing with Sen. William Fulbright, through federal legislation in 1961. In the process Storey helped create and earmark special intelligence-motivated scholarship programs the world around. The promise of scholarships, and also training in Western publishing practices, were tools in the quiver of recruitment for Helen Venn as well. And the CIA was then able to cultivate those sources within those foreign countries for intelligence purposes.

Tamsin twice declined to talk with me. She had noticed from materials in the public domain my interest in Frank Gibney's famous filmmaker son – Alex Gibney – who had by then partnered twice with Wright in documentary films pertaining first to the American War on Terror, and then about Scientology. They would have subsequent collaborations as well, including a dramatized film on Hulu on Wright's *Looming Tower*. Still, the relationship was something Tamsin couldn't help telling me about. When I mentioned her godfather's role in bringing Gloria Steinem to her mother's class, she suggested that my source, Charlotte Robinson, "had her own way of looking at things."

One of those things, I supposed, had been Charlotte's decision to talk to me about the letter she had written on Venn's behalf a half-century earlier, asking Frank Gibney to confirm Gloria Steinem as a speaker at the 1963 summer course.

Steinem, through an aide, declined with regrets a conversation about Frank Gibney and the role he played in her well-documented work for the Central Intelligence Agency community in the 1960s. Her schedule would not allow it. But there is much on the record about Gibney, regardless. He had a prominent role as writer in CIA-produced literature, including a book during the Cold War, *The Penkovsky Papers*, purported to be a diary kept by Oleg Penkovsky, a Soviet military officer reportedly executed as a spy for the West. But the diary later became suspect as a fiction created by Gibney for the CIA. [84]

Steinem had written a famous exposé on the world of Playboy bunnies for *Show* Magazine in the early 1960s, virtually launching her career. Gibney was editor of the magazine at the time, and she had, through connections he helped develop, traveled to CIA-funded youth festivals in Europe, helping to distribute American propaganda to students there. Among the materials was a newspaper she produced that carried an article on anti-communism by John McCloy.[85]

Helen Venn's relationship to the work of the Congress for Cultural Freedom and to other intelligence front organizations was deeply rooted, and Wright's appearance within her class was testimony to his insider connections as well, it seemed. His relationships with Venn would not end with her course, or her reference on his AUC scholarship application, given after he'd only met her six weeks before.

I would discover later that Helen Venn's assistance had also been sought by an associate of Wright's in an effort to export the publishing procedures curriculum to Rice University in Texas, beginning in 1978. Venn would become a director of the Rice Publishing Procedures Course, founded by journalist and writer – and former Army intelligence officer – William Broyles Jr., a prominent alumnus of Houston's Rice University. Broyles protégé, Michael Levy, a former *Philadelphia Magazine* editor, was also a founding director. Levy had hired Broyles as his first editor when Levy founded the cultural magazine *Texas Monthly* in Austin in 1973. Broyles was editor at *Texas Monthly* in 1980 when Lawrence Wright was hired there as a staff writer. It was Wright's first major job in journalism and the first that hadn't been directly tied to or funded by the Ford Foundation. It was *Texas Monthly* that published the magazine story that was preface to Wright's memoir.

* * *

Wright didn't describe the origins of his decision to attend the little summer course. His casual reference made it sound like a diversion as he wrestled with his important decision about military service and the killing fields of Vietnam.

It wasn't the first time I'd seen him labor in his writing to lay down an impression, sometimes by downplaying the importance of this or that. He'd tried often in his memoir to strike his stance with the common man, not only his rejection of his father's world, but even in a description, for example, of his job during summers home from Tulane University, working nights at the freight yard of the East Dallas Trucking Company, loading trucks with tow-motors, ostensibly working among the rowdy common laborers on the warehouse floor.

One afternoon I took time to pull the threads of history for that little trucking company and its affiliations, tracking down incorporation papers and a website posted by former company employees. I noted that the owner of the company – Harvey "Bum" Bright – would later add a more high-profile business venture to his portfolio – the Dallas Cowboys NFL team. A Texas oil millionaire investor, Bright was also on the board of directors of Republic National Bank – one of its major shareholders – deep within the thicket of the intelligence world of Robert Storey and Karl Hoblitzelle, inhabited by the major movers and shakers of Dallas. He was also a visitor at Wright's father's storefront bank. Bum Bright didn't seem like the kind of "boss" you'd neglect to mention, especially as a famous friend of his father's. But I was learning that little things Wright omitted from his omnibus memoir seemed every bit as important as what he'd left in.

* * *

Wright had acknowledged showing more interest in philosophy than in English and writing during his final year in college, testing his own philosophical values – including his conscience, he said – against the musings and perspectives of Kierkegaard. He eschewed journalism all together, along with the traditional paths that carried most writers to major publications.

Andy Antippas, his last English professor at Tulane, told me that he never came to know Wright well – it was a large survey course, not a writing class – though Wright had on occasion gotten back in touch with him over the years. He said he'd never known anything about the little Radcliffe summer course, but did remember – before becoming a "reference" for Wright in his application for his conscientious objector job teaching English at American University in Cairo – that he had discussed AUC with him.

Antippas, like Helen Venn, had been listed as a reference for Wright. He couldn't recall being contacted about the reference or ever writing a letter for Wright. But he did remembered talking to him previously, before Wright's graduation, about AUC.

He vividly recalled Wright sitting in his office one afternoon not long before graduation, his chin in his hand, his elbow on the table, talking about plans after graduation, military deferment options, and said they had discussed American University in Cairo, where Antippas, a first-year professor at Tulane at the time, had himself planned to attend grad school a couple of years earlier.

He remembered telling Wright about his own experience after deciding against a graduate teaching position at AUC. He said he had accepted the post, but got a call from the State Department that year, warning him that violence against Greeks had escalated in Egypt. He decided to go to graduate school at Johns Hopkins instead. He remembered also that Wright had later written a story about him in the Tulane alumni magazine that was not only unflattering, but had "…gotten a number of things wrong." He said he held no hard feelings about that, though.[86]

Antippas told me that in the days of his application to AUC in the mid-1960s, he'd been well aware of the intelligence connections there and CIA recruiting efforts in academia, and had in fact been "a ready and willing candidate," he said, to serve intelligence community interests in the Middle East. "But no one took me up on the offer," he said.

He'd never talked to Wright, that he recalled, about intelligence work. And the fact that Antippas had a somewhat famous cousin who was deeply involved in the U.S. State Department's Cold War intelligence program – particularly in Vietnam – had had no bearing on his own interest in American University in Cairo; he told me later that he and his cousin barely knew each other.[87]

The more I looked, the more Wright's fanciful stories of his college years had seemed often to favor narrative convenience over fact. He'd written about the racial controversies at Tulane during the annual senior prom, which was held that year on a segregated riverboat, producing student protests. Yet the dance had featured singer Dionne Warwick for the prom performance. Wright wrote that he'd been on a social committee for the event and that he'd been personally dispatched to pick up Dionne Warwick at the airport and to drive her to a hotel the night before the dance. But once at the hotel, he said, the night manager had refused her a room because of her race, prompting Wright, he claimed, to angrily challenge the manager and persuade him to give her accommodation.

Hank Albarelli did some digging and reached people that Dionne Warwick had worked with around those years, talking casually, he said, about New Orleans events. He said that while no one he spoke with remembered any such incident like Wright described in 1968, the story seemed unlikely. "They told me that she and her entourage were very well aware of the segregated hotels in New Orleans in those years, and all over the South at the time, and would never have booked one."

"Besides," Hank told me, "Her band traveled with her. They wouldn't have sent Dionne out alone on the road, to be picked up by some college student at the airport. They said it just wouldn't have happened, no way."

Little details in an investigation are cumulative – circumstantial often – but they can add up to a consistent theme. The blurred lines between what was factual and what was the building of a personal identity, a persona Wright seemed to be creating about himself, were becoming more distinct. By the time Joe Taglieri and I headed to Boston to the Schlesinger Library to examine and photograph records from the Radcliffe Publishing Course archives, we had plenty of reasons to believe that there were other signposts we'd missed on the road to Radcliffe – how the journey had come about, and how important it was to Wright's real story.

* * *

It took a week to examine boxes of files dating back into the 1950s and to the beginning of Helen Venn's tenure as director and builder of the Radcliffe Course. Sometime after she retired, the course itself had been packed up and moved to Columbia University. But the records of the years of its history at Radcliffe, archived at the Harvard library and partially catalogued, became a roadmap.

We'd taken a small apartment on the other side of the Charles River, in a blue-collar neighborhood, and Joe and I rode the bus into Harvard Square, the first to arrive each morning and the last out each evening. We'd split up the workload, occasionally sharing a find or two that was interesting, but mostly working alone. We looked for class lists of graduates and programs for speakers, at correspondence, and though some student records were withheld for privacy, there were many not excluded. Over the first three days we found the class from each summer course over 20 years – and each group of folders revealed material from that year. In each we found class lists identifying every student, elements of their applications, where they had attended college, their backgrounds, research details used in reviewing applications – and soliciting them. We found a class list for every class over those years – except one. The class list for 1969 – the year Wright attended.

We discussed the oddity that the one list we were most interested in should be missing. Bad luck, it seemed. But late the next day we pulled a brown file folder from a box of records for a different class year, and noticed some thin, typed sheets of paper on the bottom, folded, crumpled and creased. It was the missing class list, somehow not only crammed in the wrong box but then jammed down between unrelated folders. It seemed an unlikely carelessness, given the table-top-only handling of archive materials at Schlesinger Library, and constant and watchful attention by the librarians. The materials for the course had been carefully organized and catalogued at some point in the past with a finder's aid for archival research purposes. It was a reference tool more valuable than we realized at the time.

We carefully opened the aging onion-skin pages to photograph them. Beyond the notations on Wright's membership in the class there was another name that would later prove significant to us – Margaret Stone. Her father, we learned, was Shepard Stone – the American journalist and former *New York Times* reporter who was dispatched by the State Department to Berlin to become John McCloy's public affairs liaison and chief spokesperson, after McCloy was appointed by President Truman as High Commissioner for the occupation of Germany at the end of WWII.[88]

Stone had gone on to become a close confidant of McCloy's and deeply involved with banks and foundations that McCloy had directed. He was heavily involved with the U.S. State Department programs tied to the Central Intelligence Agency, which worked with privately held or anonymously created front organizations that funded the CIA's clandestine projects. They included not only the Ford Foundation, where Stone was a high-level executive, but two important foundations in Texas and another in Boston that channeled money into secret propaganda programs involving the CIA-influenced publishing world.[89]

More importantly, just 18 months before Wright and Stone's daughter became classmates at the Radcliffe summer course, Shepard Stone had taken over as the head of the American Committee for Cultural Freedom and its parent organization the Congress for Cultural Freedom (CCF) – the beating heart of the cultural cold war propaganda program, both domestic and foreign. It served as a privately-funded front organization for the Central Intelligence Agency and the U.S. State Department's more clandestine propaganda operations. The CCF became a principal mechanism behind the money-laundering banks, front foundations and other organizations that secretly shoveled money into the CCF's media infiltration efforts – and kept secret the Committee's ties to journalists, writers, artists, and to the publishing industry.

Margaret Stone later married Gordon MacDonald, a scientist who, among other things, designed high-tech surveillance systems for the CIA, including motion-triggered landmines protecting border perimeters during the Vietnam War. In 1994 he was awarded the Seal Medallion, the agency's highest civilian honor. [90] His wife became a senior writer involved in security matters for Mitre Corporation, the CIA contractor for which her husband worked.

* * *

Robert Storey was not only a public participant in these patriotic-driven anti-communist intelligence operations, he had helped create them. The tentacles reached deeply into America's legal and business communities.

As I probed congressional reports and reporting about front foundations funding CIA intelligence networks and operations, most particularly the massive media infiltration and subversion that was a hallmark of recruiting within the American cultural milieu, I began to recognize what a significant role Storey and his co-founder of the Southwestern Legal Foundation, Karl Hoblitzelle, had played in this secret propaganda war.

Front foundations that hid the intelligence community's role in pushing the anti-leftist and anti-communist perspectives of the American elite before the public, domestic and foreign, had included something called the Independence Foundation, based in Boston, which had been exposed in the mid-1960s as a dummy foundation to launder money into CIA programs. Its principal officer was a prominent Boston lawyer, Paul Hellmuth, of the Boston law firm Hale and Dorr.[91] He was also a trustee of the University of Notre Dame, and a trustee of the Brown Foundation, identified by members of the National Student Association in 1967 as a CIA front providing funding for their organization, naming Hellmuth as their CIA contact.[92]

When I had told Charlotte Robinson of my interest in Helen Venn's connections with the intelligence community, she had made a point of noting that Richard Venn had held prominent "but somewhat controversial" roles, with the Boston Museum of Fine Art. I was unsure of the significance. He had been a director of special projects at the Museum and later a director of educational programs there. Then I discovered that Hellmuth was one of his close associates and a museum trustee.

The Independence Foundation, and a Texas-based dummy foundation for the CIA, the mysterious Kentfield Fund – which a Texas newspaper reporter in the late 1960s tracked to a telephone answering service in Dallas – were simply money-laundering operations.[93] But those like the Hoblitzelle Foundation and the Southwestern Legal Foundation in Dallas, and the Hobby Foundation in Houston, were legitimate foundations, and still a part of this secret world – the same one that had subverted the leadership of the National Student Association and virtually controlled the student organization's international activities going back to the late 1940s.[94]

The Congress for Cultural Freedom and the private intelligence network to which Wright's own father was so closely connected, were branches of the same tree. And the Radcliffe Publishing Procedures Course, and the American University in Cairo, were part of that same network. Under those strictures, coincidence seemed a feeble way to explain how Wright should land at both.

As I realized how the Road to Radcliffe had taken Wright to Egypt and deeply into this elite world of intelligence connections, from which he emerged eventually as a prominent and influential journalist, I still found myself wondering one other thing.

Whatever happened to the shiny red MG convertible? It hadn't driven itself back to Texas. It was one of those questions to which I wouldn't find an answer. On the more important questions over Wright's path to a prolific journalistic career, the answers would come more readily.

CHAPTER FIVE

AN AMERICAN OUTPOST

Designs follow patterns, and they repeat themselves. I was looking for patterns. If Helen Venn's role in Lawrence Wright's journey into journalism was no accident, if his conscientious objector award and matriculation to American University in Cairo were not chance events, then what was the purpose? I was already seeing evidence that all were tied to clandestine programs of recruiting into publishing and educational arenas. Had Wright been ushered into the world of the cultural Cold War, a world that has shadowed democratic-inspired journalism with its own dark versions of truth? [95]

Wright's journey to Boston and to New York and then to Cairo in the summer of '69 was filled with coincidences – and clues. His conscientious objector approval preceded a string of lucky events: a mysterious list of qualified overseas service organizations handed him at the U.N., his chance meeting an hour later with Christopher Thoron, the fact that AUC needed teachers desperately at the precise moment of Wright's own desperate need – his two-week deadline looming to find a public service job – and then his hasty approval from the draft board despite strict requirements for Selective Service waivers for conscientious objectors.

On the surface his story, as he told it, seemed as plausible as any, and in 1986 his account had circulated to good reviews, even from the *New York Times*. A believable self-portrait of a young man in the throes of conscience casting about in his disappointment over American patriotism and militarism and reflecting on his rejection of his father's patriotic world. How many similar stories were played out by the tens of thousands in that era among young men who – in the common world that Wright pretended was his own – were wrestling with that evolving American culture of the 1960s?

But was it believable, and was it likely? Moreover, was his account true or – as the steadily mounting evidence suggested – narrative fiction? How did Wright – if his memoir was indeed a cover story designed to protect clandestine relationships and hide the assistance in his career by a network of patriotic, elite and influential anti-communists – fit into that picture?

There was a trail. And there were resources to uncover its destination.

To understand the direct role that the friends and associates of Wright's father would play in the intelligence networks of psychological warfare would require a journey through time, and deeply into the lives of this intelligence community's most prominent players. Sometimes the clues lay hidden behind events obscured by time, in brief mentions within the interior of a news story on another subject, a casual reference in a public coverage of such mundane things as weddings, or parties, or public speaking engagements, small fragments from which to construct a roadmap. And as this journey continued, what would emerge was a landscape of imperial authority – a patrician protectorate of influence and control of which intelligence was only a part, and propaganda a tool, and in which powerful interests in Texas would play a prominent role.

* * *

As I began to dig for clues in the archives of history, looking for evidence of intelligence ties beyond those I found at the Radcliffe Publishing Course, I noted that in the summer of 1966 – three years before Lawrence Wright's travels from Radcliffe to Cairo, there was an *espionage* scandal in the Egyptian capital.

The government in Cairo under President Gamal Abdel Nasser banned distribution of an Arabic literary magazine called *Hiwar*. The magazine, the government said, was a front operation for the Central Intelligence Agency's pro-west, anti-communist propaganda.[96]

In fact, *Hiwar* was directly funded by the Congress for Cultural Freedom, itself a front organization for the CIA into which money had been funneled secretly by private foundations, some of them dummy corporations controlled by the CIA, others legitimate foundations whose leadership included prominent business figures. Several hailed from Texas, including those tied directly or indirectly to Wright's father and his father's mentor, friend and boss, Robert Storey, and their Dallas protégé Karl Hoblitzelle.

The disclosures over *Hiwar* made only minor mention in newspapers in the U.S., but they became significant, contributing to rising tensions between the U.S. and Egypt that preceded the Israeli-Arab conflict in 1967, Egypt's increased alignments with and aid from the Soviet Union, and its suspension of diplomatic relations with the U.S. in June of 1967. The action by Nassar stopped distribution of the popular Arabic literary journal that had been launched in the early 1960s, ostensibly as a way to bring new Arabic writers and their literary explorations to people throughout the Middle East – and the Western world. It had been much praised in its work, particularly among Westerners.

The banning of *Hiwar* evolved from the exposure of the identifiable existence of a sophisticated media intelligence and propaganda operation in the Middle East run by the CIA with funding through front organizations that included the Ford Foundation. The magazine had played an important role in spreading Western ideology and culture throughout the Middle East as part of the U.S. Psychological Strategy Board's larger psychological warfare program directed by C.D. Jackson, a writer and editor within the Time-Life empire, and a veteran of WWII military intelligence activities. [97]

Those propaganda efforts, the world would learn eventually, used writers, artists and other cultural figures, witting and unwitting, and organizations with which they interacted as part of a global strategy to influence public opinion through clandestine efforts to control the narrative on Western culture and values.

How deeply that U.S. intelligence community was weaving itself into the fabric of Middle East politics and building a spy network has never been fully visible – particularly with regard to the American University in Cairo – which began life in Egypt as an Episcopal ministry shortly after World War I. It's conversion into an intelligence outpost was often hinted at but always denied. Even within the past five years published criticisms of the American University in Cairo for suspected links to the CIA were briskly and quickly refuted and rebuffed by university and State Department officials there. But the clues to the CIA's interest in AUC had been building long before Lawrence Wright accepted his sudden and, he said, unexpected appointment to a teaching position at AUC.

In fact, AUC had long been an important outpost in the intelligence network dating to the CIA's earliest days. Allen Dulles, director of the early CIA, and his brother, former Secretary of State under President Eisenhower and long an influential government advisor, John Foster Dulles paid special attention to AUC. Most significantly AUC was also on the radar of John J. McCloy – the "Chairman of the American Establishment," as the *New York Times* characterized him. His son, John McCloy Jr., would later become a long-term trustee of American University in Cairo. There were other close intelligence connections. Ambassador Frank G. Wisner II, who long served as an advisor to the AUC board of trustees, is the son of Frank Gardiner Wisner, CIA and State Department operative, director of the CIA's Office of Policy Coordination and propaganda programs under Allen Dulles. Indiana University Chancellor Herman B. Welles was also an honorary member of the board.

The Dulles brothers' law firm, Sullivan and Cromwell in New York, and John McCloy's law firm, Milbank, Tweed, Hadley & McCloy, were both deeply involved in the American intelligence communities during the Cold War, and benefited from those relationships in their representations of the oil industry and other companies around the world. The Rockefellers were clients of McCloy's firm. The Dulles firm represented major energy clients and related industry, including, before the war, the German chemical and pharmaceutical giant I.G. Farben, known as "the Devil's chemist," for manufacture of Zyklon B gas, used to murder at least a million people in Nazi concentration camps. Its principal executives would escape prosecution, or receive light sentences, later commuted.[98]

Those coinciding interests – intelligence and oil – would merge in ways that would be reflected in intelligence training, recruiting and outreach programs at American University in Cairo – just as they had at dozens of universities in the U.S. and other countries, again supported by foundations and banks affiliated with and controlled by this power elite. The Ford Foundation became a major supporter of those efforts, channeling millions of dollars into intelligence operations, as did the U.S. State Department through its United States Aid for International Development (USAID) programs and its related scholarships and cultural exchange programs in which Storey was so active.[99]

* * *

As I probed records of AUC going back into the '60s, I confirmed Wright's own acknowledgement in his memoir that AUC's president during Wright's teaching fellowship had been publicly outed as an operative with the CIA. Christopher Thoron – the executive director of AUC's New York office when Wright said he wandered in off the street – had then taken over from AUC dean and interim president Richard Crabbs, who signed Wright's original grant applications.[100] As I explored, I found records of USAID's extensive assistance programs and contributor funding of the English Language Institute (ELI)– a major Western culture initiative in the region for recruiting witting and unwitting intelligence assets, headquartered out of AUC.[101]

I also found a copy of a report by an Inspector General for the Central Intelligence Agency, analyzing the fiscal efficacy – not a positive report in this case – of CIA training programs and missions being run out of the university in the era of Wright's attendance.

Studying trustee minutes over decades, researching other records of the university, including books written about its history, I would find detailed records of AUC's interrelationship with U.S. foreign policy and intelligence gathering.[102] The AUC university press would become an active publisher of both Arabic and English-language editions of books distributed across the Middle East that supported a positive view of the U.S. amid controversy over America's big-footed imperialism and "pollution" of Arabic and Islamic cultures through western media.

Ford Foundation grants helped sustain the university's reputation within Egyptian culture as a place where students from throughout the Middle East could learn in English about English-based cultural ideas. It was under McCloy's tenure as a leader of the Ford Foundation that such anti-communist intelligence interests appear to have first flowered there.

In addition to the Ford Foundation, John McCloy would lead numerous organizations with ties to the intelligence community, including the Rockefeller Foundation, and particularly the Council on Foreign Relations. All of those in one way or another had ties to AUC. So would McCloy's immediate predecessor in the German occupation after the war, Lucius Clay. McCloy would lead the World Bank in developing lending and reparations agreements after the world war. And as he participated in the development of the first "civilian" U.S. intelligence agency, he would endorse the type of clandestine intelligence that required "black bag" jobs: civil disruption, assassination, and funding of right-wing dictators in Latin America, Africa, Asia, the Middle East and elsewhere.[103] The CIA would conduct proactive campaigns of political interference in democratically-elected foreign regimes that opposed U.S. foreign policy. And evidence would surface in the public record of its involvement in domestic political events.

McCloy's perspective on the functions and ethics of intelligence collection and espionage, according to biographer Kai Bird, stemmed from McCloy's years of investigating an incident of sabotage just prior to World War I on Black Tom Island, New Jersey. Train cars loaded with a reported two million tons of munitions, worth $20 million then, were destroyed in an explosion carried out by German spies, killing four, injuring others. He pursued and eventually won a reparations lawsuit with Germany that he'd taken on shortly after his graduation from law school. The experience took him deep into the world of German and foreign espionage activities, and that knowledge would become a factor in his influence over how the original CIA was created, including in the language of the charters that created its authority.

McCloy's path would cross repeatedly with Robert G. Storey – the never-mentioned political and ideological influence in Wright's own personal history – who would help develop the clandestine network of which McCloy, former CIA director William Donovan, and the Dulles brothers also were principal architects.

Programs over which Robert G. Storey was influential included particularly scholarship and exchange opportunities for politically-attractive students from politically or culturally-active families in targeted areas seen as susceptible to communist influence in Latin America, Asia, Africa, Europe as well as the Middle East. Those programs became tools not only at AUC, but at other American universities in Beirut and lesser Middle East outposts – and also in universities across the U.S. The creation by Storey and Karl Hoblitzelle of the Southwestern Legal Foundation – whose focus went beyond national and international law to the interests of Texas and international oil industries – would be an active player in both the politics and intelligence arenas of influence over Middle East oil and its related political future over the next 50 years.

* * *

While Storey and John McCloy shared close relationships with others in the intelligence community, particularly with Allen Dulles before and after his appointment as director of the newly-minted CIA – their direct interaction, at least from the public record – appears limited. Government records on Robert Storey in connection with the CIA through declassified materials proved very spotty at best. Freedom of Information requests on Storey – as they would on Wright's father – turned up at times with denials for "national security" reasons. But records in university archives, presidential papers and donations of private collections by related parties, were often of more help. I traveled to Amherst where McCloy's own personal papers were archived and spent days exploring his correspondence, diaries, and other materials for links to the Texas foundations and clandestine operations supporting the Cold War.

Records showed that McCloy traveled to Texas in the 1950s and 60s to attend both Southwestern Legal Foundation events and meetings with members of the Dallas Citizens Council and the Dallas Council on World Affairs – all of which had direct links to the public-private intelligence community that was so active in Dallas. Records of his direct interactions with Storey were harder to find.

Storey was the author of books on legal and political matters and president of the American and International bar associations. He had served as dean of the Southern Methodist University law school and on the U.S. Civil Rights Commission and the Hoover Commission. Storey has also been chairman of the State Department's Board of Foreign Scholarship, where he worked closely with the dean of Radcliffe College, Bernice Cronkhite. His influence was evident throughout the Warren Commission investigation, including McCloy's appointment to the Warren Commission itself. Yet he, like John McCloy, maintained a relatively low public profile for someone so active in the foreign policy affairs of state.

Storey had enlisted in World War I. He had studied law sufficiently to pass the Texas bar and had become involved in Republic National Bank, the Texas oil and gas industry, as well as the academies of law in Texas, particularly in Dallas. He had founded Lakewood State Bank and Trust, where he had hired Wright's father in 1960. Storey had enlisted in the military for World War II and become involved in intelligence operations, including parachuting at one point behind enemy lines in occupied France for intelligence purposes.[104] He prosecuted war criminals.

McCloy had served actively in the military leading up to World War I and contributed his service in WWII as Assistant Secretary of War under Henry Stimson. He became an advisor to President Roosevelt, oversaw the internment of Japanese Americans during WWII and opposed under President Truman the dropping of the atomic bombs on Japan. He also served with Robert Storey on the Hoover Commission for the reorganization of the federal executive, and he and Storey would both be influences in decisions in the nation's intelligence and counterintelligence directions.

Their extensive connections in law, banking and business were what led each to the post-war disposition of fascist Germany and made them influential – by virtue of prosecution decisions made during and after the

Nuremberg war crimes trials by Storey, as executive trial prosecutor, and by McCloy as High Commissioner for the occupation of Germany. Both men played major roles in the formation of the Office of Strategic Services (OSS), the precursor to the CIA.

Though he maintained a low profile before the general public, in spite of his powerful influence in government affairs, McCloy like Storey was deeply entrenched in the elite circles of American business, law, banking and academia. He served roles on international disarmament, and became an advisor to President Kennedy. He served along with Allen Dulles on the Warren Commission in its investigation of Kennedy's assassination. Robert Storey, who was influential in the appointment of members to the Commission, worked in Texas through the state's Attorney General to prevent a separate, independent, Texas-based homicide investigation of Kennedy's murder.

Storey's intimate involvement in the CIA-linked Republic National Bank of Dallas and his close partnership with Karl Hoblitzelle, who made millions through his ownership of theatres in Texas and later in the oil and gas industry, and became Republic's chairman emeritus, were also significant in the development of the secret funding of the publishing propaganda network. By the time it was exposed in 1968, hundreds of millions in funding from the Hoblitzelle Foundation had secretly supported the Congress for Cultural Freedom, the operative arm for foreign and U.S. propaganda campaigns developed by the CIA through entities like the Franklin Books program, through the work of individuals like Helen "Doily" Venn, and through academic scholarships and exchange programs to bring anti-communists to positions of authority and influence within American and foreign cultures.[105] The money would send major American literary figures like Dwight Macdonald and Robert Lowell into the psychological battlefields of culture, even as they participated in leftist protests, causes and organizations. Moreover, it would fuel a secret relationship with the titans of American publishing. [106]

* * *

Hiwar magazine's purpose as a front for CIA propaganda was exposed through revelations about its funding from the Congress for Cultural Freedom and that private organization's direct relationships to the Central Intelligence Agency – though less clear at the time was the participation of the Ford Foundation and by the powerful network of anti-communists that included McCloy and Storey.

The medium through which this influence and shadow-government was extended required more than social encouragement, politics and hope. It required intelligence and information, and allies in both the media and the CIA where cultural programs originated. For this private network of conservative anti-communists, the CIA's operation capabilities allowed them to command a virtual private army that conducted foreign policy outside the strictures of open government.

Later, those intelligence ties would take different forms, and in the 1990s the network of influence would involve a growing list of private intelligence and security firms that include in their work close links to journalists. CIA-funded Palantir, Blackwater and the Stratfor security firm in Austin, Texas, which describes itself as a geopolitical publisher, are among them, offering risk intelligence for business and political clients, and working closely with intelligence sources. It's founder, George Friedman, and partner and former CIA intelligence officer Fred Burton, I would find, maintained close ties with Wright and heavily promoted his book *Looming Tower*.[107]

Stratfor had drawn unwanted attention after its computer emails were hacked in 2011 and given to Wikileaks, showing the firm had engaged in spying on community activists on behalf of corporate clients.

Hank Albarelli would later tap sources within the intelligence community to explore Wright's association with Stratfor. That relationship involved more than Stratfor's promotion of Wright's book, *Looming Tower*. His anonymous source, Hank said, indicated 'intelligence sharing," between Wright and Stratfor intelligence gatherers. What other such relationships Wright might have had never surfaced.

Recognizing those links to Wright would have been virtually impossible, and the unspoken secrets of Radcliffe Publishing Procedures Course likely never revealed, but for Wright's own cover story – so close to the truth. But finding the backstory would prove more complicated. And it necessitated understanding AUC's relationship to the CIA.

* * *

Uncovering the tracks that explained Wright's intelligence connections and the intrigue that was created by the powerful cadre of men around John McCloy, Robert Storey and their establishment friends, involved understanding McCloy's own experience as a young and ambitious attorney who came to the perspective that protecting the American way of life required a good deal of secrecy – especially over the intelligence community's media interests.[108]

Those hidden media ties may have begun with patriotic gestures and concerns, but manipulation of the American cultural system by virtue of political propaganda, disinformation, and news media subterfuge fostered by these secret agendas reflected at times the very sorts of anti-democratic practices employed by America's ideological and political enemies, deployed by us against them.

While that secrecy eventually eroded around the world – with significant parts of the network exposed beginning in 1967 in *Ramparts* magazine's accounts of the National Student Associations secret CIA relationships – its most effective audience for propaganda had become not foreign nationals but the American public itself, which was in the dark about those inappropriate relationships.

The creation of a propaganda success story required the recruitment of writers, editors, media owners, publishers and others who either cooperated with the American spy network wittingly, sympathetically, or unwittingly. As I pulled apart these associations, I began to find the missing pieces of the puzzle. But the question remained.

Where exactly did Wright fit within that picture?

***

It seemed that Lawrence Wright was coming to a point of involvement in that elite network as a writer and journalist, with the promises of privilege and access that came with it, just as the evidence of that network's powerful influence was surfacing within the public realm. The unmasking of the intelligence ties and motives of the magazine *Hiwar* was among the first of those incidents.

Founded in the early 1960s, *Hiwar* had billed itself as an Arabic literary journal that offered opportunities to publish and to contribute to the social and political commentary of the region. It also paid writers well for the privilege and at the same time created a format for the advancement of those writers and their ideas. But the money to found and operate the magazine came from minions of the American spy agency.[109]

In April, 1966 the *New York Times* detailed the growing role of the Central Intelligence Agency in sophisticated U.S. spying techniques around the globe – including the development of high-altitude surveillance. The *Times* noted at the bottom of its story the secret funding and influence over the content of foreign magazines and books to sway public opinion in foreign countries and at home. *Encounter* magazine and *The Paris Review* served the CIA's cultural purposes in Europe, and the courting and promotion of poets like Robert Lowell and writers like Dwight Macdonald – if not always productive for the agency – served another. They were parts of a whole, like the funding for Jackson Pollock channeled through the New York Museum of Modern Art, and the funding and close CIA ties to the Boston Museum of Fine Arts – where Helen Venn's husband Richard held an influential position – and worked closely with Hellmuth, the prominent Boston attorney on the museum's board, who directed other Boston-based, CIA linked foundations.[110] The scraps of history were telling but were obscure, and never cohesive to explaining the whole story, since they were reported piecemeal, periodically. Journalism, as always, in a hurry, and a step out of context.

Other stories exposed other bits of the foundation funding mechanisms and its behind-the-scenes work in creation of cultural activities in the arts that encouraged anti-communism, in cooperation with other efforts to dissuade the world from communist economic and social ideas. Subsequent stories would shed light directly on the involvement of Texas organizations like the Hoblitzelle Foundation, the M.D. Anderson Foundation and the Hobby Foundation – the latter created by the owners of the *Houston Chronicle* – and the hundreds of millions of dollars channeled through those foundations into psychological warfare programs of the CIA.

Tantalizing connections to other Texas players would surface as well, to federal judges in Texas, Sarah Evans Hughes, and Leon Jaworski, who had also worked on the Nuremberg Trials prosecution team and had close ties to Storey and the Hoblitzelle and Hobby foundations, and to other foundations in the aggressive and well-connected Texas banking community.

* * *

As the country emerged from World War II with the mantle of international responsibilities on its shoulders, its unelected leadership – those in positions of power in finance and law – were also driven by fears of what the world might look like for them, and others in power elite, should communism spread. Development of a civilian intelligence organization that included ideological warfare was a response to those fears. A system designed to involve universities, publishing houses, international cultural exchanges, student organizations, scholarship programs, to develop "assets" within the American media cooperatives that supported these ideological goals helped produce a multi-pronged intelligence juggernaut. But, could those who created this patriotic fervor be trusted to remain democratic?

As the American propaganda network was exposed for its operations around the world – promoting of literary journals like *Hiwar* in Beirut and *Encounter* in Europe, Radio Free Europe to broadcast propaganda into the Soviet bloc, related programs involving university presses in the U.S. and abroad, and the coopting of student organizations in the U.S., Asia, Africa and the European continent – parts and pieces of the propaganda machine became visible.

When *Ramparts* published in 1967 their startling exposé of the CIA infiltration of the National Student Association, the CIA's suitcases full of cash, political intrigue surrounding their assistance, the foundation grants, and sophisticated recruiting programs creating academic opportunity, they created a corporation of influence. While the exposés were more widely reported after public testimony in congressional hearings, it was not until the book *Patriotic Betrayal* by Karen Paget that the depth of the intelligence community's involvement in student movements and the cultural upheavals of the '60s was fully detailed.

The intelligence community's use of such opportunities was reflective of a patriotism corrupted by power, demonstrated by its secret recruiting of witting and unwitting leaders of the National Student Association. Paget notes the influence of former military intelligence officers who had served in the war, at the initiation of the NSA. It speaks to the lengths to which those influential in this "deep state" would go to develop intelligence assets as weapons in its anti-communist psychological warfare. It was aggressive and purposeful, and hidden for a reason that extended beyond counterespionage, into actions that endangered a democratic society.

History suggests and in part documents that the web of influence created by this public-private intelligence partnership began in earnest around the German occupation and in the wake of the Nuremberg war crimes trials. Robert Storey and John McCloy were both decision-makers over which suspected war criminals would be prosecuted, who would escape prosecution, and who among the convicted would be pardoned later. Those decisions, history now shows, became the fertile soil in which the American intelligence community took root.

If the seeds of an orchestrated public-private intelligence community – a deep state of governance outside the control of the democratic electorate – were planted in one spot, it was in Nuremberg amid the associations that were formed there in the post-war occupation of Germany and the rebuilding of Europe. Those influences were to flower in a post-war reaction to the horrors and brutality of the war and the genocide that it spawned. But they also nurtured the growth of post-war American imperialism. [111]

As I came to appreciate that history, I could see more clearly how important the institutions of intelligence had become in the Cold War, from the creation of a worldwide cultural propaganda network to the use of institutions like the American University in Cairo as intelligence outposts. In that context, Wright's own path from Radcliffe to AUC had a deeper meaning. And, his fabrications in explaining that story began to make sense. I felt I had turned over something significant.

* * *

I asked Jeffrey Marck, a long-time U.S. expatriate, translator and teacher of English in Cairo, to visit the American University in Cairo archives to request records on military conscientious objectors who performed their public service requirements at AUC from the 1960s and 70s. He identified Wright as one of those conscientious objectors and asked the archivists for related records. There were still five years remaining in the university's 50-year privacy rule for students, but archivists agreed to release some of Wright's student records because he was a public figure.

As noted, those records were informative for what they did and did not include. Missing were the chains of notifications and approvals, authorizations, and reports to the Dallas draft board recording that the requirements for C.O. public service were being met. Other C.O.s who also found positions at AUC in that era, or those of which we became aware from our inquiries, showed direct communications by the university with their draft boards. But there was no letter in the file to or from the Dallas draft board showing Wright's successful completion of his two years of mandatory service, or recording the draft board's approval for Wright's service as an AUC English teacher. Nor anything else.

What the records did show was that Wright's initial application in New York for the AUC English Language Institute teaching fellowship – the university's most well-funded department, supported by generous Ford Foundation grants and USAID assistance – was dated September 8 – well over a month after the Radcliffe Publishing Procedures Course had ended. [112] His formal application was apparently filled out at AUC in late September, at least eight weeks after he'd indicated he'd received his notice of approval for conscientious objector status. And a memorandum on his financial award for the English Language Institute's TEFL program – Teaching English as a Foreign Language – would prove interesting as well.

The records would show several interesting things, in fact. Wright, who had married in Greece the summer after he left the U.S. to teach at AUC, was joined by his wife Roberta Murphy as a graduate fellow in the linguistics programs at AUC that next year. She was also admitted to the graduate program on a Ford Foundation grant for a two-year program that would have ended in 1972, a year after Wright's own. But Roberta would leave the program prematurely, some months before Wright's program ended.[113]

A note to Wright within the file indicated that his wife had been granted permission to finish her graduate degree remotely, with a research paper. Christopher Thoron had assured Wright in a memo that the university would pick up the cost of air fare for Roberta to return to the United States, apparently over an illness in her family.

The record included a TEFL award Letter for Wright's fellowship appointment – signed by a member of the board of trustees on September 18, 1969 – outlining payments for his 12 hours of teaching weekly, a stipend paid in Egyptian pounds, an annual study grant of $1,500, and free graduate tuition and reimbursement for expenses.

The documents would also contradict Wright's story in his memoir that he flew from New York's JFK Airport directly to Cairo after returning to Manhattan on a hurried roundtrip by bus from Boston, following his application and acceptance the day earlier at AUC's New York office.

The university financial award notes an expense reimbursement for Wright's travel to Cairo, not from JFK airport, but from Boston's Logan Airport, with "44 pounds of excess baggage," also reimbursed. Wright signed the documents on September 22, ostensibly well-after he was in Cairo teaching English. It all seemed back-dated.

His fellowship application would reveal a bit of youthful hyperbole as well. He listed his interests as "scuba diving" and "bull riding" and claimed that he was qualified following his undergraduate degree at Tulane to teach not only English, but also philosophy – and archeology.

Most importantly, the records also exposed another flaw in his story of his two-year C.O. public service duty. His tenure at AUC was approved from September 1, 1969 through June 15, 1971, a full three months short of his Selective Service public service requirement.[114]

But that didn't seem to be a concern to anyone. There was no communication between the Dallas draft board and the university concerning Wright's community service fulfillment, anyway.

* * *

There was a lot going on in the summer of 1969 as Wright was preparing to depart from the United States to Cairo to absent himself from concerns of military service in Vietnam, and the patriot nature of his family's environment, and to find himself as a writer.

The Stonewall riots in New York occurred in June that year while he was attending the Radcliffe course. The Apollo 11 astronauts landed on the moon in July. Woodstock was unfolding in upper New York state in August, the same month that Hurricane Camille killed 250 people along the Gulf Coast. *Life* magazine that summer published the photos of nearly 250 American servicemen who had been killed in Vietnam in a single week. John Lennon released his worldwide hit "Give Peace a Chance." Ho Chi Min died in early September.

A month after Wright arrived in Cairo, the U.S. launched diplomatic talks with the Soviet Union in attempts to bring the Israeli-Arab conflict to a close. There were airstrikes on September 11, 1969 along the Sinai Peninsula and against anti-aircraft installations along the Suez Canal. Air raids over Cairo were frequent in the month that Wright arrived in Cairo – without a visa. He couldn't get one in Egypt, either, since the American Embassy had been closed, though AUC was the "de facto" embassy during the conflict.

Wright would record in his memoir a solo weekend camping trip he took in the winter of 1969. He rented a camel and tent and went off into the desert to experience the solitude. But during the night, he wrote later, he saw distant "orange flashes" from bombings by Israeli jets, apparently hitting the industrial district of Helwan outside Cairo. He described seeing tiny black images of Israeli jets "buzzing like bees" in the distant (and dark) sky. [115]

But raids by the Israelis on industrial targets in Egypt, after American-made F-4s gave Israel full air supremacy over the Egyptian air force, had not occurred until early 1970, at least two months after Wright's supposed observations. Once again, his timeline was flawed – even if his night vision of distant aircraft seemed particularly acute.

The events in the world, the upheavals of cultural ideas of the late 1960s in the U.S., the exposures in the late 1960s of the CIA's infiltration of the media, political, social and student organizations around the world, was being reported for the first time. He didn't mention them. The media that reviewed his accounts never noticed.

CHAPTER SIX

THE FOUNDATIONS OF LOYALTY

The year that Lawrence Wright's *In the New World* was circulating through America's literary culture, I was investigating a quadruple homicide that had gone cold after eight years of unsuccessful police investigation. I used information from sources in the underworld to turn up a suspect, and wound up on the inside of a revived multi-jurisdictional police investigation into the high-profile crime.

It was heady business for a former teenage cop reporter from a gritty upstate daily. Front page stuff. It might have been a long way from the journalistic influence of Lawrence Wright and his literary world. But it brought with it the kind of street credentials that led to better stories – the kind where you find the serious lessons in journalism, both principle and practice, that will test you.

As I pondered Wright's path, I wondered about his own lessons and who had taught them. For one thing, questions about his fealty and loyalty to the truth were seemingly littered throughout his work. I parsed numbers and probed timelines to come to that conclusion. I dug into documents from his graduate studies program and found where the numbers contradicted his narrative. There were many small contractions, false shadings, what appeared as outright fabrications. I began to lose count.

He had told his readers that the American University in Cairo was desperate for English teachers. But the records, gleaned from the university's own archives in Cairo, showed that, in the fall of 1969, teaching fellowships like the one under which Wright was hired were in high demand. The Ford Foundation-sponsored program had 95 inquiries that year for graduate assistance teaching positions, and it received 56 formal applications for those assistantships. Yet there were only 20 positions available. So, while Wright waltzed in the door of AUC's New York office and out again with a fellowship in his pocket in a matter of hours, the majority of applicants who made formal applications that year had been rejected. [116]

It was one of many such stories in Wright's personal history that just didn't add up.

I pondered the improbability of this story as I studied Lawrence Wright's career, his life, his friends, his path, his stated values of religious indifference and rationalism. What had he learned about truth and impartiality, the value of not prejudging, but letting the facts speak for themselves to tell a larger truth. Of listening to people with no preconceived notion or judgment. I started looking for the answers in his writing itself.

He had come to see reportorial "objectivity" – and he was not alone – as outdated in many ways, certainly in narrative non-fiction, and he said as much in his memoir. It was irrelevant to the new boundaries of the new journalism to which he was gravitating, and he made a case for the subjective observer. He wanted a wider use of the personal pronoun, and to inject himself into the story. Many times, he used the tools of a good novelist, telling stories believably and skillfully. Yet he also demonstrated a dangerous willingness to shade the truth, to guide his story toward a pre-conceived notion of what that story might be. I saw it in *Going Clear*, in *Looming Tower*, in his *New Yorker* stories, and most clearly in his memoir of his early life amid the turmoil of the political and social upheavals of the 1960s-80s.

He had hidden from his readers the important influences that paved the path for his journey to become a writer. In doing so, he had hidden also his loyalties to a powerful and influential intelligence network engaged since the Cold War in propagandizing the American public and selling the virtues of Western capitalism to the world.

How deeply, I wondered, did that fealty go. I was looking for clues.

Was Wright, as a writer and journalist of growing influence, with the power of major media behind him, loyal to the truth, or to something else? Despite his protestations, was he loyal to the ideologies of his father's world, those of Robert Storey and Allen Dulles and the private networks of intelligence, instead of independent journalism? They created an architecture of manipulation that infiltrated student organizations, cultivated and placed journalists in positions of trust, recruited and coopted writers, artists, musicians, actors and their enablers to the cause of Western imperialism around the world. And he had traveled on that shadowy underground railway himself, and gotten off at several stops. [117]

The evidence of that network can be seen in the CIA's recruitment of anthropologists, sociologists and political scientists on the campuses of academia across the country and around the world as part of its Cold War strategy. Yet the depth to which its intentions and interests were woven into the fabric of everyday American life made it nearly invisible to those outside these elite networks.[118]

I would come to see that in the value of all of those witting and unwitting assets throughout the universe of American intelligence influence, few were so valuable as a journalist who could be counted on to be loyal to the foundations of a deep state – an oligarchy of influence whose realms of powers far exceeded those granted by any American electorate. Was that the network's attraction to the talents Wright possessed? And if so, what was his attraction to them?

* * *

As high commissioner of the German occupation after World War II, John McCloy guided the cultural messages of Western ideology: democracy in place of communism or socialism, distrust of Soviet ideology and the realities of totalitarian Soviet society, exposing the threat that communist ideas represented within the American culture, and creating an urgency over their exorcism.

According to his biographer, McCloy's power and influence revolved in part around his skills as a negotiator. He was a reasonable man from comfortable beginnings who moved easily among the elite and was respected within those circles. Every president from Roosevelt through Ronald Reagan turned to McCloy for well-connected leadership. [119]

Yet, there were apparently others who were paying attention to McCloy's tendency toward public reticence and thinking perhaps about the newsreel images in theaters in the American heartland, and the nation's new international posture, possessor of an atomic weapon, able and willing to wage a psychological war over a way of life.

McCloy arrived in Germany in 1949, where he replaced Military High Commissioner Gen. Lucius Clay amid Clay's more *aggressive* suggestions toward the Soviets in Berlin involving standoffs with tanks and direct confrontations before Clay's imposition of the famous Berlin Airlift. [120]

As McCloy stepped onto this international stage, *New York Times* reporter Shepard Stone, who had developed early ties to the American intelligence community, was dispatched to Berlin to help organize public communications for McCloy and assist with his public appearances. It would launch a career-long partnership across several institutions.

At the time he was named to the position, McCloy was leading the World Bank in its post-war reconstruction lending efforts. He had become close to the Rockefeller family and taken over as chairman of Chase Manhattan Bank. He was a trustee, and then chairman, of the Ford Foundation, and he would hold similar positions with the Rockefeller Foundation, while becoming chairman of the highly influential Council on Foreign Relations.

Stone had followed McCloy from Germany through each of those organizations and would serve in executive positions in the process, playing a major role at the Ford Foundation as head of International Affairs. Stone helped direct its financial support of projects and programs that were front operations for the CIA; chief among them were those that provided hundreds of millions of dollars in secret funding for the vast network of cultural propaganda organized under the CIA's secret intelligence network.

Organized through linked foundations, banks and other organizations, the CIA was seeking loyal allies in the worlds of not only journalism, but of the social sciences and eventually, most visibly, within student politics. The CIA's operation and manipulation of student peace and political organizations would become a flash point of Cold War cultural intelligence from the late 1940s forward. Exposure of those relationships by the Church Committee in 1976 left an impression that Congress had outlawed the CIA's practice of using reporters' credentials as cover for international spying, and co-opting student leaders for intelligence purposes. Of course, those programs continued. Whatever changes occurred had simply driven those practices further underground.

* * *

In the CIA's international propaganda efforts, the Congress for Cultural Freedom played a pivotal role, operating as an independent private organization, for all public purposes dedicated to the free speech and expression not found in communist countries. But the secret funding, encouragement and development of writers and artists as cultural figures to carry the messages of the CIA and the intelligence elite – wittingly or unwittingly – about Western culture, made the approach almost indistinguishable from their communist adversaries. Some writers and artists and celebrities were seduced by opportunities that ranged from scholarships to publication, to speaking tours to participant roles in international political affairs, and promotion within the arts.[121] The CIA's assistance of 'acceptable' writers as representatives – and influencers – of this Cold War cultural landscape, would color, censor, promote or deny literary and cultural creativity, altering the direction cultural movements, ideas, and communications might have taken, for good or ill, in their absence.

The Ford Foundation's financial support, directly and indirectly through its contributions to organizations like the CCF – and to academic publishing and publishing and media in general – was mimicked on a more clandestine basis by organizations like the Texas foundations created by Texas billionaire Karl Hoblitzelle and protege Robert Storey. While the Ford resources were huge, the Texas foundations also wielded significant financial clout. The $500 million in Hoblitzelle funding for the Congress for Cultural Freedom is the equivalent of nearly $5 billion today.

The Hoblitzelle Foundation's vast resources sprang from the wealth-yielding business ventures of Karl Hoblitzelle, chairman emeritus of Republic National Bank in Dallas, who built vaudeville theatres in 1930s Texas, and later turned them into the Interstate movie theatre chain. Hoblitzelle compiled wealth in oil and gas and was a co-founder, with Robert Storey, of the Southwestern Legal Foundation. His own foundation had a list of high-profile trustees in Texas that included Federal Judge Sarah T. Hughes, who administered the oath of office to President Lyndon Johnson aboard Air Force One in the aftermath of Kennedy's murder, and Leon Jaworski, who served with Storey in the Nuremberg trials, held roles in CIA-funding foundations, and later became special prosecutor in the Watergate affair.

Those trustees, whose fiduciary roles to the trust would compel them to explore the uses of funds granted to recipients by the foundation, never raised questions, according to any available record, about the use of hundreds of millions of dollars from the Hoblitzelle Foundation to fund the Congress for Cultural Freedom as it published CIA propaganda. The CIA-inspired Franklin Books Program – the publisher of books worldwide under a cover of independence, but whose operations involving the CIA's foreign policy interests, were coordinated by the U.S. State Department.[122] Helen Venn was their liaison and recruiter, and brought into the fold many prominent individuals within the media world. Her friend and associate Frederick Praeger, a publisher of educational texts and a Franklin Books executive was a frequent speaker at Venn's classes, a compatriot in cultural propaganda. He was also a member in the late 1960s of the State Department's Board of Foreign Scholarships, of which Robert Storey was chairman.

The Hoblitzelle Foundation disclosures of secret intelligence funding was not the only Texas foundation so assisting. That Texas would play an outsized role in all of that was the result of many factors, but the wealth generated by oil was key. The Hobby Foundation in Houston, where Leon Jaworski served as attorney and advisor and which was created by the family that published the *Houston Chronicle*, was another contributor to such programs.

Foundations like these, and established philanthropies like the Farfield Fund, were the providers of the suitcases full of laundered cash used by CIA operatives to ply foreign policy goals outside of the control of Congress, the judiciary or the executive branch of government. These mechanisms of influence reached across the country from the Texas plains to the Ivy League coast, across oceans, across continents, and across America's cultural landscape.

When U.S. Rep. Wright Patman of Texas, in 1964, disclosed the CIA's use of such fronts for propaganda purposes – inadvertently, but in a public forum – the *New York Times* editorialized against the practice:

"The use of Government intelligence funds to get foundations to underwrite institutions, organizations, magazines and newspapers abroad is a distortion of (the) C.I.A.'s mission on gathering and evaluating information. It means operating behind a mask to introduce governmental direction into cultural and scientific spheres where it does not belong – at least not in a democracy like ours."[123]

And yet, it would seem, the owners and at least some of the management of the *New York Times* had themselves been fully aware of the CIA's Cold War disinformation and intelligence campaigns, and compliantly helpful, even giving berths and briefings to agency players all along. Where was the truth?

* * *

In mid-1967 – as Wright was on a summer break from Tulane before his senior year, backpacking around Europe, Turkey and the Middle East – Shepard Stone was named president of the international Congress for Cultural Freedom and its domestic counterpart, the American Committee for Cultural Freedom.

Stone's quiet appointment occurred even as *Ramparts* magazine was first disclosing to the public that leaders of the National Student Association, instead of being independent in their goals for student activism in democracy, and in world peace and freedom campaigns, were instead paid by and controlled by the CIA to promote anti-communist goals among world youth, and counter similar campaigns by the Soviet Union.

The disclosures of the existence of front organizations in the private sector and secret funding of the NSA and other organizations resulted in deeply critical responses over the coordination of anti-communist books and other publications using private and university presses both domestic and foreign, funded by the CIA, to prosecute anti-communism.

Magazines and broadcast programing like those controlled by the Congress for Cultural Freedom and the foundations that supported it – Radio

Free Europe, *Encounter* magazine, *Paris Review* – when confronted with criticism that those relationships were contrary to a free and independent press and to a democracy based on truthful discourse – the CIA pushed back.

Thomas Braden, a journalist who became a top assistant to Allen Dulles and who directed the International Operations program overseeing cultural propaganda operations against the Soviets, was later a newspaper publisher and political candidate in California. He wrote a defense of the CIA's propaganda efforts in *The Saturday Evening Post* in 1967, calling them essential to defending American security. If such clandestine manipulation was "immoral," he wrote, then he was "glad that the CIA was immoral."[124]

But the readers of the *Post*, that icon of homespun America journalism, knew nothing of the *Post's* own relationship to the spy agency, nor of Braden's fundamental involvement in the programs he had helped craft and deploy.

I could not shake the idea that those programs had limited free expression and the promotion of peace, tolerance and the common good – not to mention coloring forever the literary expression of a half-century. I had written as a college journalist about student associations of the era, only to see now that the NSA and the vast student movements around the world in the 1960s and 70s where not what they had appeared – interested in a more democratic union and individual liberty.

As Andrew Rubin, a Georgetown University English professor, noted in his book, *Archives of Authority: Empire, Culture, and the Cold War*, those manipulations changed the nature and output of world literature, causing certain writers to be favored and their path to publication supported; others, who held other perspectives, were diminished or ignored or their access to reach an audience was undermined, depending on their cultural and ideological perspectives.

As the disclosures of CIA secret manipulations published in *Ramparts* broadened in 1967 and 1968, the issues became the subject of congressional inquiries, hearings and commentary, and produced corollary reporting elsewhere that disclosed other parts of the secretive efforts by this unseen intelligence community to control public perspectives. [125]

But the use of banks, private foundations, law firms and other organizations as sources of influence, recruiting and espionage funding was evidence of a "classified" network of surveillance and intelligence operations. It extended beyond government authority but used the resources of government, that included domestic intelligence gathering – statutorily illegal for the CIA – as points of departure from the perspectives so carefully sewn into the consciousness of the American public about the Cold War threat to the nation.

As author Karen Paget pointed out, the combination of protecting America and American interests – and the elite network of communities that controlled those interests – may have been motivated by American values. But the methods and tactics of those communities still betrayed the intentions of democratic freedoms, and in its hands-on acts of regime change and the destruction of self-determination in foreign countries, had mirrored the totalitarians anti-communists decried.

During this era of unrest, powerful private individuals like John Mc-Cloy and Robert Storey were able to coordinate foundation resources and those of the State Department's U.S. Aid for International Development (USAID), to create a coordinated plan for protecting the infrastructures of power and the entitlements of their elite establishment. Those institutions, more than democracy itself, became America.

It was out of this environment and the programs that composed the substructure of this network that Lawrence Wright's career as a journalist would be launched. I could eventually see his roadmap in my sleep.

He would go from the safety and convenience of a Ford Foundation-paid fellowship for graduate school that covered his public service requirements at AUC directly to a string of obscure magazine jobs – financed through the Ford Foundation. I had also found these publications to be under the surveillance of the FBI's later discredited CoIntelPro network ideological surveillance – and sometimes intimidation – directed at liberal and certainly socialist-oriented publications. That surveillance had occurred throughout Wright's employment at each.[126]

The magazines were considered "progressive" magazines – two of which covered racial segregation and racial relations in education and the third which was a spawning ground for "activist" journalism, reporting on sensitive social issues. As writers and academics have noted repeatedly about the Ford Foundation, it was often considered curious that this elite and very politically-conservative organization gave financial support to liberal organizations, liberal causes, and liberal publications, including those that promoted a leftist agenda, even as the FBI was watching them for evidence of subversive "anti-American" behavior.

But there were good reasons for that.[127] Such funding opened doors to intelligence gathering from within, as well as the opportunities for subtle influence and potential disruption. And some of the publications – like the unique magazine for which Wright worked – had associations in which this intelligence network was interested. I found it curious that Lawrence Wright's career should begin at a magazine dedicated to reporting on matters of race relations in the United States – a volatile area of coverage in which the little magazine, at the end of its life, had begun to stand out.

I would find it even more curious that the magazine's archived files at the Amistad Research Center in New Orleans would show that the information on one of *Race Relations Reporter*'s past employees – who was destined to become the most famous of its staff writers – would appear to have been excised from the records of this historically-significant little magazine.

The archives included records of all its former staff members dating to inception, of its activities in covering segregation and integration, its negotiations for support from the Ford Foundation and other foundations. It included correspondence between the magazine's well-respected director Jim Leeson and McGeorge Bundy, former national security advisor to President Kennedy and then head of the Ford Foundation. Bundy's brother, William, was a CIA agent and advisor to President Lyndon Johnson, and later an assistant Secretary of State in Asia. And the little magazine was well-known among that elite circle of political influence.

There were in these files letters of hires, dismissals and the detail that spelled out the magazine's administrative history. The records seemed intact, chronological and complete, as best we could tell, except that Lawrence Wright's employee file, and all references to him were missing entirely. "Almost," said Joe Taglieri, who spent days reviewing those files by hand, "as if it has been purged." But if the files had been removed, a few things were missed. His service dates were recorded in payroll disbursements and expense claims tied to story projects.

It was not the only place we would find Wright's records to have seemingly "disappeared."

* * *

As Wright recorded his experience at AUC, he noted the air of "espionage" that existed around the university at the time – given that Egypt had cozied up to the Soviet Union and Cairo was awash with Soviet interests. He acknowledged casually "vague" rumors of a CIA presence at the university in Cairo, and described encounters with Soviets who he presumed could possibly be agents. Other than his date-questionable foray into the desert to camp, where he said he witnessed air strikes outside Cairo, he said little of the Egypt-Israeli conflict itself, nor what a crucial role people around AUC had played in those events, nor the battles underway to minimize the Soviets' spheres of influence there.

John McCloy, U.S. State Department records now show, negotiated privately with Egyptian president Gamal Abdel Nasser and maintained a personal relationship with him. McCloy's law firm also played a major role in the legal wrangling around the creation of the Organization of Petroleum Exporting Countries (OPEC). And his son, John McCloy II, would become a longtime trustee of AUC, beginning in the mid-1970s. He remains on the board of trustees. McCloy's relationship and oversight of the Ford Foundation was instrumental in its support for AUC, even as he and McGeorge Bundy sought to blunt evidence of its CIA connections. It was all a close circle.

It continued to puzzle me that Wright's reflections in his memoir never mention his father's benefactor and mentor, Robert Storey. Here was the founder and chairman of the bank where Donald Wright made his career. He was cofounder and president of the Southwestern Legal Foundation where Wright's father served on the investment committee – a fiduciary position requiring his knowledge of the foundation's financial activities. Storey's son, Charles, who was deeply involved in his father's legal and banking ventures, had become a close friend of Wright's father. He was quoted in Donald Wright's obituary saying Wright's father "could have been mayor" of Dallas. [128]All that passed silently under Wright's radar, despite the fact that the Southwestern Legal Foundation – which had its own extensive interest in oil and gas and particularly in the industry's international legal affairs, particularly in the Middle East – was another of the CIA-connected organizations that would play a role in Lawrence Wright's career.

Still, it would be the Ford Foundation itself, with its links to American foreign policy through the State Department and the Central Intelligence Agency, that would be a primary player itself in Wright's career – supporter of not only his graduate studies but of the first three magazines at which Wright worked.

I found additional perspective by studying the creation in the mid-1950s of something called the International Congress of Jurists – patterned much the same way as the Congress for Cultural Freedom had been developed, only focused on the legal communities of lawyers, judges and law school academics around the world. Storey was deeply involved, traveling the world to lead conferences and ICJ organizational meetings.

The ICJ reflected direct efforts by McCloy, Storey, and others within that elite and powerful intelligence network – which included Eli Whitney Debevoise, a prominent New York lawyer with close connections to McCloy, stemming from Debevoise's service as a deputy high commissioner for the German occupation – to hide CIA programs using these foundations and other means to supply under-the-table money for a range of anti-communist Cold War tactics affecting multiple professions and interests. [129]

McCloy was himself directly involved through the Ford Foundation in supplying grants for covert CIA purposes. One of those grants was $250,000 in the mid 1950s to the Southwestern Legal Foundation to support its international legal work, including the recruiting of Western allies and the promotion of Western cultural influence for propaganda purposes. [130]

Covert CIA funding of the ICJ, just as with the CIA's puppeteering of the National Student Association, when exposed in 1967, prompted investigations. The ICJ developments resulted in direct inquires by the Lyndon Johnson administration into the spy agency's relationships with foundations. But it should not have taken much investigation, since prominent supporters of Johnson in Texas were directly connected to those foundation fronts. [131]

The International Congress of Jurists was a priority project of Robert Storey when he was president of the American Bar Association in the mid 1950s and was also closely promoted by McCloy through the Ford Foundation. It received support from the Houston, Texas-based M.D. Anderson Foundation – where Leon Jaworski served as an attorney – contributing a quarter-million dollars to the ICJ operations, including its recruitment of legal scholars and practitioners in India and Asia who were screened for their political perspectives. The money helped fund international meetings of the group, through which this web of Western cultural promotion was battling communist influences. Some of those conferences, including an organizational gathering in India, drew Storey's direct personal participation.[132]

* * *

Wright's wife, Roberta, would take an early leave from Cairo and AUC's English Language Institute to return home and Wright would follow shortly thereafter, his degrees and his teaching assignment – if not the full two years of his Selective Service commitment – having concluded.

A review of a Ford Foundation grant to American University in Cairo, dated June 28, 1965, found among documents in the university's archived records, showed the Foundation had earmarked $308,000 for the university's English Language Institute for a term of three years – equivalent to some $3.6 million in today's dollars. In addition to his Ford-paid tuition, Wright was making 400 Egyptian pounds per month as a teaching assistant – higher than the typical wage of a college professor at other universities in Egypt.

The grant was typical of the Foundation's substantial support over the life of ELI, but didn't reflect all funds Ford spent to promote English language education in the Middle East through AUC and other institutions. The Foundation was engaged with both the State Department and the Central Intelligence Agency in developing a substrata of English language education throughout the Middle East and around the world, also providing personnel and academic contacts through linguistics programs at UCLA, Indiana University, Notre Dame and other U.S. universities.[133]

Grant documents describe the ambition of the Teaching English as a Foreign Language (TEFL) program and of the ELI program as encouraging proliferation of teaching centers and labs in the Arabic world, to encourage Arab grade school and secondary school teachers to acquire those skills, and bring their students into the Western orbit. It was an elaborate plan, and it has continued over the ensuing decades.

Wright would move on in the wake of his AUC experience but would not stray far from Ford Foundation associations as he looked for a job in journalism in 1971. A friend of his wife would help lead him to the series of positions at Ford-supported little magazines while he established himself as a writer in the emerging cultural changes in journalism.

* * *

Roberta Wright's family lived in the south, and Wright would first try the *Charlotte Observer*, a respected American newspaper where Roberta's friend, journalist and author Frye Galliard was then working. Galliard had served as an assistant editor at *Race Relations Reporter* and when the *Observer* turned Wright down for lack of experience – he ended up hired by the magazine under editor Jim Leeson.

Galliard had left the magazine when it appeared it was about to close for lack of funding. Its Ford Foundation grant was being reviewed and was later terminated.

Based in a Victorian-style house adjacent to the Vanderbilt University campus in Nashville, the operation was best known as a "news agency" resource for other journalists because of its unique staff of librarians – larger than the magazine's reporting staff – which gleaned from newspapers and magazines around the country, daily, the most extensive and up-to-date clipping files in the country reporting on American racial issues.

The Race Relations Information Center, under which RRR had been converted in 1969 from a newsletter to a newsprint-style magazine, had a long history of support by the Ford Foundation. By the time Wright arrived as a novice reporter, the RRIC had received more than a half-million dollars in Ford's support. [134]

Galliard worked for the magazine as it converted from its newsletter format, and published eight feature pieces in its first two years. He worked with Steve Nickeson, who later became editorial director and managing editor under Leeson. Galliard, a student at Vanderbilt and politically active there, had left the magazine in early 1972 to go back to North Carolina to work for the editor of the *Charlotte Observer*, Colbert (Pete) McKnight. McKnight was a founding trustee of the Race Relations Reporter affiliate, Southern Education Reporting Service, and its own newsletter, *Southern School News*, also Ford supported.

When I tracked Nickeson down on a Native American reservation in New Mexico, he told me that he had himself hired Wright for the job, but later became disillusioned about his work and attitudes. He said he found him "arrogant," especially for a novice writer, "something of a prima donna," he said. But he said it was clear that Leeson was more disturbed by Wright's cultural perspectives. He said Leeson fired Wright because he felt he was a racist, something that Wright himself – as noted earlier– generally acknowledged in his memoir, but characterized as "unconscious racism," born of his Texas upbringing. Wright would complain in his memoir, however, that he suffered from what today is described as 'replacement theory' – that, as a white male, racial and gender issues were costing him opportunities.

As *Race Relations Reporter* began to explore more sensitive subjects, particularly concerning treatment of Native Americans in the U.S., and to explore difficult racial controversies going beyond segregation – Ford Foundation decided to channel its funds elsewhere. It would continue to support *Southern School News*, where Wright would work for a time after losing his job at *Race Relations Reporter*.

Galliard had been quoted in a story in the *New York Times* in 1972 about the threat to Race Relations Reporter's survival after the Ford Foundation's exit, saying without additional support it would fold. And his prediction was correct. While the Clark Foundation rescued the magazine temporarily, the loss of Ford support killed it. [135]

* * *

Because of Wright's father's connections not only to the Central Intelligence apparatus, but the FBI as well, and knowing that the FBI had done routine surveillance of periodicals and writers behind J. Edgar Hoover's own anxieties about communist subversion and liberal-left media, I had wondered if *Race Relations Reporter* had been a target during Wright's tenure. Many magazines had been subjects of the FBI's notorious – and illegal – domestic espionage program, CoIntelPro.

A Freedom of Information request netted more than 800 pages of documents related to the surveillance of periodicals and included *Race Relations Reporter*. The FBI had tracked not only content but distribution – determining who was subscribing and reading target periodicals, what bookstores and newsstands were selling them, and what the political interests – particularly liberal perspectives – of its readers and subscribers might be.

Documents show they did so by creating relationships with magazine circulation managers who supplied lists of subscribers and vendors, and, in particular, bookstores that sold *liberal* periodicals.

Race Relations Reporter, it turned out, was of particular interest for the FBI as it probed racial unrest and radical organizations like the Black Panther Party, among others. The interest in RRR seemed tied in part to one of its trustees, Carlton Goodlett, the owner of the Black newspaper, the *Sun-Reporter*, in San Francisco. His racial activism and close ties to the Black Power movements, – and his friendship with the American radical Angela Davis – seemed an obvious explanation.

* * *

Wright's tenure at *RRR* was relatively short; he wrote a number of articles but after losing the job and moving to *Southern School News*, he worked on freelance assignments, and later landed a position with *The Progressive* magazine out of its Washington bureau. *Progressive* – another target of CoIntelPro – had become a career destination for a number of up-and-coming journalists over the years. It also received charitable grants – another connection Wright would have to the organizations that had been successfully used by John McCloy, McGeorge Bundy, Shepard Stone and others as a conduit for secret funding for CIA media and intelligence projects.

I noticed that former *New York Times* reporter Judith Miller, a Pulitzer winner for contributions to coverage of Al Qaeda, was at the same time a writer and editor with *The Progressive* and, like Wright, a rising star in journalism. She would cover national security and other issues for the *Times*, but would see her journalistic stars dim after she published stories in the paper about Iraq's alleged possession of weapons of mass destruction. The stories were wrong and she later left the paper under a cloud, going to work for a think-tank that had been founded by former CIA director William Casey.[136]

Wright, in time, would find his "breakthrough" piece in a freelance story he wrote for *Look* Magazine in 1979 – a publication that itself had long-standing ties to the American intelligence community – about astronauts who had walked on the moon. In the course of that research, he said later in interviews, he flew to Austin to conduct an interview and ended up in the company of a restaurant critic for *Texas Monthly* magazine – to apply for a job as a staff writer with the growing and popular magazine.

Curiously, though Wright never acknowledged it, there were other connections to *Texas Monthly* from Wright's own history in his foundation-supported path to a writing career.

The magazine – which became a nationally-recognized literary journal in the genre of slick east coast publications – had been founded in 1973 by Michael Levy, a Dallas native, who had worked his way through a series of jobs that led to a position at *Philadelphia Magazine*, and his subsequent founding of *Texas Monthly*. The culture-oriented magazine with a Texas perspective would grow to a circulation of more than two million.

Levy hired a co-founding editor for the magazine, William Broyles Jr., then an inexperienced journalist, and it was Broyles who six years later would endorse Wright as a new and upcoming staff writer for *Texas Monthly* in 1979.

As I researched those transitions, I noticed an advertisement that had been placed in the pages of *Texas Monthly* in 1978, about enrollment for a new summer course to be offered at Houston's Rice University, where Broyles had distinguished himself as a student. He joined the Marines afterward, went to Vietnam as an officer, and was decorated for his service in, among other things, intelligence operations involving Vietnamese refugees.[137]

That summer course for which Broyles – and Michael Levy – would become founding directors, would end up lasting for 20 years as the Rice Publishing Procedures Course. The expertise for developing the course would come from Lawrence Wright's friend and mentor – Helen Venn – his former instructor for the Radcliffe Publishing course, and reference for his AUC and Ford fellowship applications. Venn was listed with Broyles and Levy as one of the course's original directors.

Another famous alumni of *Texas Monthly*, Daniel Okrent, would also turn up as an original trustee for the Rice University clone of Venn's Radcliffe course. Okrent, the now-famed editor, author, historian and screenwriter, joined *Texas Monthly* not long after its founding by Michael Levy in 1978.

Okrent would go on to a stellar career as an editor and writer for major U.S publishers including Harcourt, Brace, Jovanovic, and Alfred A.

Knopf. Named in 2003 as the first "public editor" of the *New York Times*, he would serve also as an editor-at-large for *Time* magazine, as managing editor for *Life* magazine, and as a writer for *Esquire*. He was a finalist in 2007 for a Pulitzer in history, for his book on Prohibition.

Helen Venn would have other close connections with those who would also connect with Lawrence Wright, including principals of influential U.S. counter-culture magazine *Rolling Stone*. The magazine's founder, Jann Wenner, was a speaker at the Radcliffe publishing course in the summer of 1971, and was a frequent correspondent with Venn.

Archives for Venn's course at Harvard's Radcliffe Institute at Schlesinger Library include a photograph, never before published, of Venn in 1978 with Michael Levy and two of Jann Wenner's co-publishers, Donald Welsh and D. Claeys Bahrenburg. Levy is pictured kneeing, as if kissing Venn's ring. Welsh and Bahrenburg became co-founders with Wenner of *Outside Magazine* in 1978, the same year that they, and Levy, attended Venn's publishing course in Cambridge – and the same year that Levy founded *Texas Monthly*.

Broyles, like Lawrence Wright, would go on to have a much broader literary career. He became an author and screenwriter – helping pen screenplays for directors Steven Spielberg, Ron Howard and Robert Zemeckis, among others, as well as for the Tom Hanks' movies *Castaway, Apollo 13,* and *Saving Private Ryan*. In the Clint Eastwood film, *Flags of our Fathers,* Broyles shared screenwriting credits with former Scientologist Paul Haggis – the man who would later become what Wright called his "donkey," who carried his story in his account on the Church of Scientology.

The investigation was turning over clues to a small and separate world within which Wright was circulating. The cross connections and Cold War loyalties that gave it structure would become like a maze built of coincidence, twisting its way in and out of the world of the Cultural Cold War. In truth, I was coming to see, there was little coincidence about it at all. And despite the exposure of the CIA's hand in student politics, and within the media, those disclosures did not, as supposed, disinfect the agency from its clandestine domestic influence. Though the agency had pledged to stop using journalistic cover for agents, or to recruit reporters as informants within the nation's newsrooms, or infiltrate domestic institutions and organizations, it didn't stop. It just went further underground.

Chapter Seven

The Media Lothario

Writers of non-fiction narratives develop a relationship with their readers through the power of language and well-crafted and well-reasoned ideas; and, if they are honest, truthful, committed to describing as accurately as possible what they have seen and learned, supporting it with well-documented fact, that relationship becomes one of trust, which leads to respect.

The respect that comes of this compact between writer and reader is typically what drives reputation – success in the arena of cultural writing – and the incumbent praise that may come to authors who we revere is a natural thing. But there are other paths to success. Insider connections, promotion, undisclosed support – things that if publicly known could also become a factor in that formula for respect.

Lawrence Wright's own acceptance within the media milieu has been extraordinarily positive. From small and obscure publications like *Race Relations Reporter* and *The Progressive*, he moved over the period of five years to one of the nation's newest and culturally smart magazines, *Texas Monthly*. From there his memoir pushed him into the headier world of New York journalism, to *Rolling Stone* magazine, and finally to *The New Yorker*.

Today his work is generally accepted at face value – seldom if ever examined critically by reviewers, critics or commentators.

That was certainly the case of his book on Scientology; his work on Al Qaeda and terrorism was not only accepted, but almost reverentially appraised by the media itself. Wright is more than a journalist and author, of course; he has celebrity status and has become the subject of stories and commentary himself. But his treatment by the mainstream media has been more than polite; it's been almost uniformly uncritical – with a few international exceptions.

More recently, early one morning, I watched as Wright was introduced as a guest of the MSNBC *Morning Joe* television show. He'd been invited to talk about his recent novel, on a fictional pandemic that – the commentators effused – seemed eerily "prescient." It's a term that has so often been attached to Wright's work that it has become a part of his public persona. Whether it was his screenplay for the movie *The Siege,* which predicted a New York terrorist attack two years before 9/11, or his pandemic creation, that "ahead of the curve" writing and reporting most often made me wonder what kind of access to intelligence Wright may have been afforded. For a reporter, access can make the difference on timing. And timing is everything.

As I examined Lawrence Wright's increasingly detailed history, I found a different face from that which was turned outward toward the media at large – and which accounted for the praise with which he had been received. He was, it began to seem, a product of the media's own self-adulation and promotion. Was it just the warm personality of his interaction with people, his unassuming nature? Given the descriptions I had heard of him by those who were not part of the media fan club, that seemed less likely.

On top of that, I had seen personally that the famed author was not above distorting the truth. He had repeatedly, serially, done so with me, beginning from the time I first approached him and asked to talk with him about his book *Going Clear.* He went to his twitter account to warn his friends to "beware," that he was being stalked by a "reporter/PI" hired by the Church.[138] Over time he dropped the "reporter" description, and claimed I was not a journalist but a private investigator. We had had an email exchange when I first asked him for a conversation about the Church's criticisms of his book and about the defection of a principal source for his work, ex-Scientologist and active critic-apostate Mark Rathbun, who had challenged Wright's characterizations after publication on important issues. In that email Wright had – with exclamation marks expressing his incredulity – asked *"Are you a private investigator?!?"*

I explained that I was a long-time reporter, freelancing.

I wondered how he had come to that conclusion – but quickly unraveled that minor mystery. My friend and former source, private investigator Rick Johnson, had noted on his website my work with his students involving pro bono investigations in the public interest.[139]

Wright had assumed or interpreted what he read into what he wanted to believe. I had not written the reference on Rick's website to that work, but it wasn't ambiguous. If Wright had carried his inquiries further, he would have seen who I was – and who I was not.

Wright would subsequently, frequently and willfully repeat the misnomer – long after he knew it wasn't true. In 2018, in an interview for a local publication in Austin, responding to a question about his book on Scientology, he was quoted as saying that an "incompetent" private investigator had shown up at an appearance of Wright's small band to ask for an autograph. I had indeed used that opportunity to talk with him. But by that time, I had long identified myself as a reporter, working to investigate matters that I wanted to talk with him about. He knew that when he autographed his book for me, with the note, "…you know the story."

* * *

In fact, by then I knew little of the story. But as I pondered this casual disinformation, I wondered how he had dealt with claims of errors in his work. I would find few corrections. But a piece he had written in 1994 – two years after former *New Yorker* editor Tina Brown had hired him as a contributing editor – in which he acknowledged that he had not checked the facts in a story before publishing his assertions – stood out. It involved a story on recovered memory syndrome, and in it he described court testimony from a clinical professor of psychiatry, Dr. Roland Summit of the Harbor-UCLA Medical Center. He detailed in his story what that testimony had been.

But the correction – and a published, if very obscure, apology from Wright – came after a complaint that the account had been fabricated. [140]The doctor had never testified in the case, and instead, the supposed "testimony" had been created by Wright by extracting information about the subject from other sources. Wright's story was also criticized for vastly exaggerating the number of questionable recovered memory syndrome cases in the U.S., a number of critics contended he'd pulled from thin air. [141]

Mistakes happen. Writers are human. But the willingness to write a detailed account of an incident that never happened – an assumption of facts, unchecked – raises natural questions about the consistency of a reporter's due diligence. What of the many personal stories Wright had told in his books and magazine pieces that didn't seem to add up? Maybe no one had called them to question. One of them in particular would stick with me throughout the investigation, and I would never find the key to the story's truthfulness.

In his memoir Wright described an event in his young life involving a cousin, who like his father was also known as Don Wright. The young man, whose mother had passed when he was a young boy, had been orphaned when his father – Wright's uncle – had died unexpectedly. Wright wrote that his father had insisted at the funeral that the young Don Wright come to live with his family in Dallas. And he spent a year there before going out on his own, Wright wrote.

He attended the same high school that Wright attended, Woodrow Wilson High in east Dallas, and I found his photo in a yearbook. But he apparently dropped out after his junior year. Wright wrote that his cousin got a job at the O'Neal Funeral Home in Dallas, and among his duties was driving the ambulance for the city-county emergency service that O'Neal's had provided under a county contract. It was an O'Neal ambulance that had carried President Kennedy's body to Air Force One in 1963. And it was the O'Neal ambulance service that in 1964 had a contract with the Dallas County jail to provide ambulance transportation for inmates – which then included Lee Harvey Oswald's killer, Jack Ruby.[142]

In the course of that work, Wright wrote, his cousin was called upon to transport Ruby to the hospital after Ruby – following his conviction and death-penalty sentence in 1964 for the murder of Oswald – had injured himself at the jail by ramming his head into the wall. Wright said his cousin recounted to the family his conversations with Ruby as they traveled back and forth to the hospital together several times, whenever Ruby needed medical care. Wright dutifully reported in his memoir, some 20 years later – using quotes he'd not personally heard – that Ruby had told young Don Wright that "…they are feeding me cancer."

But the dramatic quote wasn't enough. He extrapolated on his cousin watching Ruby's health fail. Wright wrote:

> Soon he (Ruby) began to deteriorate, becoming markedly thinner, more Oswald-like. Don watched him waste away with every successive ambulance ride. It was sad, but Don had an orphan's attitude toward death and wouldn't waste his sentiment on a man he couldn't save.[143]

It was another story that didn't add up. The timeline was all wrong.

I wanted to ask Don Wright about that myself, but I discovered that he was hard to find. The church in Kansas – in this era of identity theft concerns – refused me information about his baptism date, date of birth, or his full name. For the longest time, I couldn't find a middle initial.

But eventually I would confirm part of Wright's story. An old city directory in Dallas revealed that Don Wright had an apartment in a small complex in East Dallas in 1964, and it listed his employer as O'Neal Funeral Home. But he was only at that address during that year, and in 1965 and afterward, I could not locate him in Dallas or the surrounding area.

I dug into Ruby's arrest and his tenure at the Dallas County jail, where he remained after his death sentence for Oswald's murder as his conviction was being appealed. He would still be there when he died of cancer in January, 1967. I wondered if it was possible that young Don Wright had truly had the opportunity, as Wright had written, to develop a conversational relationship with Ruby during trips back and forth to the hospital.

I studied jail records and reports from the time and tried to track down entry logs to no avail. I read archival accounts of individuals who interacted with Ruby when they worked at the jail. And I noticed two things that raised questions about Wright's story.

There were records from the jail that indicated that Ruby had been treated for a cut on his head at the jail the night he injured himself – but they indicated he had not been transported to the hospital. I found reports from a nationally-known and controversial psychiatrist, Louis Jolyon West – who had deep and long-questionable ties to the CIA and its infamous MK-Ultra LSD behavioral-control experiments. He had been called in to examine Ruby in jail, and had, however, referenced in paperwork a hospital visit. There were contradictions, and the jail record seemed the most reliable. Ruby had been treated only at the jail, his physician had written.

But there was another set of facts that failed to fit as well. Ruby was seldom transported to the hospital from the jail during his three and a half years there, and when he was transported, there or elsewhere, security was extremely tight. Photographs of the era show him flanked by two sheriff's deputies on one of those trips, in the back seat of a police sedan. The need to transport Ruby by ambulance during a cancer-caused illness would have been nearly non-existent – for a very good reason.

Ruby's terminal diagnosis of cancer didn't occur until late December 1966, just days before he succumbed to a pulmonary embolism at Dallas' Parkview Hospital – a blood clot, it was reported, caused by "undetected lung cancer." He had not shown any symptoms or indication of the disease until two weeks before he died.

I wondered how Ruby could have happened to have that conversation with Wright's cousin under those circumstances. By the time Ruby's cancer was discovered, Don Wright had already enlisted in the military, served in Vietnam, been injured and returned home, according to Wright's account.

Wright's story didn't seem to hold together. But he wasn't going to talk about that. And after I did locate individuals named Don Wright in Texas, the right age, and attempted repeatedly to inquire, none responded. I never located Wright's cousin to ask him about his experience with Jack Ruby, or how that story could possibly be true. But I did find his middle initial.[144]

* * *

In time, I approached *Looming Tower* and started first with review pieces that had been written about it. The reviews were impressive, laudatory. Only a few of the reviews I found questioned Wright's conclusions or observations from his five-year reporting journey into the realities of Al Qaeda and terrorism. A veteran of war correspondence, Dexter Filkins at the *New York Times* said he thought Wright should have written more about the hijackers on 9/11, and he also expressed doubt about Wright's use of direct quotes in his book. It wasn't exactly a call-out on a fundamental issue. But Filkins wrote:

> My other complaint is more substantive. Through the enormous amount of legwork, he has done, tracking down people who worked with bin Laden and Zawahiri over the years, Wright has drawn up verbatim reconstructions of entire conversations, some of which took place more than a decade ago. Many of these conversations are riveting. Still, in some cases, it's hard to believe that memories are that good.[145]

Memories are not that good. And reporting quotes that are remembered by others should be handled clearly that way – quoting the speakers as they recount their recollections.

But Wright's handling of that material improved his narrative flow, as Filkins suggested, made it a better read and gave the appearance of more insider access than Wright actually had. But creating quotes is cheating, and any reporter with a truthful relationship with their reader will realize that fabricating quotes is dishonest, not literary. For Wright to remember what he may have heard or said himself at some point in time might be subject to flawed recollection, but at least he would be quoting his own recollection in terms as accurate as possible – and confessing the possible flaws in such recollection. In these cases, he clearly created words to fit his narrative, and give it the aura, if not the substance, of truth.

Wright's practice of doing so has littered his work throughout his career, I would find. It might clutter the narrative to quote an individual recounting his recollection of a conversation between other parties. But to put words in the mouth of someone, without making it clear that they were not the words spoken, denies the reader the opportunity to evaluate the credibility of that recollection.

Still, Wright's quotes were offered as fact. To pretend that the words he described were those that were spoken is either illusion, or delusion. Wright, at one point, quoted in English what supposedly had been said in a cave a decade earlier and ostensibly spoken in Pashtun. Though he claimed more than 600 interviews for *Looming Tower* over a period of about five years, his notes are often scant when it comes to the actual source of his information for those quotes.

Journalists who come to their best work as writers have often also served as an editor at some point along the way. It is valuable training that is hard to duplicate. When reviewing the work of others and working to make stories tight and ensure their accuracy, editor's learn little tricks from which to test a writer's attention to detail. One of those is to be on the lookout for quotes that have multiple attribution. For example, a specific quote followed by "they said."

Wright does it frequently in his work, and it surprised me that it seemed neglectfully ignored by his fact-checkers and editors in numerous stories by Wright in *The New Yorker,* and in his book-length manuscripts. He describes in *Looming Tower* a conversation from 1985 – two decades earlier – between an Afghan military commander, Islamic jihad recruiters there, and a professor who had arrived at the commander's camp with Arab recruits. The commander rejects the two recruits because of a Soviet retreat. As Wright described the incident, the decision prompted a response from the recruits, which he quotes (and failed to source.)

"'If they have withdrawn, aren't we at least supposed to chase them?' *they asked."*

How many times had I seen the same thing? Unless the recruits had answered exactly the same, in chorus, how could he attribute the quote to *"they said."* And, how would he know? A copy editor would have questioned those conclusions just that way. Which one of them said it? What was the exact quote? I wondered if Dexter Filkins' observation had prompted a reaction from Wright. But attempts to reach Filkins were unsuccessful. His review had otherwise been as complimentary as others.

But while publications across the country wrote positive reviews, not everyone agreed over the reliability of Wright's reporting. His book stirred up vigorous commentary on social media on both sides of the fence, and his critics there sensed that his work had been crafted to endorse the "official story" of what had happened on 9/11. Some termed his book "propaganda."

The entire Pulitzer-winning effort had been far less about what happened on 9/11, than about a perspective that Osama bin Laden had created the Al Qaeda terrorist network to exist as dangerous cells around the world and that this terrorist organization was active, laying in wait and a continuing and imminent threat to America. And of course, it delved into what had also been reported earlier – including in a 2003 Congressional report – that outlined a breakdown in communication between the FBI and the CIA over terrorists involved in 9/11 who were under surveillance by the agencies while inside the country, and working toward the World Trade Center attack.

Wright's reporting, as Filkins had noted, simply added more detail – and color – to what had already been reported about that. A non-fiction narrative – with some apparently fictional exceptions.

Jason Burke, a war correspondent for the *Guardian* newspaper in London covered Afghanistan and the fighting there beginning in the late 1980s, and wrote a book about Islam and Al Qaeda. He reviewed Wright's book in 2006 and raised critical questions over Wright's "certainty" on a number of supposed facts about Al Qaeda, the war on terror, and even Wright's own sourcing. He had worked with UK documentarian Adam Curtis on a film about the War on Terror that questioned much of what the American public, and the world, was being told about Al Qaeda. Wright himself referred to a dinner he had with Curtis in London in which he said he offered to show a skeptical Curtis Al Qaeda's "incorporation papers." [146]

Burke's review opened with a description of Al Qaeda as something far less understood than most people believed. It seemed in high contrast to Wright's analysis.

"We know something exists," Burke wrote about Al Qaeda in 2006 in his review, "though what is continually debated. The evidence of its existence is limited to internet sites, intermittent statements and bomb attacks which are linked, with varying degrees of justification, to 'al-Qaeda' by the perpetrators, by the victims or by a variety of other actors." [147]

Burke commended Wright for his on-the-ground reporting in the Middle East, his lengthy list of sources and noted that, while a lot of what the book covered had been earlier reported, Wright's account had added "new detail" to what was known about certain events. Yet he also noted the absence of reliable information to develop that kind of detail. He noted that all reporters in the region had faced huge challenges in determining what was true, and what was rumor, propaganda, or planted information.

"The sole sources of information are selected leaks from 'intelligence sources' of dubious reliability," he wrote about reporting in that environment. "The result is a wash of information, most of it barely worth the few pulses of electronic energy that its dissemination requires."

Specifically, Burke quarreled with Wright's sourcing and citation of "evidence" in *Looming Tower* that supported his arguments.

"Bizarrely," Burke noted, "Wright repeats still-unproven allegations of visits by key al-Qaeda figures to Baghdad. Sketchy references tell us that at least one of the sources is badly-flawed American magazine articles."

He added:

"And when Wright says that Ayman al-Zawahiri, bin Laden's closest collaborator, and Abu al-Zarqawi, the Jordanian militant recently killed in Iraq, set up Ansar ul-Islam, he is in error. Interviews with Ansar members in Iraq in 2002 told me that the group was, in various forms, extant from the mid- to late-Nineties. And, when Wright says al-Zawahiri and al-Zarqawi may have set up the group with the aid of Iraqi intelligence, he is repeating something that is dangerous, very probably false and certainly unsubstantiated. Wright is so unhappy with this apparent 'fact' that he adds a rare asterisked footnote on the page, saying this 'supposition' is based on information from Ayad Allawi, a leader of the Iraqi opposition before the 2003 war who was a conduit for many of the least accurate elements of the prewar claims about WMD."[148]

Burke wondered in print why Wright would include it. But when I read his assessment, I thought of Wright's time under his Ford Foundation-paid days that led to *The Progressive* where he worked with Judith Miller – who had been forced to resign from the *New York Times*, it was reported, over her allegedly inaccurate reporting on the existence of weapons of mass destruction in Iraq – an issue that was a significant catalyst to the U.S. invasion of Iraq. Ayad Allawi had been among her sources on those stories, it was reported.

* * *

In the course of Wright's research into the terrorism of Osama bin Laden, in January, 2004, he published an article in *The New Yorker* talking about time he spent in Saudi Arabia in bin Laden's home town of Jeddah. The circumstances caught my eye.

I was, by the time I read the story, deep into the history of his father's friend, employer-mentor-associate Robert Storey, and the extensive links to intelligence programs all around Wright's early career. I had tracked the links between the Central Intelligence Agency's private support network – from banks like Karl Hoblitzelle's and Fred Florence's Republic National Bank to Riggs Bank, linked through another former Republic president, Lewellyn Jennings. Riggs had been a conduit in the CIA's Iran-Contra scandal. The pieces were creating a picture, and Texas and the connections of Storey, Hoblitzelle and related foundations were important contributors to the anti-communist political espionage that existed in the country. As I recognized Wright's familial intelligence affiliations, it made me wonder who else had noticed.

What caught my eye was Wright's notation in his story that, in trying to do research about bin Laden, he had been denied a visa into Saudi Arabia for over a year. The story implied that Western journalists who might write critically of the Saudi royal family could incur such difficulties. But he had found a work-around. More precisely, a work permit at the *Saudi Gazette*, an English language newspaper for expatriate workers, published by Saudi Arabia's most popular national newspaper, whose editor had hired Wright for a few months, as Wright detailed it, helping train young reporters there in journalism.

The story described working with the novices and the opportunities the job offered him to do interviews in Jeddah about bin Laden. It was a convenient opportunity, and I wondered how he had managed to come by it. I looked into the editors who had hired him, and as I looked, I stumbled across an obscure reference in a file at Wikileaks. Among the millions of documents that WikiLeaks's Julian Assange had published were confidential U.S. State Department cables. I found there the names of the editors who had hired Wright and whom he had worked through at the *Saudi Gazette*. Both had been the object of intelligence debriefings on the Saudi government by a State Department official. The cables had been designated "*confidential*" and pointedly warned against disclosing the identities of the informants – by then in the public domain. One of the cables, among a series of reports on contact with Saudi media over gathering intelligence on the Saudi government, read:

Over coffee in a Jeddah Starbucks, the chief editor of the English-language "Saudi Gazette," Mohammed al-Shoukany, and deputy editor Abdallah al-Shehri (protect both) elaborated on the changes in the Saudi media environment. "The government is pushing this new openness as a means of countering the extremists," al-Shoukany told Riyadh press office. "It's still all about the War of Ideas here, and the American programming on MBC and Rotana is winning over ordinary Saudis in a way that 'Al Hurra' and other U.S. propaganda never could. Saudis are now very interested in the outside world, and everybody wants to study in the U.S. if they can. They are fascinated by U.S. culture in a way they never were before."[149]

The editors were among seven identified as "protected" sources who were privately providing intelligence information, according to the memorandums. I had wondered, logistically, how a single reporter over five years had physically managed to track down 600 interviews, across language and geographic barriers, and then stumble upon sources with intelligence ties and win their assistance. Was it all just coincidence and good luck, or extremely skilled and efficient reporting? Or, did Lawrence Wright have inside help from the intelligence community, public and private – something more than his friends at the Stratfor intelligence operations in Austin might provide – in his massive inquiries into bin Laden and the terrorist organizations that had become the new focus of threats against America in the post-Cold War world. How did he have time in all that to spend a few months schooling young Saudis in the art of reporting?

CHAPTER EIGHT

GOING CLEAR ON LAWRENCE WRIGHT

T
he history of the Church of Scientology is replete with controversy, and anyone who is inclined to pursue information about that controversy will find it. What they are far less likely to find are the details of the Church's response, corrective actions, legislative initiatives, its systematic work against discrimination, and its work with attorneys, lobbying and public relations firms, other clergy, and the string of favorable court decisions that explain the story behind the story of a long history of attacks.

At points in its history, and some of them still recent, governments in a number of countries prohibited the practice of Scientology. In three of Australia's six states, Scientologists were forbidden to have Church materials in their homes. When found, they were destroyed. The Church successfully fought such discrimination over a period of years, and in 1983 sealed the issue through a lawsuit.[150] The suit led to a high court decision over arguments for the Church's recognition, represented by Australia's former solicitor general and Queen's Counsel, overturning such discrimination.[151]

Scientologists there and in other countries were not allowed to send their children to public schools. They were discriminated against in employment. And of the decisions behind those restrictions on religious freedom, many had been inspired by a conspiracy of intent that included the US Central Intelligence Agency, the Federal Bureau of Investigation, intelligence operations in the United Kingdom, Germany, Spain and other countries, and through Interpol – leading to the Church's *Freedom* magazine exposé of ties between top Interpol officials and Nazi war criminals.[152]

In almost all of those earlier cases of what the Church called official "suppression" of the religion, court rulings would over time change the landscape, removing many of the more insidious restrictions against them, though there were and are still intelligence operations ongoing in Germany, Russia, Hungary and elsewhere that seek to limit Scientologists' right to freely practice their beliefs. In Wright's accounts in *Going Clear*, little of that is mentioned.

The Church's fight for human rights – especially in the arenas of mental health – as it has documented, have been supported by prominent and influential individuals not only in the U.S. but in countries around the world. They include the United Nations Commission on Human Rights and its special rapporteur, and the Citizen's Commission on Human Rights, which the Church co-founded with Thomas Szasz,[153] a prominent psychiatrist critical of institutional psychiatry.[154]

But when Lawrence Wright characterized the Church as a potentially "dangerous" entity, which he concluded was not entitled to its status in the U.S. as a tax-exempt charitable organization, he was echoing sentiments expressed long ago by governments that had less interest in religious freedom than in political control. Wright never got into those issues in *Going Clear*.

David Miscavige himself would note at one point that these most recent attacks on the religion – from major media outlets including *The New Yorker*, HBO and A&E Networks and their airing of attacks by former Scientologist and actress Leah Remini – were "nothing" compared to the existential threats against the Church in the past. Yet it is clear that Wright's book, the reporting by the *St. Petersburg Times*, (now the *Tampa Bay Times*), and television programs like Leah Remini's now-cancelled *The Aftermath*, have captured the Church's attention and raised its ire.

Yet some of those stories circulating behind the scenes, over its reactions, never surfaced, like one account of Leah Remini's motives in attacks toward Church officials – the supposed "aftermath" of a request to appoint her to a position within the Church's executive staff as a senior advisor to David Miscavige.[155] Her defection, contend Church insiders who were aware of the issue, was more tied to that rejection, and attempts to draw attention to herself, than to her feelings about – or past practices within – Scientology.[156]

Still, the Church's frustration over its inability to get a fair hearing from those media outlets – and to share evidence and information to mitigate unrestrained and often fabricated or unsubstantiated accusations against it – has consumed enormous amounts of time, effort and money. But the attacks have failed to threaten the Church's survival – as earlier attacks had done – when they were motivated by the same government interests that eventually outlawed discrimination against the religion.

In those days, from February, 1954 when the Church was founded in Los Angeles, and on into the 1980s – and even to the present day in Russia – Scientologists have faced foreign government's willing to arrest and imprison Scientology leaders over their beliefs, as happened in Spain. In the 1960s and 70s members were refused passage into the United Kingdom and were subjects of intelligence activities against them elsewhere. Even within the United States, in a nation that declares that its foundation is based on religious and intellectual freedoms, the IRS's Criminal Investigation Unit in Los Angeles engaged in illegal conduct and constitutional violations that included jimmying open trunks of executive vehicles, break-ins and thefts at the Church and efforts to suborn perjury from Church staff.[157] The FBI's CoIntelPro program of politically-inspired surveillance and smear campaigns included the Church, its founder, and its activities.[158]

More recently, the drama has played out as a war of words, most of them spilled across the Internet in blog postings and websites, but also in newspaper articles, magazine stories and books like Wright's. Both the Church and those who inveigh against it have published attacks against each other, and a lot of it hasn't been pretty. The public media was heavily influenced by the work of Lawrence Wright and Alex Gibney – and evidence of this is borne out by the extensive hate-inspired commentary across the blogosphere that proliferated afterward, and endures.

The Church has complained about the religious intolerance promoted by its critics and assailed major news outlets for their refusal to tell both sides of the story. And it has characterized its critics as liars, criminals and unreliable sources, noting in some cases what it calls "criminal" conduct.

On the last count, the Church has demonstrated ample evidence to document those assertions, but has had difficulty getting major media outlets to listen, or respond.

As I tried to sort through the truth of it all, I wondered how much sorting Lawrence Wright had done as he transitioned from neutral observer – if he ever was – to become essentially the apostate's champion, turning his book *Going Clear* into a compendium of the arguments of the apostates and of other Church critics. He leaned heavily on his predecessors – though his publicists and marketers, I could see, were leaning heavily instead on the catch-words of the journalistic culture: "investigative reporting," an "in-depth investigation," a "unique" look – none of which appeared to me to be true.

Lawrence Wright had chosen sides. And Paul Haggis – Wright's "donkey" – was certainly the vehicle to which he owed that passage. Yet, as Marty Rathbun, Wright's principal source, himself said publicly later, he and Haggis sought to manipulate Haggis's status as a "former scientologist' for personal gain – including renewed attention to a fading career. Wright – coincidentally – happened along at the right time to make Haggis's defection of far higher profile.

With Wright wedded to Haggis' story, divorced from Rathbun's criticisms for misrepresentations of factual material, yet subsequently tied to both, Rathbun's defection and outing of Haggis was only a precursor to further embarrassment in store for Wright over his unflagging support for Haggis, even as his credibility waned. When Haggis was accused of a violent sexual assault in Italy in 2022 – with four other sexual assault allegations pending in a civil suit – Wright was still quick to offer his support. He suggested on social media after Haggis' arrest that "maybe" Scientology was behind it.[159]

In November of 2022, a civil jury found Haggis responsible for the rape and sexual assault of a New York publicist, and he was ordered to pay $10 million in damages. Haggis denied the accusations in the civil trial, and in the accusations of rape in Italy, which led to an official investigation but did not result in criminal charges.

As I burrowed deeper into Wright's transactions with his sources, it seemed he was picking sources based on perspective. It was a warning sign that belied characterizations of the book as investigative. I saw how heavily he had leaned on other authors – including his close personal friend Janet Reitman of *Rolling Stone* magazine, a former Mideast war correspondent who published her book on Scientology just after Wright published his piece in the *New Yorker*, and as he was first courting, unsuccessfully, celebrity members.

His approach included actress Anne Archer and her son Tommy Davis, who was then on the Church's communications staff, and would be among those who eventually confronted Wright and his editor at *The New Yorker*, David Remnick. They warned of errors and misconceptions Wright was about to publish in the magazine as a precedent – the "foreword" more or less – to the story he would write in his book.

Later, as I saw photos posted online by apostates as he socialized with them, I wondered how much of that was simply getting to know his sources and how much reflected his home-boy relationship, so to speak. He was becoming their champion. And they were looking to reach a much bigger audience. He had leaned heavily on Marty Rathbun, as Rathbun would say himself. As I examined Rathbun's later confessions over the handling of the IRS "war," and the ethics of HBO's promotion of similar false accusations in Alex Gibney's documentary – despite being advised well in advance of contrary documentation – Wright's source relationships looked troubled.

Rathbun – from everything I would learn inside the Church, and could observe myself – was no one's fool, but at the same time someone who could change horses in mid-stream without so much as a ripple. His first loyalty had not been to the Church, but to its teachings. His other loyalties were murkier.[160]

He clearly saw his own behaviors – adhering to the principles of Scientology while abandoning the Church itself and trying to form his own "independent" version of the religion – with a righteous innocence that belied a temper. I didn't see him as the sort of principal source that Wright – even then, in the wake of his epic accounts of Al Qaeda in *Looming Tower* – should have trusted to either be truthful, or to hold the apostate line. I think Rathbun had too much conscience for the latter, and too much volatility for the former. And it didn't take long after Wright's book debuted for Rathbun to level criticism. He had expected an investigative take-down of the Church, but that wasn't what Wright produced. The first thing Rathbun did after Wright published *Going Clear* was to trash this new apostate champion and his work – by posting a very bad review of Wright's book.

* * *

Apostates – primarily excommunicated members the Church says it removed from the clergy for cause – make up the largest number, the most vocal, and the most well-financed of its critics (excepting perhaps its old nemeses the Eli Lilly Pharmaceutical Company).[161] Together they have posted online nearly as many words as L. Ron Hubbard wrote in his lifetime – and he holds the Guinness World Record for the most prolific published writer of all time.

They also became the source and substance of online postings by ex-journalist, Tony Ortega, former reporter and editor for a chain of "alternative" weekly newspapers under the *New Times* banner that first planted its flag in Arizona, with the *Phoenix New Times*, and then expanded the *New Times* chain, ending up acquiring a New York presence when it bought the vaunted *Village Voice*.

Ortega dropped out of Columbia University's journalism school despite winning a John Jay scholarship there – apparently earned on the strength of a First Amendment fight between his high school newspaper and efforts by school administrators to censor inflammatory content. The matter gained national attention when the American Civil Liberties Union stepped in resist 'censorship.' He went on to lesser rungs on the journalism ladder and would later flout mainstream ethics for journalists by fabricating stories. He had on more than one occasion, while working for alternative weeklies, published fictitious "news" stories in those newspapers under his own byline and sometimes under another name. One of his fabrications published in *New Times L.A.*, was a lurid falsehood written by Ortega under a pseudonym about two actual rape victims supposedly participating in a television reality show – with sex offenders. The story was re-reported by other news outlets before it was finally exposed by the *Hollywood Reporter* as a fake that he'd written himself– but only after Ortega first claimed in print that the pseudo-anonymous reporter was "fired" for the incident.

On another occasion Ortega published front page claims in a *New Times* paper in Kansas City that contended that unknown civil war veterans were buried beneath a site where a city construction project had gotten underway, halting the project and requiring public explanations in a press conference by city officials who, with readers, had also been fooled. I wondered what other such incidents had just never come to light.

But Ortega's supervising editors proved forgiving, if not complicit, in these deceptions. Curiously, or not, Ortega later grew close to the alternative newspaper chain's owners, two men who would later acquire New York's *Village Voice*, the grandfather of alternative newspapers, and then envelop it in scandal.

Owners Michael Larkin and James Lacey went quickly through a string of experienced editors at the *Voice*, but each served only a short tenure and resigned over questions about the new owner's intentions and practices. Ortega, recruited from another of the chain's small papers, was finally named as editor. He would later use that status – "former editor of *The Village Voice*" – as cachet with the mainstream press when he assumed a self-appointed role of chief reporting "authority" on the Church, a sham of self-promotion but readily subscribed to by reporters at papers all over the country – and across the globe – including recently a by-line for Ortega in *Rolling Stone* magazine. None have mentioned his fall from grace at the *Voice* immediately after new owners took over, nor his past fabrications, or his long-standing financial support by Church critics.

The owners who had promoted Ortega from fabricator to facilitator of their financial plan for *The Village Voice*, would both later be indicted and charged by the U.S. Justice Department with money laundering and sex trafficking for allegedly using the *Voice's* "adult personals" classified pages online as a forum to facilitate prostitution. The charges would include allegations of child sex trafficking. The owners incorporated the *Voice's* personals ads into *Backpage.com*, and when authorities began investigating allegations of underage sex trafficking – they insisted the ads were carefully screened. Child sex traffickers used code words, but the owners and Ortega said they used algorithms to screen out pedophiles and such providers. But the *Voice's owners*, the Justice Department charged later, had instead left such lucrative sex trafficking ads in place. Ortega had become a public voice for the paper's owners, making and publishing such excuses – rather than claims[162]

Ortega's credentials to be editor were challenged by a number of longtime and well-known *Village Voice* journalists, most prominently investigative legend Wayne Barrett. In an interview a year before Barrett's death, he talked with L. A. Rivera, a former *New York Daily News* reporter and writer who freelanced for *Freedom* magazine; Barrett made clear that he considered Ortega unqualified as an editor – and that as a journalist Ortega was unrestrained by ethical anchors.[163] Rivera would hear similar tales from another famous former *Voice* reporter, Gay Talese.

Ortega later drew controversy onto his own shoulders when he used the editorial pages of the paper – an institution that had helped spawn "New Journalism" and the elevation of first-person narrative journalism that Wright had said he wanted to practice – to belittle and misrepresent a growing chorus of critics, protestors and even picketers outside the paper's office.

The pickets had organized to bring heat onto the *Voice's* owners and editors as sex-trafficking facilitators and had tried with little success to shut it down before the Justice Department later did it for them. *Backpage.com* had by then become extremely lucrative, generating, the Justice Department estimated later, some $500 million in revenues.

Facing financial pressures stemming from the controversies, falling revenue from the changes in the news industry affecting all publications, and other factors, the owners sold the paper in 2013. The new editors promptly fired Ortega, something never mentioned, I would note, when reporters from mainstream news organizations used Ortega as a "source" on matters pertaining to the Church, nor when HBO and A&E Network would treat him as a credible guest on anti-Scientology programming.

Ortega's former bosses at *New Times* publications, Lacey and Larkin, and Carl Ferrer, the CEO of *Backpage.com*, were among seven individuals eventually charged criminally over their alleged facilitation of prostitution and sex trafficking through the site, which they had separated from the *Village Voice,* and continued to produce independently, after the paper was sold. Ferrer pleaded guilty in 2018 to some of the government's charges, and in late 2021 Lacey and Larkin saw a mistrial declared by a judge in the government's case. Prosecutors refiled charges and a new trial was ordered for February 2022.[164] A book published in 2022 detailed the case.[165] Prosecutors said they reviewed all aspects of the operation, but did not disclose if Ortega's role in defending the publication came under scrutiny.

During Ortega's tenure at the *Voice,* he began using its pages to publish a regular column about Scientology. He had sometime earlier written about the Church while working for a weekly in L.A. and Karin Pouw, a spokesperson for the church, had met with him. She later dropped discussions with him when his intentions became clear, she said. Co-workers at the *Voice* would later describe his blog about the Church as an "obsession," that few others on the paper were interested in. They also said it had led him to neglect more serious editorial duties.[166]

After his firing, and with the help of the Church's more vigorous apostates – some of whom had been removed for theft and profiteering from parishioner's contributions, the Church noted publicly – he began focusing solely on an independent blog site he called the "Underground Bunker." Its black and white images of what looks to be a Nazi communications center have attacked almost daily the Church and its practitioners, trading on the Hollywood celebrity interest surrounding some of the Church's members to sell web advertising.

Ortega complained about the contracting by the Church's *Freedom* magazine with professional and experienced journalists and about anyone else who might question the mainstream and tabloid reporting surrounding the Church. That included any skeptics of the *St. Petersburg Times* coverage, the work by Wright and Gibney, and the major entertainment networks that facilitated and promoted what the Church saw as "attacks." Ortega had come to represent the core of what Church executives came to call the "posse" of apostates. They were former members who fueled controversy with lawsuits and legal claims. They had testified in each other's legal cases brought against the Church, and in some cases – as with several of the sources Wright used in *Going Clear* – had became "professional" witnesses on behalf of attorneys regularly suing the Church.

Where the apostates would find success, however, was within the media – most particularly in 2009 with the *St. Petersburg Times*, which had campaigned against Scientology since the Church first located its land base and spiritual headquarters at Clearwater, Florida in the late 1970s. The stories the apostates told then provided the impetus if not the basis for other writings about the Church, including Wright's. And at the center of that was Marty Rathbun, and his ex-friend Mike Rinder.

Both Rathbun and Rinder were among the most prominent and central members of that "posse." The Church, in their satiric version of the *New Yorker* magazine, called them "A Posse of Lunatics." Both had risen in rank as members of the Sea Organization over two decades. Rathbun had higher-level duties with the executive staff, though Rinder, an Australian assigned to the communications staff, had been involved longer. Both were removed from their posts within the Church over misconduct that included lying and violence toward others. Some of those allegations are public, but Church executives would tell me more in private.[167] The Church detailed many of the issues in online postings, along with grievances toward former Sea Organization members who have used their former positions as platforms to – the Church says – "profit from their criticisms."[168]

Despite the questions raised about their own conduct, and especially about past incidents in which both had been called to question for lying,[169] Rathbun and to a lesser degree Rinder, would become principal sources for the *St. Petersburg Times* 2009 exposés about the Church – a set of stories by writers Joe Childs and Thomas Tobin. The reporters had been offered access to Church officials, including to the Church's leader David Miscavige, to refute allegations. In the end, on instructions from editors, they said, they proceeded to press without those perspectives.[170]

It was Rathbun who in 2011 and 2012 would become a chief source for Lawrence Wright, and a secret intermediary with Wright's film-director and former Scientologist source Paul Haggis, who, Rathbun has since said publicly, orchestrated his own resignation from the Church as documented in email exchanges and Rathbun's subsequent confessions – over what he had claimed was political support by the Church for anti-gay legislation in California – Proposition 8. – by the Church. It was something the Church has not only denied but documented to the contrary, noting that to do so – engaging in political activity – would put its hard-won status as a non-profit organization at risk.

Yet Wright built the credibility of his source Haggis around that contention, and as recently as 2022 it was cited by the *New York Times* – in a story about Haggis's arrest on suspicion of sexual assault in Italy, later dismissed – as fact.[171]

* * *

As I dug into the history of attacks against Scientology and compared it to what Lawrence Wright had written about the Church, it became increasingly "clear" that he had stopped far short of any real investigation – or else had decided to ignore those things that might have better explained the controversy about the Church, or put it in context, or challenged what his "posse" of apostates had told him.

I said as much to Tony Ortega one night in Denver at a small atheist organization's headquarters in a semi-industrial part of town. Ortega had produced a book about the Church and another of its critics, Paulette Cooper, a sometimes-troubled public relations agent and freelance writer for, among others, the *National Enquirer*, who had taken on the Church in a book years earlier, and wound up in a contentious dispute that left her in trouble with the law over accusations of a bomb threat – its origins disputed – and a threat against Henry Kissinger. It was a scenario where almost no one seemed to have clean hands, including some within the Church.[172]

Ortega's pejorative assertions about journalists who might have the temerity to look at the world from inside the Church's *Freedom* magazine was echoed many times in his blog site – where sometimes he would generate – or so it appeared – hundreds of comments a day, all of them antagonistic, as if representing large numbers of anti-Scientology critics. How many of these were, or are legitimate, and how many might have been generated for appearances sake as so-called "sock-puppets," is hard to discover.

I recall, however, one of those strings of comments, which I read after Ortega posted on his blog that Jim Lynch, a former editor with the *Chicago Sun-Times* and a well-respected newsman who had worked for *Freedom*, had died of a sudden illness. Ortega's readers posted comments filled with vicious invective and name-calling directed toward Lynch, and his family, and toward the Church. They mocked him in death.

I had noted a similarity before in Ortega's followers in the vehemence of some of their comments, but this particular string stood out, a sort of uniform expression of hatred – all except for one lonely comment, from a real-world journalist who wrote that he had known Jim Lynch in Chicago. He described him as a decent, honest man and a fine journalist and expressed shock at the words of Ortega's commentators.

If anything, that stuck with me. I never met Jim Lynch, though he was still working for *Freedom* magazine out of Florida when I first started talking with Church executives. He'd made many friends among the clergy staff. And it was later clear that his death brought them all a deep sense of loss, and grief.

Over several years, in the wake of Wright's book – he never mentions Ortega, though Gibney included Ortega in his film – I would watch as mainstream publications accepted him at face value. When Marty Rathbun took a hard U-turn in his apostate support – outing Ortega as being a paid front man for the apostates – Ortega would turn his blog into a forum of anti-Rathbun rhetoric. The feud among the apostates would fuel other fires. But it would not affect Wright or his willingness to rely on their version of events. It seems apparent now that he didn't worry about it. Who was going to question his assessments of Scientology, which he had termed "among the most stigmatized religions in the world."

Yet it also appeared, shortly after the book was published, that this could have been a miscalculation.

Rathbun, Wright's most prominent and principal source, had operated behind the scenes advising Paul Haggis and helping him manage his "coming out" as an ex-Scientologist and critic, even as Haggis was "allowing" Wright to bring forth his well-rehearsed story. But Rathbun would recognize in the immediate wake of the book's publication that he'd been had. Wright was not the investigative reporter he thought he was. Instead of using Rathbun as the source authority on matters he had some actual knowledge about – most principally the Church's fight with the IRS over its status as a tax-exempt organization – Wright had gotten it all wrong and Rathbun didn't seem to understand why. Much like the Church itself, Rathbun had found that Wright didn't like the story he was told. Regardless of what was true, Wright, like author Russell Miller before him, had found a better story.

Rathbun, as a central figure in the network of apostates attacking the Church, was able to help them succeed by attracting media attention that eventually morphed into a national and international spotlight through Wright's book and Alex Gibney's "documentary" film. As the ripples of angst about the Church, encouraged by Wright's book, spread, they were manifest in hate speech, discriminatory language and incidents of violence. A woman, inspired by what she had seen and read, aimed her car at the front window of the Church of Scientology in Austin, Texas, the city where Wright lives. She crashed into the nursery area, which was mercifully absent children that morning.[173]

In Sydney, Australia, a young man tried to stop his mother from attending a Scientology session at the Church there. He attempted to stop her from going inside and then stabbed a young Sea Org member to death outside. There were other incidents, if less dramatic. The media coverage had created a frenzy of intolerance. And in the U.S., following the film, both Gibney and Wright personally worked behind the scenes to try to convince the IRS to reopen the Church's tax exemption and overturn it.

Neither act is within the traditional role of independent journalists, or even documentarians. But despite the pair's influence with the media and public, they were not successful.

What was ironic, inexplicable, and inescapable was that any credentials as independent journalists were already discredited by their shared history. They were both products of the same elite media circles, both deeply tied to America's intelligence Deep State and its many private partners, both tied in one way or another to the clandestine activities of the Cultural Cold War, and to individuals directly involved in the CIA's illegal domestic political and social influence tactics. And they had ended up joined at the hip in influencing perspectives on terrorism – and oddly – on the Church of Scientology.

Yet, they've never breathed a word of those influences.[174]

When Gibney turned *Going Clear* into a documentary – without, he bragged, doing any inquires on his own – it was apparent that differing points of view would be almost entirely absent. He denied the Church an opportunity to know what "accusations" he intended to levy in his film, and declined to meet with Church officials – unless they would grant an on-camera interview with David Miscavige.

When he and Wright encouraged me to broker an interview with the Church's ecclesiastical leader, and I handed them the letter explaining the Church's denial, they barely looked it over and had nothing else to say. They were only interested in getting the camera moment. They had their story and the only one that worked for them was the story they wanted to sell – a sort of shared existential perspective that had been formed in both, it would seem, by elements within their families and their ties to that elite network of the cultural cold war – with its predatory interest in journalism as propaganda.

At least that was what the landscape looked like from where I stood.

* * *

The Church, founded by writer, philosopher and humanitarian L. Ron Hubbard, has been written about endlessly over the decades since its inception in the 1950s following the publication of Hubbard's best-selling book *Dianetics: The Modern Science of Mental Health*. *Dianetics* would prompt widespread attention in the U.S. and eventually around the world, affecting the thinking of millions.

The most controversial reactions to his theories and postulations on mental health came from the mental health industry itself. This reception surprised Hubbard and also readers of *Dianetics* who saw Hubbard's work as offering some compatible alternatives to psychiatry's own controversial treatments – ranging from lobotomies, physical and chemical restraints, electro-shock and less-than-efficacious, often dangerous, pharmaceutical solutions.

The history surrounding those issues has been captured in massive archives and documented by the Church. There is little question that the escalating antagonism from psychiatry toward Hubbard's perspectives was more about preserving the psychiatric communities' dominion over mental health 'science', than about any fault in Hubbard's research. He had clearly struck a nerve. The campaign that he started subsequently, to expose the dangers of psychiatric guesswork, continues by the Church today. [175]

Dianetics laid out the foundations of Hubbard's conclusions about the relationship between the mind, body and spirit, and while it was not the "bible" of Scientology's form and practice, it informed the structure of what would become the Church. What would strike me as I reviewed the Church's arguments on the intent, motive and practices of its critics – the apostate community – was that even those who spoke most vehemently against the organization itself most often continued to practice what they had learned in their study of Scientology and what Hubbard had devised and taught. They remained Scientologists in independent ways. Their grievances it appears were with the administration of the Church itself. Not with its message.

* * *

In a long career as a reporter, I was no stranger to controversy. It was within the boundaries of strong opinions on controversial matters that I often found stories. I had embraced controversial subjects, from investigating human rights abuses and injustices in state and federal prisons and probing corporate misconduct and even murder investigations and wrongful convictions to looking deeply into corrupt practices within both the private and the public sectors. I had traveled through uncomfortable places probing the world of police, the legal community, the judiciary at large. The pain and the angst that had surrounded the Columbine High School massacre had itself led me to the heart of controversy's most damaging venues. And so, I was not put off by the accusations that surrounded Scientology. It was easy to find criticism, anger toward the Church, and accusations that were often outrageous in their implications. And as I probed those, I also met and discussed with individual Scientologists the attraction to their religion, commentary gathered from Australia to Hungary, across the U.S., and points in between.

As I grew closer to Church executives in Los Angeles, more doors were opened. I traveled to the UK on two occasions, to the annual meeting of International Association of Scientologists at Saint Hill, where Hubbard did much of his work on his concepts on religion and its nature. I would meet David Miscavige there, on stage, on that first trip. We had our picture taken together and I told him then I saw some spaces in the narrative about the Church that raised questions. Later, I would realize that it was Miscavige who was opening those doors, from afar.

I was to learn early on that within the Church there was more than a "can do" attitude, and it was coupled with a work ethic like I had seldom seen anywhere else. I had spent a half year working among some of the hardest-working people I'd seen before, Amish carpenters. But these clergy members were motivated by a positivity that was unfamiliar. They could get things done, and on short notice, applying long hours and a dedication to the task. My first trip to the UK for an annual international Scientology event demonstrated that.

I got an unexpected call early on a Thursday morning from the *Freedom* office in L.A. It was Karin Pouw, church spokesperson, and she asked me in her gentle French accent if I could go to the UK. I was surprised by the invitation, and I asked her when she was suggesting I go.

"Today," she said. "Do you have a passport ... and a tuxedo?"

I had neither. The flight was just a few hours away. She said she thought that I could make it, though I didn't know how. But, with help from a friendly tailor and the intercession of a Sea Org member from the local Church in Denver, I found a one-hour passport renewal office, bought a tuxedo, had it taken in, and made the flight to New York and on to London with minutes to spare. I was to see that kind of efficiency many times over.

But sometimes – most particularly in decisions on how to react to the criticism of apostates and the major media onslaughts that followed – I would also see its opposite. And I would observe an almost naive expectation that the media the Church was dealing with had an obligation to "be fair" – and if simply given the documentation that corrected the record, they would do so.

But as I would see in legal correspondence shared with me – including a letter from HBO attorney Stephanie Abrutyn to Anthony Glassman, who was representing the Church in communication with the film network's airing of Gibney's *Going Clear* – there was little concern demostrated over fairness.[176] In another letter in response to complaints to HBO executive Sheila Nevins over Gibney's film, the network suggested that since the Church had its own media, it could tell its own side of the story there. That may have been part of what stimulated the decision by the Church to launch its own international television network in 2018. It had determined that it would tell its own story, to anyone who cared to listen.

* * *

In the course of working closely with professionals who contracted with the Church, and in working with Church members and its clergy, I never saw the kinds of antagonism or disrespect for the law and social convention that have been described by the most embittered of apostates. I found the people I met almost antithetic to those ideas.

But I did see passionate attitudes, and on a few occasions, disagreements between Sea Org members that might echo down the hall and sometimes rise to the level of shouting. It was similar to things I had witnessed in every newsroom I was in, where the press of deadline sometimes piqued tempers. One afternoon I heard loud voices down the hall at the Scientology Media Productions studio on Sunset Boulevard where I was working that day, and as a Sea Org member walked past the office from that direction, I remarked about it.

"Everything okay?" I asked.

He stopped by the door. "We're like family around here," he said. "We work, we get tired, we argue, we make up." He smiled.

I understood what he meant. I'd worked some long hours among them all, watched their dedication to their jobs, and their unity in their understanding that the Church's history reflected a fight for acceptance, for the tolerance owed to any sincere religion – including this, the world's youngest major religion. I'd seen their patience as well and respect in their treatment of others.

I was reminded of that as I looked through memos and files and saw to my surprise that many valedictions to individual staff from Miscavige were signed "Love, David." There was a camaraderie that made the accusations of physical punishment and even violence completely suspect.

Working occasionally out of the Hollywood office of *Freedom* magazine over the course of several years, doing research and investigation, I discovered other things that told a story behind the story of the controversy around the Church, things that offered a different perspective on that history, including conversations with clergy members who had spent years as in-house editors and writers for *Freedom* magazine.

One of them, Tom Whittle, who served as editor, was a journalism graduate from Syracuse University before becoming part of the Church and he had worked for investigative columnist and American journalistic legend Jack Anderson. A number of others had journalism degrees or past experience and other journalism training. A former investigative colleague of mine recalled an IRE convention event at which Tom had bought dinner one night for nearly a dozen journalists, including the heart of the Indianapolis Star's investigative team – regaling them with stories of journalistic adventures with Anderson. [177]

In researching the magazine's history – particularly after reading criticisms of *Freedom*'s work from Tony Ortega – I discovered a long litany of powerful stories, domestic and international, that were as proficient in investigative reporting as those I'd seen at major papers. One had exposed the brutal practices of government contractors who used patients confined in a network of South African mental health facilities as a source of slave labor. The exposure embarrassed the South African government and led to reforms – and also to the banning for a time of *Freedom* magazine there.

The magazine had also documented and exposed illegal domestic activities by the U.S. Central Intelligence Agency, using hard-to-uncover records of the spy agency to expose classified and secret programs involving, among other things, the testing of biological agents on the streets of New York among unwitting citizens. To expose the practices, staff members pieced together records of receipts for materials purchased to find a suitcase modified and equipped to "puff" chemical agents into the air on crowded American streets. [178]

Freedom had also led the way in exposing mind-control experiments by CIA-paid psychiatrists Sidney Gottlieb and by Louis Jolyon West – who was Jack Ruby's jailhouse analyst. And it published in excerpts a book by New Orleans prosecutor Jim Garrison – the only person to bring a criminal case in Kennedy's killing – and another by Air Force Col. Fletcher Prouty, a chief of operations for the Joint Chiefs of Staff during the Kennedy administration. Prouty, whose book exposed behind the scenes details leading up to the assassination, later became the model for Oliver Stone's CIA informant in his movie *JFK*. He was an early adopter of the notion of a conspiracy in the assassination of President Kennedy involving the government's intelligence "networks."

Freedom's exposés on the CIA were noted and reported at the time by the *New York Times*, , the *Washington Post*, by the major wire services and other national newspapers, here and abroad. Those stories, I would find, had also been filed away in the once-classified archives of the CIA, now revealed in FOIA documents that show the extent to which the CIA, the FBI, and the IRS had built intelligence files, conducted surveillance, and closely monitored media reports on the Church since the 1950s.

During the Nixon presidency, those agencies had been used to investigate those on Nixon's "enemies list," including the Church. *Freedom* unearthed documents showing the IRS participated in creating unfounded accusations about Scientology, its motives and intents. The IRS had done the same with other Nixon enemies, most especially organizations on racial justice. Even actors like Paul Newman and Lucille Ball were targeted.[179] The attitudes reflected in such calculated domestic attacks against perceived ideological enemies, were no different from the Cold War propaganda programs created against the nation's foreign enemies. Government records would demonstrate that similarity.

The Church itself, as has seldom been reported, was one of the most active organizations in the country pushing for open records legislation in the late 1960s and thereafter. *Freedom* magazine had been among the vanguard of early adopters and most proficient users of the federal Freedom of Information Act, passed in 1967. The Church's decades-long war with the Internal Revenue Service over its charitable organization status began about the time that the act was passed, and its subsequent litigation over FOIA access helped define the act and improve its impact on open government and the right of citizens to access government records.

But none of that history was mentioned in Wright's book, or Gibney's documentary.

Eventually, my education on the Church would include hours of discussions and conversations with a friend of L. Ron Hubbard and later trustee of his estate, Norman Starkey. In his deep South African accent he told me about Hubbard's early welcome into his home country and Rhodesia. He described how the Church's founder was later expelled from both countries for publicly advocating an end to apartheid practices and constitutional changes allowing for "one man, one vote" among all citizens, regardless of race.

Starkey's own colorful stories of mentoring by Hubbard unfolded in multiple venues, during long sessions reviewing Church history in *Freedom* magazine's offices on its Scientology Media Productions studio lot and later as we walked through the grounds of the Church's Gold Base near Helmet, California. It was the same place where Lawrence Wright had contended that the Church had run a punishment camp – a virtual prison, he had insisted – for errant clergy members. Wright had built the subtitle of his book, "the prison of belief," around that concept, though he had never seen evidence or physical proof that it existed.[180]

I found no prison camp there.

What I did find was a clean, well-lighted place, full of people who seemed to be enthusiastic about their work, and open to talking about it. The accommodations were well-appointed and pristine, and some areas were elegant, with state-of-the-art film and sound production studios, recreation facilities, a golf course shared with the community for events.

Starkey had served aboard *The Apollo*, the ship Hubbard had used to center his Church and to facilitate its growth in the early 1970s. We talked about that as Norman escorted me on a tour of the house that was built by the Church after Hubbard had passed. The house, he said, was a realization of what the Church's founder had described as "ideal" and a model of the one Hubbard had once planned to build himself. Through room after room, I saw the history unfold in artifacts, and more brightly as Norman recalled his time with Hubbard around the world.

That evening he recounted a story that I found more revealing.

Sometime after Norman had joined Hubbard and weathered with him some storms of controversy, the Church's founder named Starkey as captain of *The Apollo*. The ship was in port at the time and Hubbard – an officer with the U.S. Navy during WWII, who would later teach Starkey the intricacies of captaining – ordered him to take the ship out from its dockage.

Norman described rushing up the gangway to the bridge, worried and upset. He had no idea how to pilot the ship, and didn't know what to do. Hubbard had told him that in a past life he had had the necessary experience, to trust himself. But he said he was terrified. Yet he went to take his post. When he arrived on the bridge, his worry evaporated.

"I was very relieved," he said with a broad grin on his face, "to find there was a licensed harbor pilot already at the helm – ready to take the ship to deep water."

In fact, Starkey, as a respected member of the Church and confidant of Hubbard, would later bear witness to its passage through some very deep waters.

The stories describing Hubbard's life and character in no way resembled the often-mocking portrait painted in the unauthorized "biography" of Hubbard as written by British journalist Russell Miller. Like so many other "outside" works, Miller's book reflected only the perspectives of critics. Wright had leaned heavily on Miller's work – at times even lifting passages that he only lightly rewrote – just as he and Gibney had leaned on the tabloidesque stories told by the apostates to form the foundation of their peculiar truths.

I began to wonder why Wright hadn't worked harder to win the trust of these same Church executives and officials and members of the clergy who had seen first-hand the development of the Church, in its first generation, who had contributed and sacrificed for it, and dedicated their lives to it. He had missed a fascinating story. When Wright made his first attempts to talk with Church members, according to records of those contacts, the Church had opened their doors to him. But as it became apparent that he had an agenda – as had become apparent with Miller, the *St. Petersburg Times*, and Ortega before Wright – those doors began to close. [181]

Wright's plan to understand why people believed what they believed about Scientology (a question he never answered in the book) wasn't a plan that would take him inside the true story of the Church's history. Wright made a choice. But it didn't seem to be one driven by journalistic ethics, nor honesty, but by a willingness to participate in a deception. Haggis may have been Wright's "donkey," but Wright became Haggis' mule – carrying the script the Oscar-winning director and screenwriter, with the help of Marty Rathbun and the apostates, had crafted about Scientology, and himself.

In Wright's characterizations of the few conversations that he had with current members of the Church within the celebrity community – beyond Paul Haggis – his tone tended to mock their positive comments about the Church. If Wright came to the story as a skeptic with perspectives already formed, as it appeared, there was little the Church could do, I thought, to overcome the prejudice that he was helping to feed – except through transparency.

I had proposed that same proposition to Wright – transparency. What did he have to say about these things? But he refused to discuss it.

* * *

Early in my investigation as I explored deeply Wright's contentions in *Going Clear*, I also looked at the more technical aspects of his work – including his evaluation of sources. This was long before I discovered Wright's curious and culpable associations with the private intelligence networks involving his father and his father's close associates, as I have amply illustrated in previous chapters.

As I examined the reporting and approach to *Going Clear*, noting anomalies going beyond questions of who was interviewed, who wasn't, to the accounts that Wright had relied on, I found some interesting contradictions. He had recounted some fantastic stories told to him by individuals who had gotten into trouble before over fabrications. One of his sources – anonymously cited, but easily identifiable as Garry Scarff – had made up a story about losing family members in the Jonestown massacre in Guyana in 1978. But Wright didn't disclose that information. He also convinced Wright that he'd been forced by the Church to participate in a bank robbery to pay off a debt he supposedly owed for church services. No record of any such bank robbery could be found, yet apparently without testing that story – the when and where of it – Wright published the story.

The Church has noted in public that Wright has never offered to identify the bank, the time and date this allegedly happened and evidence to support the accusation. It would have been a damning accusation – if it were true. So, why didn't Wright drive that point home by documenting it. And if he couldn't, where were the fact checkers?

I had read with belated interest Wright's original story in *The New Yorker* on film director and Scientology apostate Paul Haggis and later, as noted before, had expressed concern about the Church of Scientology's parody in *Freedom* magazine in response. It had been cleverly done. But, mocking the story instead of attacking its factual underpinnings seemed to misjudge the issues and treat them too lightly. However high-minded and droll that satirical response might have been, it was something that would in the elite and closeted circles of journalists, particularly those who moved within the orbit of The *New Yorker*, be viewed as just another bit of Scientology "agitprop." The story of a bank robbery – a federal offense – seemed like a good place to attack factual failures. Bank thefts don't go unnoticed. Where was the FBI and police report?

But no one in the media was listening to the Church's responses.

Over time I would map out a number of alternate approaches to Wright's factual shadow dance. But before that occurred, I had already discovered other significant concerns about accuracy and especially, from the viewpoint of any critical analysis about Wright's book by independent reviewers, I wondered what questions they had raised in the major papers and magazines reviewing Wright's work.

As I gathered the reviews, I turned my attention to one in particular, by Charles McGrath, who had worked with Wright at *The New Yorker* as its fiction editor, and then later was named editor of the *New York Times Book Review*. I called him to ask him why, in his "review" and profile sketch of Wright as author, he had pointed to none of the obvious shortcomings of the book, including the inaccuracies that stemmed from Wright's narrative design.

But while he graciously responded, he was without satisfactory answers; we talked about the limit of a reviewer's responsibility when I asked why, in his review, didn't he note that Wright had in places simply lifted whole sentences and phrases, verbatim or almost verbatim, from the works of others; why didn't his review raise critical comment about the use of direct quotes that Wright never heard himself, and could not document in any way but through long-ago recollections of individuals who had already declared their antagonism toward the Church? What about the bank robbery tale, raised and dropped. Was it appropriate for a reviewer at the *New York Times* to assume the arguments in *Going Clear* were factual, with no skepticism? What did reviewers do, if not point to flaws as well as finesse by an author?

Moreover, as noted earlier, I asked McGrath directly about his decision to travel to Texas and be a guest in Wright's home while he was writing his story. It certainly raised questions about the "rules" for reviewers of books that existed at the *Times* – policies that are designed to encourage independence or at least disclosure. And, the fact that McGrath's son, Ben, also a *New Yorker* writer, was a good friend of Wright, raised for me the appearance of conflicts of interest in McGrath's review. It was clearly an assignment that reflected a different sort of ethic than the one described in the *Times'* own ethics policy.

If nothing else, the discussion and policy violations provided a window on the cozy, self-protective and elite world of journalism at the stratum at which *The New Yorker*, the *Times*, major print publications, major book publishers, and television networks, practice their brand of journalism upon the American public. It is a momentous responsibility for the nation's paper of record, and for its most influential "literary" magazine as well.

That would come home to me ever more strongly, the deeper I looked into the sourcing within Wright's book and the treacherous territory he had entered when he began to socialize with his sources, to promote their ideas independently, to fail to do his due diligence on the "other side" of the story, and to fail to apply any objective standard in his narrative. Wright had approached his subject with a perspective that gave way to agenda. And no one had called him on it.

Certainly not Charles McGrath and the *New York Times*.

* * *

There is an oft-quoted phrase in the practice of journalism that cannot be more true: "A journalist is only as good as his sources."

There were, even in journalism's better days, still more reporters who turned to official sources, official descriptions and the usual suspects than those who did more than keep a rolodex file, who built sources the way the Amish build houses and barns, with strong foundations, working with trust and respect.

In the changes that have gripped American journalism over the last two decades, where hedge funds buy out magazines they don't know how to run, and where the elite of the media world are made into celebrities, the great reporters like a Wayne Barrett or a Jimmy Breslin, may seem harder and harder to find. But the symbiotic relationship between journalists and their sources – the chemistry that is reflected upon in the clichéd and hackneyed phrase about co-dependency – itself carries deeper implications. Those kinds of skills don't just happen and they come only after a journalist has worked the corners of difficult stories, taken risks, particularly on unpopular topics, and explored those stories from numerous angles – including the human side.

Source work on routine journalism – casual sourcing – may be straight-forward, the finding of an expert or reliance on a spokesperson for a comment. But investigative reporting, getting behind the scenes and into the room where a story is unfolding, requires more than lucky timing. It takes trust. And trust takes knowing who your sources are – no matter which side of right or wrong they might be on – and what you can expect from them. That trust becomes a two-way street, a way of life.

How had Lawrence Wright come to that bedrock knowledge that, in producing an "investigative" piece, the relationships with principal sources require a deeper understanding, a probing and honesty that creates trust. This is especially important where controversy is involved, where individuals targeted in an investigative story can be miscast as the result of falsehoods created by a source, or where reporters don't explore deeply enough the factual underpinnings behind what they are being told.

It goes beyond granting to the source a certain faith in their truthfulness – at least to the point of exploring their story. It goes to the importance of knowing that a principal source is not going to change their story, including whistleblowers pressured to remember things differently later, or after publication tell you that you got it wrong.

A reporter must thoroughly understand the relationship with the source, especially one that is crucial and central to your story. If that story produces controversy – as Lawrence Wright's *Going Clear* did throughout the country and in other parts of the world, even to the point of producing violent reaction directed against Scientologists – you must be sure that your source understands what you are reporting and has an opportunity to have input on its accuracy, so that they don't back up on you later, or dispute that understanding, when the story is in print.

But that is exactly what happened to Lawrence Wright in *Going Clear*. And his friends in the media have ignored it.

* * *

Wright didn't discover that he had been manipulated by his source Paul Haggis on his *New Yorker* story that preceded his book, and he wasn't careful enough in his work to avoid another principal source from criticizing what Wright wrote as inaccurate.

I was thinking about that specifically on that night in Austin, where Wright lives, as I waited outside the downtown Violet Crown Theatre as he was about to host a local showing of the *Going Clear* documentary that filmmaker Alex Gibney created from Wright's book.

It was the third time I had come to ask Wright, once again, to talk to me about the accumulating questions I had, both about what he had written about the Church, and about those things I was just beginning to discover about his personal history.

I was thinking about his source work on *Going Clear* because I intended to ask him that night about the bad review on his book from someone who had every reason to have expected an accurate depiction of the Church of Scientology and the controversy. The review written by Marty Rathbun.

Most particularly, Rathbun posted his review on a blog site that he'd published since 2008 in which he had broadly criticized the Church. Now he turned his heavy criticism toward Wright for painting false portraits of the Church and most particularly for creating a misleading portrait of the Church's efforts to resolve its conflict with the Internal Revenue Service and its investigations over the Church's eligibility as a tax-exempt organization.

The IRS had settled the question itself in 1993, after the Church had delivered what amounted to box-car loads of documents to the IRS for its review. Church executives made available to the IRS any and all financial records of the Church – down to a piece of paper, the Church's corporate secretary had told me, with 47-cents in coin taped to it – and it was from its extensive review of that material – the most complicated such case in the agency's history – that the IRS finally decommissioned its investigation and affirmed the Church's not-for-profit status.

But Wright's book had told a different story.

Wright adhered to some of what Rathbun had told him, but only in part, the story of David Miscavige personally initiating contact with the IRS commissioner at the time – despite objections of the Church's lawyers – and taking matters in hand to settle them. Rathbun had a minor role in the process, but had been witness to some events and knew details.

Wright, Rathbun asserted in his scathing review, had created his own version of how the settlement came about and with his documentary partner Alex Gibney publicized a claim that the Church had "bullied" the IRS into a settlement, overwhelming the federal agency by filing endless lawsuits, creating such legal bottlenecks and expense that the IRS had no choice but to capitulate. It was no more accurate than Wright's assertions that the Church had no status as a religion, or that it was the obligation of the IRS to determine if the Church was a legitimate religion or not. Neither of course was true.

* * *

It wasn't that Wright's book contained no balance at all. In one portion Wright quoted and paraphrased testimony of a Franciscan and Harvard Divinity School graduate, Frank Flinn, who had opined in court proceedings and elsewhere his belief that the Church's conduct – even if it had created a rehabilitation center within the Church for clergy who were troubled and even if it required members to do manual labor – was not much different from other religious orders.

But Wright's selective and allegedly "false" reporting, particularly about the reasons the IRS granted the Church the tax status it sought, were too much for Rathbun. And he had spoken out. [182]

Monique Yingling, the Church's primary tax attorney and corporate counsel, who has represented the Church of Scientology since before its 1993 settlement with the IRS and whose late husband, Gerald Feffer, a former U.S. deputy attorney general, was directly involved in the resolution of the IRS investigation into the Church as the case was settled, also scoffed at the descriptions by Wright and by Alex Gibney in his film, tagging them as "ludicrous."

In a letter to Jay Ward Brown, an attorney for Home Box Office, Yingling complained that HBO – which had backed and aired Gibney's film on the Church for millions of viewers – had ignored repeatedly the Church's concerns over blatant inaccuracies, particularly about the IRS. But neither HBO, nor Gibney, nor Wright himself were interested in hearing what the Church had to say, just as *The New Yorker,* under editor David Remnick, had not been interested in the arguments that the Church had made about Wright's own inaccuracies and failure to fact check them. Wright himself had recounted in an almost mocking tone a bathroom conversation he'd had with Remnick about using material that the Church had provided to the magazine – to try to correct errors and defend against accusations – and turned it against them.[183]

But of all the errors that had occurred in Wright's reporting – and there were more than 200, as the Church has documented repeatedly in online postings – the IRS account was among the most egregious.

Yingling noted the farcical nature of Wright and Gibney's account, and detailed the errors.

"Contrary to Gibney's and his fellow propagandist Lawrence Wright's assertions, the IRS had no authority to adjudicate whether Scientology

is a religion, much less for such a determination to confer upon it 'the vast protections of the First Amendment,'" she wrote, "The only branch of government competent to address that question is the judiciary, and there are 50 years of uniform judicial precedent confirming that Scientology indeed is a bona fide religion protected by the First Amendment."[184]

She added, "No rational person can seriously believe that an emerging religious denomination could cow our most powerful and most feared federal bureaucracy and 'make its knees buckle,' as Gibney claims. The truth is exactly the opposite, for it is the Church that was the victim of the IRS."

She noted that both the Church and its founder had been on the Nixon IRS enemies list, and were both subjected to "malicious prosecutions at then-President Nixon's direction."

Wright's distortions or misunderstanding of the story, despite being advised in advance – both by the Church and by his own source Marty Rathbun – of errors easily corrected, seemed willful. For Wright, they served one function: to capture a perspective on the Church that reinforced the idea that it is highly litigious, suing any and all critics, at the drop of a hat, using intimidation tactics, and using the courts to silence critics and perpetuate what Wright has characterized as a "business scheme" rather than a religion. That in fact is something long ago rejected by American and foreign courts. The Church, executives have pointed out, hasn't sued anyone for more than 25 years.[185]

I had met Rathbun later, long after he had written his review of Wright's handling of factual matters, and had listened to him recount some of the detail behind Wright's interviews and contacts with a group of "apostates" – particularly and primarily its most vehement critics, among whom Rathbun had long been associated. It amounted to a recantation of most of what the critics had so publicly contended about the Church.

* * *

That night in the intimate setting of the Violet Crown Theatre in Austin, two years earlier, almost like a gathering of invited friends with not more than 100 people in the elevated seats before the big screen, Wright took the stage and introduced Alex Gibney's version of his book, and said he would take questions at the end.

I was afforded the last question and I asked him then about the review of his book by Marty Rathbun, his chief source. Why I wanted to know would his principal source render such a bad review, criticizing his accuracy and failure to tell the complete story?

The question seemed to catch him off guard for a change. But he paused for only a few moments before he looked up at the audience and gave them his boyish smile.

"Well, do you expect me to respond to every bad review?"

He laughed out loud. And the audience laughed with him.

But the question hung in the air and still does. He's never bothered to answer it.

* * *

Wright's relationship with Rathbun had been a direct one and Rathbun's influence on what Wright had written was obvious. He had been a source throughout the telling of the story, acting as a guide to Wright about matters to which Wright would have little access beyond what had been on the public record. And yet Wright appears to have never discovered that Rathbun had been the secret catalyst to Haggis' "coming out" as a celebrity defector from the Church – something that had long been a goal of the apostate crowd.[186]

Rathbun had been a more influential source than his former close associate within the Church, Mike Rinder – who a former editor at *Freedom* had told me once grabbed her by the throat in a fit of rage and had to be pulled away by others as he tried to choke her. Another senior staff member had also been attacked by Rinder who had delivered a sucker punch, he said, in a similar incident of allegedly unprovoked violence. Rinder was another of Wright's trusted sources. He had ignored the accusations of violence against Rinder and Rathbun, but accepted at face value their own accusations about alleged violence by others. The selectivity was convenient.[187]

But when Rathbun began to criticize Wright's work – for distorting badly the account of the IRS settlement, for repeating unsubstantiated accounts of misconduct by the Church and its founder, and primarily for failing to deeply investigate the Church as he had expected Wright to do – it prompted Wright to stop communicating with Rathbun.

He no longer needed him.

CHAPTER 9

THE CIA AND THE
JOURNALISTIC IMPERATIVE

Psychological warfare and systemic propaganda – concepts that evolved in sophistication after their contributions to the horrors of the second world war, framed by fears of conquests and subjugations by totalitarians – were primary motivators in decisions to manipulate the American journalistic and cultural communities from the very formation of the "civilian" Central Intelligence Agency in the early 1950s.[188]

The message of psychological warfare – conveyed by and through the independent popular press, history has shown – was more important than the integrity of the democratic free press to those like Allen Dulles, who directed and shaped the CIA in its formative years, and to the politically-influential individuals who helped him create it. At least this was true for the patriots who had weathered the storms of war, on and off battlefields, and sought to keep the country on a new permanent war footing – even if that war was to be one of endless wariness over the existential nuclear threat, outbreaks of regional wars, and U.S. generated political disruption around the world. And that required a kind of new-speak, the language of fear and exceptionalism.[189]

Americans have been taught that the free press is a place where reporters and editors have a free hand, protected under the Constitution, to responsibly explore the truth about government, politics, society, culture, business and more, answering to no one but the public. But because of its manipulation by private interests, it has never lived up to the ideals of the "Fourth Estate."[190] While it has reported factually on matters of day-to-day life and assumed accountability in many cases for its reporting, especially in local communities on local issues, the fracturing of news and sources within the amorphous Internet have made the journalistic environment an even more perfect partner for the hydra-headed intelligence networks. This "deep state" environment of distrust and the intelligence network's continued interest in shaping public opinion – and public policy – is one highly susceptible to disinformation. [191]

The press as it has existed and evolved under the watchful eye of what C. Wright Mills called "the power elite," has been unenthusiastic about reporting on itself, and the influences that have shaped it, and over acknowledging its own distortions of history. Our "Citizen Kanes" and the subsequent inheritors of their mass media empires – have crafted history on their own whim and inclination, mostly to protect and preserve this status quo – despite its awkward burdens of incumbent racism, sexism and religious bigotry and its deafness to the commonweal.

The American press, already yellowed and tarnished by sensationalism, began to know – and justify – a new kind of self-censorship and cooperation with external influences with the advent of World War II, and the dawn of the Cold War. In the world war, the free press came to assess new lines of ethical responsibility, weighing a journalist's duty to the truth when it clashed with the media's perceived duty toward a patriotic political philosophy, blurring lines on all sides. When propaganda became the mortar that held these political perspectives together, the foundations of historical truth cracked. Now, certain of those truths – Vietnam, Iraq, Al Qaeda, our own sense of who we are as Americans, as citizens of the world, even some of the most cherished stories of our culture – cannot be trusted. This is the legacy of a journalism that has lost its way.

* * *

As I probed the history of the CIA's relations with journalists, as propounded by the press itself, I saw that Nelson Poynter and fellow Hoosier newsman Lowell Mellette[192] became part of that patriotic blurring by assuming direct censorship of Hollywood film production during the Franklin Roosevelt administration, beginning during the buildup to WWII. It was then that Poynter and Mellette helped shape messages for American theater audiences in films that first portrayed communist Russia as an ally, and later as a mortal enemy.[193]

Their narrow imprint of permissibility was the stamp of approval needed by every film Hollywood would make from the late 1930s into and beyond the half-decade of war that followed; and, in the process, rules and perspectives they established would linger and color the literature of film for decades to come, reflecting the government's interest in the medium for national security and the promotion of its own cultural values, the world around.

But – I would note in the course of investigation – Nelson Poynter's relationship to the CIA and the intelligence community and the cultural Cold War went far deeper than that. He had been a deputy to one of the creators of the OSS, and the CIA, William "Wild Bill" Donovan.[194] And in that role, as publicly reported, he was instrumental in the formation of the State Department's U.S. Information Agency and its powerful international tool for cultural propaganda, the Voice of America.

Powerful media figures who emerged and flourished in this environment, and whose influence was generally under the radar of public perception included the likes of C. D. Jackson, the close friend, protege and confidante of Henry Luce, the mega-millionaire owner of the Time-Life media empire who was dubbed "the most influential private citizen" in the country from the 1930s into the 1960s. Both Jackson and Luce were closely and intimately tied to the evolving intelligence community under the CIA and Dulles – as were many other journalists, authors, editors and intelligence mavens, like Shepard Stone, the former *New York Times* reporter who would play a significant role in the perpetuation of intelligence influence over the media, across its multiple forms, and across decades.

Within these circles I also found Frank Gibney, closely tied to Luce and to Jackson and through them introduced to the culture-changing media networks of the CIA, including the American cultural magazines like *Show*. Gibney edited *Show* when it published Gloria Steinem's new-journalism account of the world of Playboy Bunnies, and, as noted earlier, helped recruit her into intelligence work. Jackson, as President Franklin Roosevelt's director of Psychological Warfare, had helped design, facilitate and encourage the nation's new civilian intelligence agency's clandestine, public-private relationships with the American media. The connections were kept largely beneath the public radar.

Evidence of the CIA's propaganda campaigns did surface in the public record, but only occasionally and, incidentally, mostly when exposed by independent publications, and then forced into the public arena through mainstream reporting on Congressional hearings and federal investigations and other events that could not be buried. The disclosures in 1967-68 of the CIA's infiltration, manipulation and ideological control of the National Student Association was among the most important because it became visible. Infiltrations of labor unions and college class rooms; sociology, anthropology and political science departments at major universities, scholarship programs, and the publishing industry itself, were far less visible. Those anxious strategies, uncovered over time, generated influence and this success was evidence enough of the efficacy of this Cultural Cold War to those who were waging it. It justified the lengths they would go to fight it. It was also evidence of indifference to the collateral damage that this secret ideological warfare would have on a free and open society, and its opportunity to know the truth about itself.

* * *

To be favored as a journalist or writer by these political powerhouses – owners of the media systems that included the *New York Times, CBS, NBC, Time-Life,* major magazines like the *Saturday Evening Post,* and major book publishers like Harper & Brothers, later Harper & Row, was more than an open avenue toward success. Conversely, disfavor – the wrong perspective, too much interest in the "peoples" truth over "corporate" truth – became an impediment to developing a popular "voice" for a journalist.

And if anything illuminates Lawrence Wright's favored status as an influential American journalist today, it is the light that comes from understanding the subtle expressions of favor and disfavor among journalists. Wright's roots in the very community of individuals who created propaganda systems involving civilian intelligence should prompt exactly the sort of questions that a democratic society should ask – but fails to ask – about the independence of all its journalists.

But who is to call out that question?

To attempt to speak independently, or question the reverential treatment of the media status quo, can itself be a ticket to exclusion. And exclusion – political, social and religious – was and remains a political idea that, I would conclude, fits neatly into how Lawrence Wright and his fellow traveler Alex Gibney had composed their own reality – and shared it around the world – on the Church of Scientology and more important matters of public interest.

Both Wright and Gibney, now celebrity media figures, sons of fathers who were unquestionably tied directly and deeply in that clandestine public-private intelligence network, were mentored by undisclosed sources, and are scions of that intelligence family and inheritors of its whirlwinds. Wright was beneficiary of its foundation-supported intelligence community links to academia, and to the press. Gibney's father – and stepfather – were part of that network as well. It seems easily understood that the seeds of "appropriate" ideological perspectives grow best under the hand of those recruited to the tasks before them.

* * *

That notion of exclusion itself was reinforced and made widely public in the era of Joe McCarthy and the House Un-American Activities Committee – on which Richard Nixon served while co-authoring anti-communist legislation. The Committee inspired witch hunts against writers and journalists who refused to be forced to make political statements rejecting communism, or to kowtow to government pressure.

But the politics of exclusion had deeper roots, even in the evolution of a more independent media in the 1960s and 70s, as I would witness in newsrooms where Black voices and female voices were routinely excluded, muted or ignored.

Though history has detailed those issues in the pages of countless books and magazine articles – including a lengthy story published in 1977 in *Rolling Stone* magazine by Carl Bernstein– much of the detail of media manipulation by the intelligence community still remains obscure to readers today. [195]

Even those exposés – like Bernstein's disclosures about the CIA's media-manipulating Operation Mockingbird – were tepid in what they disclosed, and further obscured by what was left undisclosed. I would be reminded by Len Colodny – who with Robert Gettlin first exposed the prior and extensive intelligence connections of Bob Woodward in their book *Silent Coup* – that he and Gettlin reported those ties, had drawn public attention, and Woodward had not formally denied them. Bernstein, Colodny told me, has never publicly discussed his own knowledge of Woodward's alleged role in the CIA's bold manipulations of the American press, something Colodny contends that Bernstein became fully aware of and has chosen to suppress.[196]

"His story about Operation Mockingbird," Colodny said, "I think was in some ways a reminder to Woodward of what he knew and didn't disclose. Something he's held over Woodward's head."

Efforts to contact Bernstein were unsuccessful.

As Bernstein pointed out in *Rolling Stone* in 1977, the roots and the rigors of shaping public opinion became the focus of multiple and specific intelligence programs to capture loyal media. He identified close CIA connections of major American journalists like Joseph Alsop and those who employed them, such as William Paley of CBS, Barry Bingham Sr., owner of the *Louisville Courier Journal*, and owners of the cooperative press agencies like the Associated Press, UPI, NBC and many others. And it went far beyond Operation Mockingbird.

Cass Canfield, who brought publisher Harper & Row to the pinnacle of literary and cultural influence, and who served on the board of directors of the CIA front Farfield Foundation, was described by the *New York Times* in his obituary in 1986 as the "titan" of American publishing. His influence was sewn into the fabric of the country's intellectual tapestry. His CIA ties were ignored. [197]

Bernstein also failed to mention the CIA's political relationships with his own former *Washington Post* bosses – editor Ben Bradlee and the paper's owners, Philip and Katherine Graham – who Colodny and Gettlin exposed as witting participants in a myth that American journalists and the public came to believe, and adopt, about Watergate, and the resignation of Richard Nixon. They concluded that the Watergate reporting itself was yet another distortion of American history, and part of a political coup by forces tied to the intelligence community who feared Richard Nixon's own independence in the realm of American foreign policy and the politics of detente with communist leaders.

As the CIA and friends sank their patriotic talons into the civil rights of American citizens through these secret propaganda efforts – like what Bernstein had dragged out of the shadows into public view – infiltrating media organizations with witting participation of owners and cooperation of some reporters, was quietly a part of everyday life from the 1940s and well beyond its exposure in the 1970s. Like much of its foundational narrative, the agency's supposed retreat from using journalists as spies and spies as journalists was also myth. They just got better at avoiding getting caught.

In truth, such influence and manipulation from within the intelligence community has never really divorced itself from journalism. A full reading of the history of Bernstein's reporting partner in the *Washington Post's* coverage of Watergate – Colodny points out – reveals Woodward's own links to that clandestine intelligence network. He served during his time with the Office of Naval Intelligence as a White House briefer for Alexander Haig, who was a chief of staff in the Nixon White House. It occurred immediately prior to his unlikely hiring at the *Washington Post*, after only a few months reporting experience on a Maryland weekly newspaper. Hired as a novice reporter, he was assigned to its biggest story ever – suggesting those networks of journalistic influence never left us after the NSA disclosures years earlier. We know this in part, because it is the myth, and not the fact, about Woodward that persists.

* * *

Those who participated in the intelligence apparatus created under the CIA's long-time director Allen Dulles found that the value of a media with a built-in intelligence infrastructure would best facilitate the crafting of public opinion to insure anti-communism and pro-capitalist ideals. Not only that, but this media engagement helped preserve the institutional systems that the public-private intelligence community had worked so hard to develop within the universe of publishing and journalism to shape "acceptable" media output. The creation of Franklin Books, the seduction of academic presses and cooperation of established publishers all point to the intent of those programs.

And yet these clandestine operations were then, and remain now, largely unseen by the public at large, just as the infrastructure that has muddied the waters of "independent" journalism has been largely invisible as well – at least within the mainstream press.

Where those relationships have been made visible by disclosures in congressional hearings and independent reporting, they have been generated most often by radical or counter-culture publishers. And because they are outside the mainstream, the details are just as often forgotten by successive generations. Probing the details of the Church Committee hearings in the mid-1970s was simply a reminder that the revelation of journalists' ties to and payments by the CIA, were more familiar to people in the 1970s than they are today. Yet such revelations have surfaced periodically at other times – including the late 1990s after the Terry Anderson hostage ordeal exposed concerns over the CIA's infiltration and quiet influence over the press and other elements of our culture.

That would become ever-more apparent as I looked deeper into the associations of Lawrence Wright and Alex Gibney. History will repeat itself as we forget what has come before. That amnesia includes the truths discovered about control of the media, and democracy's demand for something better, those truths becoming lost through scant press attention to the issue. And now, we are confronted with a withered press, starved of its vigor, suffering the loss of its own institutional memory and its failures to resist threats to democracy raised by journalism's cooperation with the CIA, and its fellows.

Maintaining influence over the American and foreign concepts of democracy and its boogeyman-nemesis, communism, and creating favorable perspectives on the role of democratic governments in fighting the spread of communist ideology around the world, were foundational concepts in the creation of the American intelligence networks – and in its persistent, media-supported messages to the American public. I asked myself, was that process itself a kind of tyranny, an imposition on and disrespect for the governed? Was it any different really than the propaganda, as I had been taught from grade school on, that supposedly existed only under dictators and communist regimes?

John McCloy, the acknowledged "Chairman of the Establishment," in his formative study of espionage early in his law career, was comfortable with secrecy and with bold and clandestine espionage techniques.[198] He became not only an advocate of the media-intelligence relationships but also of "second story" jobs, the black-bag arts of espionage – and of secret recruiting networks to find loyalists at home and abroad. He was equally comfortable with obtaining, secretly, the help of the American media and particularly those who controlled it. And he shared those perspectives with ideologues like Robert Storey and his protégés in Texas.

Storey was dedicated to this Cold War propaganda mentality. He had from his military intelligence experience helped influence and craft secret private intelligence networks and their links to the CIA, and to British intelligence.[199] That military intelligence background included parachuting with much younger men behind enemy lines in Europe to serve intelligence objectives. He was courageous, determined and brilliant. His legacy has lived beyond his legend and has included his influential and history-changing work as executive trial counsel at Nuremburg. He carried this knowledge and insider experience into his Presidential appointments to the U.S. Civil Rights Commission, to the Board of Foreign Scholarships, and through his work with the "congresses" on international law through establishment of the International Commission of Jurists. He helped devise, and then disguise, the financial support through private foundations of a recruiting network of journalistic, literary and cultural "allies" where acceptable perspectives were valued more highly than the independence of writers within this American democracy. He'd created a cloak of cover behind which a paternalistic society would protect its citizens from truth's harder lessons. All in the name of patriotism.

Long before the days of the Kennedy assassination in Dallas – where Storey influenced the conduct of investigations in Texas and Washington into the murder – Storey had become one of the Establishment's quietly powerful, mostly behind-the-scenes, top legal counsel, private advisor and confidant. And from those associations flowed the intelligence community's domestic work within America's borders, like recruiting and developing members of the "independent" press – which has been held up as a beacon of hope for democratic ideals – to be America's own version of *Pravda*. And he's provided, at least trackable at Lakewood Bank & Trust, a haven for some of those whose intelligence service could be useful. [200]

American attitudes in the late 1930s and very early 1940s had cast Russia as an ally and had glorified the strengths of the Russian people. But those attitudes had shifted as the War in Europe was ending and the era of war crimes trials was beginning, becoming one of growing suspicions and distrust as the defeated Nazi regime was dismantled and in its place was built a Germany divided by Eastern and Western economic and governmental philosophies. McCloy played a central role in that process – as did the press, ever-more patriotic at the end of the war years and ever-more populated by those willing, in their own understanding of the New Cold war, to participate in underground campaigns for crafting public opinion.

By 1946, during the formation of the institutional structures of the Office of Strategic Services (OSS), the immediate post-war predecessor to the *civilian* Central Intelligence Agency, the marriage of intelligence and propaganda, and the inclusion and courting of powerful insiders within America's newspapers, wire services and radio commentators, had become a pillar of the espionage system's work on home soil.

It was reflected in the appointment of former *New York Times* reporter Shepard Stone to serve as John McCloy's public relations agent during McCloy's leadership over the post-war occupation of Germany and Stone's continued lifelong service to the Establishment communities in which McCloy's leadership was central.

Stone's additional work with the Ford Foundation and eventually the Congress for Cultural Freedom would be touched by Storey's ability to direct the flow of hundreds of millions in secret funds into those networks by clandestine means, much of it through the two organizations with which Storey was affiliated, the Hoblitzelle Foundation and the Southwest Legal Foundation, both keys to those connections.

I would find myself marveling, the deeper I dug, how very little of that story has ever become part of the lexicon of American journalism's understanding of itself, even though the clues are littered throughout the public record now, yet seldom put into textbooks.

Most Americans are familiar with Radio Free Europe and to a much lesser degree its sister broadcast networks in Asia, Latin America and Africa, all of which transmitted over public airwaves Western cultural ideology into communist and third-world countries – and which were launched through the CIA and the U.S. State Department's extensive intelligence-linked activities. Individuals are less familiar now with magazines like *Encounter*, which in Western Europe and throughout underground networks in Eastern Europe, promoted the idea that those Western ideologies were bulwarks on which individual freedoms and community liberties could be built – and which were the only reliable foundations for freedom.

More often, those Western cultural promotions were designed by the same individuals within the intelligence communities who were also undermining democratic initiatives in foreign countries, if they challenged the American cultural and political bias, or sought to approach democracy from different, more socialistic angles, or used "revolutionary" methods that allowed for socialistic, less-capitalistic, attitudes toward the commonweal.[201]

The best evidence of it all is found in books and studies that have come to public attention most often by independent and in some cases more independent academic publishers – recognizing that many academic presses also had close links and funding from the intelligence community and at times wittingly published CIA-authored materials. More progressive elements of the independent press – like *Ramparts, The Nation, Mother Jones,* and *I.F. Stone's Weekly* – have often led the way in exposing those connections – sometimes prompting Congressional inquiries.

Those cultural lenses through which we have come to view the world at home and abroad have a natural bias, which significantly shapes what we read, hear or watch. We are a nation of shared values as well as differences. But the depth of long-running attempts to shape the American perspective, and the evidence of that, which is routinely ignored or goes unmentioned by major media today, is legion. And this cultural propaganda, the shaping of Cold War attitudes, and attitudes on the War on Terror, has not, as the CIA's legislative charter requires, been confined to international activities.

The work of the CIA and its created network of home-shore allies went on throughout the country from the agency's founding, clearly within the domestic territory where the CIA was legally forbidden to conduct its operations. At points along the way debate surfaced over whether CIA propaganda in foreign countries would create collateral propaganda with Americans through international reporting. But those home-land concerns seldom surfaced.

Gradually through the 1950s and into the 1960s, these networks tied to the CIA became what President Harry Truman had feared and warned against when he resisted the creation of a peace-time intelligence agency with broad authorities – and what indeed became the clandestine quasi-military arm of the intelligence network supported and controlled by leaders of powerful financial institutions, foundations and academic interests. Their aims may have been patriotic in the preservation of democracy and born among the horrors of war, but they also betrayed the very democratic ideals they sought to protect – as Karen Paget so well illustrated in *Patriotic Betrayal.*

As Paget has pointed out, the CIA's infiltration of the National Student Association beginning at the end of World War II was bearing fruit in its clandestine efforts to thwart communist youth organization in the 1950s and 60s; by the early 60's its deployment of writers, like Gloria Steinem as a witting asset to promote Western propaganda at international youth festivals in Europe, were only ripples on the surface. It had created friends among loyal war veterans who supported anti-communist activities and were among the ranks of journalists. It had courted and seduced Hollywood celebrities to its work, and writers and artists. Such influential writers as Dwight MacDonald and poet Robert Lowell among them, and Lowell's close friend, poet Emily Bishop, who would become close to Lawrence Wright's sister Rosalind. It was beginning to seem like a small world, despite its many players.

For counterintelligence, the agency and its minions had also infiltrated the nation's unions, its radical political groups and the civil rights movement, in which Robert Storey would play a prominent and intercessive role through his appointment by President Kennedy to the Civil Rights Commission. It had recruited private foundations – including those operated by Storey, the mentor, friend, employer and protégé of Lawrence Wright's banker-father – to hide clandestine funding of CIA espionage.

And Wright, years later, having loosely followed a path designed by the agency and its friends, would end up in a position of trust within the American literary and journalistic communities and would do so with his own secrets still intact. The natural question was how had that been possible?

Wright, a product of this same intelligence-media network, would come, at least behind the journalistic curtain, to represent the success of that intelligence effort, a "Manchurian candidate" of a different sort, steeped in the persistent perspective of intolerance for political perspectives other than those of the intelligence networks who helped create them. The mirror that journalists are supposed to hold up to America and the world, to reflect what is frank and true about the world we live in, has never reflected the role of writers like Wright who became important and productive tools in this mission-critical offensive of the American intelligence community.

And Wright, in his prolific influence, would apparently tap all of these mediums. Awash with such evidence, I could reach no other conclusion.

* * *

It was not just like-minded individuals in journalism concurring with political and cultural leaders on the superiority of Western political thought and ideology that infected journalism and the independence of the Fourth Estate.

Individual and influential journalists – the public record has revealed in detail – have long served as conduits for intelligence gathering and in some cases were directly involved in espionage or counterespionage for the Central Intelligence Agency. I would find in the purloined State Department cables on Wikileaks many references to Republic National Bank where its vice presidents traveled the Middle East on oil-related missions and met for debriefings afterward with State Department personnel who would weave their observations into this "Deep State" intelligence matrix.[202]

The least involved journalists were those simply debriefed by intelligence operatives about what they knew and had learned working their foreign and domestic news assignments. The most involved actively gathered and shared information with case agents for the American spy network, helped to recruit foreign nationals to act as spies, and carried messages between CIA operatives and their spy network. Many were assigned based on their sympathies and loyalties to intelligence operations, others by their interests in defending democratic freedoms. Others, for the money. Regardless of origin, the impact remained the same.

Though in its creation and development, the CIA, as with its predecessor immediately after WWII, the OSS, was specifically prohibited from engaging in domestic espionage; within the borders of the U.S. and its territories, its intelligence networks in fact were involved from inception in domestic roles infiltrating journalistic organizations and winning support for such clandestine activities from publishers and media owners.

Frank Wisner, one of those instrumental in the CIA's creation, helped imagine and develop the agency's propaganda arm, which came to be nicknamed "The Mighty Wurlitzer" – a reference to Wisner's ability to play the press, and influence the public – like a church organist creating and shaping the music of a voluminous pipe organ.[203]

There were multiple propaganda efforts affecting journalists and the media, but few were widely disclosed. Operation Mockingbird was an exception and eventually became public long before Carl Bernstein famously wrote about it. Its sister programs – like the Franklin Books Program and others – recruited editors and publishers at home and abroad to write, print, produce and distribute pro-Western cultural and anti-communist propaganda around the world. Helen Venn of Radcliffe Publishing Procedures Course, as a liaison, coordinator and facilitator for the program with the State Department, was a conductor on this peculiar underground railway.[204]

Disclosures about Operation Mockingbird would come to reveal how major American media voices – like those known to everyone within the country who ever read a newspaper or heard a radio or television broadcast – often cooperated with the intelligence community to tells stories in ways that the CIA wanted them told. As I pored through trails of documentation demonstrating the larger plan, the more jaundiced and manic it seemed. Yet, it had worked.

The infiltration of American newspapers, magazines, book publishing – and the film medium of Hollywood, with its vast celebrity influence over American and foreign public perceptions – would be more extensive and less visible because of its use of witting and unwitting journalists and media owners in carrying out its intentions, under the oversight and influence of the Central Intelligence Agency.

Journalists who have written about Operation Mockingbird have described the CIA's use and recruitment of more than 400 journalists in the 1950s, 60s and 70s who, like Frank Gibney – the author of the CIA propaganda ruse published as *The Penkovsky Papers*, the purported diary of a Soviet military general executed for spying for the United States – were eager for political or financial or reasons of inclusion, to be part of this clandestine media labyrinth.

But there were other reasons for such associations as well – affecting the careers of CIA-cooperative journalists.

As Carl Bernstein wrote in *Rolling Stone* in 1977, in a fractured chorus-like and likely composite quote that cited "plural" and anonymous CIA sources:

> "One of the things we always had going for us in terms of enticing reporters," observed CIA officials who had coordinated some of the arrangements with journalists, "was that we could make them look better to their home offices. A foreign correspondent with ties to the Company (the CIA) stood a much better chance than his competitors of getting the good stories."[205]

In such light, freedom of the American press – under the democratic ideals set out under the U.S. Constitution in provisions that memorialize the basic freedoms that include the right of free speech and the freedom to practice one's religion without interference from federal or state governments – looks different under the lens we so seldom apply to the institution of journalism.

But then, as I would see in studying the differences between the public and private sides of journalist Lawrence Wright, what glitters is not gold. I would also find that the simple most important issue surrounding the survival of Scientology – the expressions of tolerance and acceptance toward it within the larger interfaith religious communities – would never be addressed in Wright's work. Why muddy up the message? [206]

* * *

Despite all the negative reflections within the Wright book and the Gibney film on the Church of Scientology, and particularly in Wright and Gibney's unwavering reliance on sources with an axe to grind, I found most particularly curious Wright's inability to answer the question that he himself had indicated at the outset of *Going Clear* he intended to answer: Why Scientologists believed as they did. I would come to see his inability to come to some conclusion as a reflection of the shallowness of his investigations.

Because he wasn't really crafting an objective investigative project – as I had told Tony Ortega that night in Denver – what he ended up accomplishing – as the Church has argued – was merely an aggregation of previous writings from outside the Church, dressed up with some interviews from former members and Paul Haggis' manufactured tale as a celebrity defector, none of whom could ever take him "inside" the organization, and left him only with those things within the Church's history that his sources had already made into fodder for criticism.

In essence he had discovered nothing new, had ignored mitigating evidence and facts that threw his apostate sources into question, and never addressed one of the major issues within the Church, which has been their battle for religious tolerance and a place at the table of religious and spiritual philosophy. Had he gone beyond the obvious, the easy, he might have found a better story, as well as answers to his questions. [207]

***

On a trip to Hungary, I had spent part of an afternoon talking with a long-time Scientologist during the opening events for a new Church of Scientology in Budapest. He said he had discovered *Dianetics* in the 1970s while traveling outside the communist bloc, and took an interest in L. Ron Hubbard's philosophy of the mind and spirit. He had taken it upon himself – since the works and the religion were banned in Hungary and other communist countries at the time – to smuggle a copy of *Dianetics* into the country and later to bring more copies for others. An underground exchange developed among individuals interested in a different sort of spirituality.

He told me his involvement in the music business led to his travels throughout Europe for concert promotions, and so he was exposed, he said, to Western books and cultural ideas that he became more curious about. The Scientology approach to religion appealed to him and he'd stayed with it until, at the end of the Cold War, as the new openness took place, he said Hungarian practitioners – like those in Australia, the UK, Germany and other places around the world who had seen severe repression – began to surface more publicly. He was celebrating the opening of the Church in Budapest as a step forward in the long fight for religious tolerance and freedom of thought there.

A few weeks after the opening ceremonies, police would initiate an investigation, close down operations for a period of time, demand documents and records, obtain court-ordered access to the facility and otherwise create an atmosphere of angst. There were candlelight protests in the streets outside after that. And I wondered how much had actually changed, except to see these Scientologists practice their faith more defiantly.

I had flown to Budapest on short notice and had made it to the airport on an overnight flight with just a half-hour before the official ceremonies began. I found a cab, rushed across the beautiful city, and walked up to greet an executive staff member from Copenhagen who'd been assigned to get me to a seat – on time – for the opening speeches.

She was small but determined and pulled me by the arm through a tightly-packed crowd, our many apologies floating uselessly forward in English as I reached a folding chair 15 rows from the stage. I'd made it more than a quarter way round the world and arrived with just five minutes to spare. She was breathless, as was I and as I squeezed into my seat, she smiled and handed me a program – then paused. "How's your Hungarian?" she asked. The program was indeed beyond my linguistic skills, as were the words of all of the speakers.

The language barrier would be overcome with a few transcripts and translators and I put together a brief story for *Freedom* magazine on the opening and the history of oppression that had existed in the country toward many religions, but that Scientologists there had worked to overcome for themselves and for all others so situated. It was characteristic of what I would find around the world. A determination by Church members to pursue their freedoms of religious belief and thought, and a dedication to make that pursuit universal within an inter-faith community.

On a trip to Washington sometime later, I would travel among a multi-faith delegation to a hearing before the United States Commission on International Religious Freedom, and listen to the arguments made by members toward tolerance, free religious expression, and cooperation among all religions – along with tales of brutal religious repression in many countries. At least, I thought, the repression of Scientology in the U.S. did not result in physical reprisals like those that occurred elsewhere, replaced with a kind of psychological warfare in which Lawrence Wright had now ridden into the fray carrying the flag of the critics – their knight in armor.

I followed delegates on that visit to the Washington National Cathedral and as a misty night rain fell outside, I watched members – Jews, Muslims, Catholics, Protestants and Scientologists – join hands in a circle of prayer that centered on the very spiritual ideas of tolerance and acceptance.

Where was this, in Lawrence Wright and Alex Gibney's assessment and examination of the Church of Scientology, I wondered? Where were the accounts of the repression and discrimination that had occurred against the religion worldwide – and which Church clergy and executives had worked so diligently and continuously to overcome? Where were the interviews and the stories about the Church's privately-funded worldwide network of disaster relief teams that have responded to untold suffering in the wake of hurricanes, earthquakes, landslides and other catastrophes.[208]

If mentioned at all by the gallery of critics who circle the periphery of the Church, it was always with derision, a mocking of the work and the people volunteering for it, efforts to cast doubts on the programs themselves. And Wright had become their standard-bearer.

Yet, the history of the Church, particularly its fight to survive, were tied directly to goals the Church's founder had long ago outlined: a world without war, without crime, absent insanity, peaceful and tolerant. He was describing an important purpose for every human being on the planet – and I found that a fascinating story in itself.

But those ideas certainly ran contrary to the permanent war footing that the nation's leadership had conceived, and crafted propaganda vehicles and closeted relationships to sustain. Hubbard's ideas in *Dianetics*, spreading across America in this same 1950s environment, espousing the opposite, leading the *New York Times* bestseller list, looked like a threat to post-war imperialism.

But that hadn't been the story that Wright and Gibney had told. The story they had told was common, misleading, emotional and pejorative, and without a shred of doubt about its conclusion. If I had learned anything from a career devoted to the day in, day out of investigative reporting, it was that the sign of fairness and of balance is in the "doubt" you introduce into the work. They had shown none.

As I explored the issues within Wright's book and the documentary that he and Gibney crafted, the increasingly narrowed focus and the elimination of mitigating information seemed deliberate, useful in creating a negative perspective about the Church.

But it was not until I discovered that Wright and Gibney had been in personal contact with members of the judiciary, with lawyers involved in Internal Revenue Service matters, and with individuals with political influence, and had campaigned to encourage a new investigation into the Church, to deny its status as a non-profit – a matter far beyond the bounds of neutral journalistic conduct and into advocacy – that there finally seemed to be no other conclusion I could reach. Wright, in all his literary garb and sway, and despite his denials, seemed to be trying to do what governments and investigative bodies had attempted to do for decades and failed. Bring down the Church.

Still – with what I had learned about both Wright and Gibney and their family connections to the tentacles of espionage of the Central Intelligence Agency, and most particularly to the elite network of private individuals and institutions that helped the CIA conduct domestic intelligence and propaganda activities – it all fit.

Everything was grounded in the politics of exclusion. Control is about exclusion. And so, for Wright – and for Gibney, in so much as he parroted without independent verification Wright's words and conclusions, reducing them to even starker images – the points of attack against the Church and its followers were nothing more than what both had learned at home and hearth – around their fathers' dinner tables, where guests included some of the most powerful men in the country.

Only those who are invited to the kind of democratic institutions of that cultural elite are welcome at table – from their publishing houses and their movie studios, to their promotion and production of cultural values and ideas to which Wright and Gibney and their mentors lay claim. They have enjoyed the powerful connections needed to distribute those ideas, and to enforce the politics of exclusion. So, for what Wright described as his investigation into "the most vilified religion" in the world, exclusion of those parts of Scientology's story that cast a more balanced light I came to believe had been the product of more than casual neglect.

I would wonder over the course of my inquiries whether the CIA could be a current antagonist of the Church, but I could find no direct evidence that this was true. The CIA had certainly tracked the organization over periods of years, both according to Church records and to declassified FOIA documents; the agency had reported on the Church and maintained intelligence about it; it had coordinated and contributed to FBI and IRS profiles that led to investigations through Interpol, the international police agency, during the Church's early years.

But what interest might the Church hold for the intelligence community at this late date, especially when entire private media companies – the Arts and Entertainment Network (A&E), HBO, and other carriers – have profited from the content that promotes religious intolerance against the Church, a rebroadcast of one-sided accounts of its world, with impunity. What need would the CIA have to inveigh against Scientology's reputation?

***

Of all the questions I could not answer, for lack of access or incomplete information, I remained particularly curious over the timing of Wright's first *New Yorker* piece on the Church, in light of the book release by his friend Janet Reitman, whose book on Scientology was published about the time of Wright's article. [209]

Even *Salon* magazine, in a 2013 review of *Going Clear* by Laura Miller, noted that while Reitman had in 2011 written a "fine" in-depth (if less pejorative) book about the Church, it was Wright whose work came with an "imprimatur" of his Pulitzer Prize and the cachet of *The New Yorker* magazine behind him – and so got much more attention. I had wondered how those coincident events might have affected his relationship with Reitman. But she, like so many others Wright had warned not to talk to me, was inaccessible.

Was his work on the Church an accident of that association, an opportunistic turn on knowledge of the work of a friend, whose own book would gain far less attention in the public press – and wouldn't lead to any documentaries or the kind of press and reviews Wright received? Or was there some other impetus issuing from his long-standing intelligence community connections and the agency's lingering interest in religions that operate outside the traditional American norms that would encourage his attention?

I would never reach definitive answers to those questions. But I could see that those associations and connections had put religion in the forefront of his literary and journalistic interests – just as it had for the CIA. He had characterized his own youthful religious experience with his conversion to "rationalism" and to his avowed interest in religious organizations and leaders, wondering consistently, he has said, why people believe what they believe. It's a question that he – or the CIA – never seems able to answer.

In Scientology's case he never even approached an answer to that question, taking an entirely different tack than the charted course he had laid out for himself in *Going Clear*'s preface – something few reviewers would note. But his works certainly reflected that of others who had taken positions on the Church that it was dangerous, illegitimate, and even perhaps a "terrorist" organization.

None of those things were ever true about Scientology, from what I could see, and I had seen a lot – perhaps more than any previous outsider, and certainly by any journalist. [210] But, I noted, it had behaved independently, stubbornly so, resistant to efforts to control, diminish or compromise its message, which included waging a war with international governments on all legitimate fronts, seeking acceptance, mounting expensive legal fights for its right to survival, working to expand the religion onto five continents and establishing congregations around the world, producing its literature and its religious tenets and teachings in more than 50 languages.

I had walked through the Church's state-of-the-art printing plants that produced constant reams of work, from printed pages to the streams of digital media. I read the plaques on the wall that honored its publishing houses for their advanced technologies and efficiencies. And I watched as the Church built an international television network that – in the words of David Miscavige – allowed the Church for the first time to "tell its own story."

Scientology's survival has depended on the dedication of clergy members and Church executives, many of whom had known and participated with Hubbard as he developed his work, developed training skills and processes, codified and clarified his knowledge into the "scripture" of the religion, and outlined his understanding of the science of the mind. In the process he had attracted millions of readers, followers and practitioners, over decades, making Scientology the most successful of new world religions.

It was from my discussions with its participants, those who had donned roman collars at one juncture to reinforce the perspective of their rightful place in the religious mien, using symbology to demonstrate the legitimacy of a human right – to choose one's own beliefs, and to be treated with tolerance for those choices – that led me to those conclusions.

Nothing I could find in Wright or Gibney's work on the Church would approach a description of members' dedication to those ideals. Instead, it would cast them in the light created by their critics, and only that light. Whatever agenda might be served by the story of the Church as told from the outside – by its critics alone, consistently negative, a drum beat picked up by a mass media where governments – under orders from courts of justice – had left off. The full and real story of Scientology and its survival, well in the wake of Wright and Gibney's one-sided work, has remained untold.

* * *

From Operation Mockingbird to the less formal arrangements between the power elite and their media influencers, the nation's intelligence community and its secret selves have compromised the American press it promoted. Its minions have included spies posing as journalists, and journalists serving as spies and informants within a network of espionage, a secret role and a secret world hidden from the public and from all except those with "a need to know" – a description that does not include the American public.

It is from the public that those crucial "deep state" secrets are kept, and from whom the truth is hidden. Where is that documentation – the loyalty oaths, the evidence of prerogative, power and patriotism, all used to justify a secret pledge to privilege, kept by a journalist who violates his promise to the public and their democracy. Where was the independence needed to pierce the veils of propaganda, of fake news, of disinformation? We see its footprints are all around us – but the documents are classified.

"If Lawrence Wright has a case agent in the CIA," Peter Dale Scott had told me during one of our conversations, "you'll never find that. It's buried too deep." [211]

But the systems and networks and connections that have supported the very things that Wright represents – with his secret connections and untold history – were and are very real. The evidence of it has surfaced, if only fractionally and infrequently, here and there. That the American press has been a willing participant in this shadow-culture, for my lifetime and longer, is something I never considered, until now.

But we are in a press and reporting environment that is ever more aptly described as lapdog, not watchdog, and in which celebrity journalists and media stars assure us as to what is or is not factual, judging by their own perspectives and dead reckoning. We are left to deduce that they themselves seldom know what the truth is – even within their own world of journalism.

Media critic Ben Bagdikian, in a 1991 analysis and snapshot of journalism and the world of media, published by *Mother Jones* magazine, noted how the expanding media monopolies of the 1980s – from which the title of his 1983 book is taken – had altered forever the journalistic landscape, and how the cozy relationships between government and the press barons had caused the American media to miss or ignore stories of major importance to the American public.[212]

Even the story of the Iran-Contra scandal, that unfolded under President Reagan's administration and which exposed once again the CIA's often brutal hand in foreign political policy and intrigue, was not "broken" by the major reporters of the major papers in the major American cities – or by their foreign correspondents in Latin America and the Middle East. It was revealed by a small, obscure independent magazine produced in Beirut.

If anything has gone clear about the world of American journalism and its hidden influences, as so starkly demonstrated by the story of Lawrence Wright's rise to a career of prominence in American letters, it is that the codes of journalism were tossed on the rag heaps of history with callous impunity, along with the idea that a reporter is only as good as his sources.

America's Society of Professional Journalists has a code published and oft-quoted that sums up the difference between the intent of honest journalism, and the more unsavory realities of its practice. It is a code that I believe Wright and Alex Gibney glibly violated, with impunity.

It reads:

"The public is entitled to as much information as possible on sources' reliability." [213]

As practiced by the mavens of intelligence propaganda, that just may be journalism's epitaph.

CHAPTER 10

THE MANCHURIAN JOURNALIST

"Manchurian Candidate" is a term that was once deeply ingrained in the lexicon of American culture. Published in 1959, *The Manchurian Candidate*, written by Richard Condon, was turned into a film in 1962 starring Frank Sinatra. The title phrase caught on as a reflection of America's anxiety about the survival of democracy and the threat of communist governments and their potential to influence American politics. Its uncomfortable subtext cast the shadow of a threat cloaked in normalcy that could rise unexpectedly to destroy the very institutions on which our culture was built.

The term has since been used to describe persons disloyal to their own country by virtue of control or influence by an outside force. As I was considering the deeper meaning of Lawrence Wright's undisclosed associations and his history with the American intelligence community, public and private, the comparison came to me: a journalist, who appeared to share the common values of those interested in democracy, hailing instead from a hidden elite and plutocratic culture that has long exercised influence over what we know and believe about our culture, about our world, as Americans; seemingly engaged in manipulating our once-respected, if never revered, mass media.

Lawrence Wright – and his fellow traveler Alex Gibney – share something powerful in that elite culture, which is the ability to influence, to be believed, to carry a credibility that belies their history of association with an intelligence network that has often and importantly acted as a puppeteer over the free press – engaging some within it in unwitting participation, compromising others. Those associations raise questions of the depth of their intimacy with the CIA's "Mighty Wurlitzer" – the agency's ability to play the media like a pipe organ to propagandize the American people and the world, in the past and now.[214]

The threads of the unseen and only partially recorded involvement of the CIA and its network of intelligence have been deeply woven into the fabric of our culture in ways that far exceed the use of newspapers, television, books, and Hollywood films to color the public perspective. Those threads were wound and unwound by those who began with a moral and perhaps noble purpose – the protection of a nation from outside forces after World War II – and in the end created a threat that was antithetical to the very ideals that a free, open, and democratic society was expected to represent.

Influential leaders within the country rise from many places, but most always from the head, foot, and heart of the American capitalist community. In the era of the CIA's creation, they brought intellectual currency to the table. They served in positions of influence and power or they worked with those who did. They survived presidents, administrations, changes in the political will of the people, and they kept others who might challenge their presence out of the seats of power.

Presidential leaders do not act alone. They are advised, influenced, and sometimes manipulated by individuals, both seen and unseen. They are accountable to the public only as the press may hold them accountable. Leaders elected by the average and common electorate, and those who rise to influence, are not granted dictatorial powers but are institutionally representative of the ideals created within the concept of a democratic society itself. Their programs and methods may have been different but were, and are, defined by boundaries. For example, Lyndon Johnson wanted to create a "Great Society" that was colorblind, tolerant, and open; Franklin Roosevelt outlined the power of fear to undermine and erode liberty and urged the resistance of tyranny and oppression. Those elected leaders have operated by the will of the people to adhere to the virtues of freedom and to use the ballot box to ensure that liberty. Yet we have often trusted patriots, and distrusted politicians, failing to see the power of those who – like those who built the infrastructure of cultural cold war propaganda – were able to change the course of history.

There is an element of illusion in what we know and understand about who has strung the bow and played the tune to which we all dance. Karen Paget skillfully detailed the CIA's infiltration and manipulation of the National Student Association for anti-communist purposes, and anthropologist and author David Price has exposed in his work the systematic infiltration of the anthropology community by this same intelligence network under the CIA.

Robert Storey was a patriot, a powerful man – a "heavy hitter" as Peter Dale Scott described him – who, despite writing books and serving as a leader in the American and international legal and academic communities, managed to maintain a low profile in the clandestine intelligence networks he helped create. Through his skillful work and intelligence John McCloy, the "Chairman of the Establishment," endured a higher profile through his presidential appointments and positions. Yet, as I pulled the threads of their involvement in helping Allen Dulles and others create this secret – and domestic – intelligence community, I would come to understand that honorable ideas don't always serve the virtue of moral and righteous democratic goals, at least in ways that contribute to the commonweal. There are always unintended consequences.

More to the point, what I would come to see is that the great Fourth Estate had itself failed in its mission in ways that go unreported. And that Lawrence Wright, for whatever role he has served in his own evolution as an important American writer and shaper of public opinion, has hardly been alone in this seeming mischief. This culture of media and communication, with its largely undisclosed ties to a clandestine intelligence network, and its passion to influence what we believe, has been peopled by many artists, writers and journalists along the way – from the poet Robert Lowell to novelists like John Updike and influential journalist Gloria Steinem, to artists like Jackson Pollock and filmmakers like John Ford, each in their own way acquiescing to the silence of secrecy and the abandonment of what every individual within the cultural community has a responsibility to respect – truth.[215]

In Middletown, USA, where my formative journalistic education began as a young police reporter amid the hard and gritty streets of an Everytown, as a witness to the interactions of Everyman, moral and immoral, I was yet another product of a flawed academic system that taught me what it would, and failed to teach me what I and others needed to know about the realities of our world – and its true history.

My elementary school there was named after a common-spoken Indiana poet, Eugene Field, and within the fire-brick walls of that small school I can recall being taught with the rest of our industrial middle-class about "communism" and how those who lived harnessed to that unhappy yoke were denied what all Americans were privileged to have, access to truth. I can still remember across those decades imagining what life was like in the Soviet Union, where repression and fear, I was taught, were the order of the day – a place where individuals were imprisoned or worse for trying to speak the truth, and where ruthless propaganda created a society built on totalitarian lies.

No textbook or teacher ever raised the possibility, that I can recall, that those elements were alive within our own culture as well; even later, in a freshly integrated high school where the friction between white and black was more than palpable, I heard nothing about the American ethic except the Pledge of Allegiance. In college in my hometown, the first inklings of more radical thought surfaced not in the classroom, but in the cultural upheavals of the late 1960s, in the wake of the killing of John and Robert Kennedy and Martin Luther King, in the music of dissent that was surfacing, in protests on the college campus. And, mostly among peers on my college newspaper and within the school's journalism department.

One of the teachers there, David Iliff, also worked a full-time job at the local morning daily newspaper as city editor. Before his journalistic career, I was told, he had been an agent with the CIA, but he never spoke of it. He was an aggressive journalist and the first to teach me respect for the craft's institutional knowledge, the techniques of gathering news and meeting deadlines, and how to resist restrictions imposed by authority.

One night he sent me to a lecture on campus by the radical Renee Davis. When I chased down a local state representative who had gotten up from his seat to shout down Davis' call for a May Day protest in Washington, D.C., and then stormed out of the auditorium, Iliff praised me for running down the street after him to get additional comment. Just a few months before, he had walked me through my first front page banner byline, coaching me over payphones, tipping me to a secret passageway in city hall to a basement lockup where I found and interviewed a pair of suspects in a gun robbery. I never wondered where his loyalties were directed. Whatever he had been before, he was a journalist first and last, and I never doubted it.

In Lawrence Wright's case, the doubt never left.

* * *

I had met numerous times with executives of the Church before the opportunity arose to sit across the table from its chairman and chief executive David Miscavige. We had talked in venues on opposite sides of the world, exchanged pleasant conversation, made note of the challenges the Church had faced. But three events had stayed with me and informed my perspectives as I gained ever more information about Scientology's history, its struggles for acceptance, and the plethora of propaganda that had been promoted about it from the outside.

At the Church's home at St. Hill Manor in England, during the annual gathering of members of the International Association of Scientologists, I found myself among a small group of members and friends at a private meeting between Miscavige and the mayor of East Grinstead – the small and very British town where L. Ron Hubbard had first made friends among the local constabulary. Hubbard had established a tradition of annual contributions to the community's local fire department, arts events, and community service organizations. After Hubbard's passing, Miscavige had continued that tradition and those contributions were made part of the annual international event, on stage.

But here, after the festivities of the evening had closed down on a damp October night, in an elegant walnut-paneled room of St. Hill Manor, the castle-like home that Hubbard had occupied, I watched unobtrusively from a corner of the room as Miscavige met with the mayor – who in earlier days had been a teacher at the school there.[216]

Miscavige had told me a story about his introduction to Scientology in a small nondescript Church office in suburban Philadelphia. He suffered badly as a young man with asthma, and it was through the techniques of Scientology that he learned to cope with the frightening aspects of the ailment that, as a young teenager, had at times led him to crawl out onto the roof of his family home at night, to lie there trying to get enough air into his lungs to stifle panic. His release from those terrors by what he learned changed his life, he said, and set him on a path that would last his lifetime – and cause him to dedicate his life to the ideas, and ideals that Hubbard had developed. Eventually it would bring him into Hubbard's inner fold, a position of unparalleled trust.

But that night, outside East Grinstead, I saw an aspect of the man that I think few have seen. He was there to thank his old teacher for the love that he had shown him as a young man who was at times bullied by peers because of his religious faith.

At the time – in the early 1970s – practitioners of the Church locally were referred to, he said, as "Sinos," and his teacher had witnessed harassment and had invited him to participate in sports that an asthmatic would have never been able to play, and where barriers between him and others had been broken. His teacher had shown him kindness and understanding and taught Miscavige a lesson about tolerance that he never forgot.

In that intimate little setting, warm and gentle, Miscavige handed to his teacher a small gift, and thanked him for the larger gift he had given him those many years before. As I stood there looking on – a position I had assumed so many times as a reporter, the quiet listener and secret sharer – I wondered to myself how Miscavige could have been characterized so differently from the man I saw render this tender affection. And I would keep looking for the answer to that question.

* * *

In author Richard Condon's concept of the "Manchurian Candidate," his central character is "brainwashed" into a role as a political assassin by a foreign power. History records that the American CIA was extensively involved in psychological research – including the use of LSD and other psychotropics, hypnosis, and torture – to determine if an individual could be induced to override their own moral and ethical codes to commit such acts. Psychiatrists like Jolyon West and Sidney Gottlieb had been under contract to the CIA to conduct such experiments,[217] and it is another interesting historical note that West was the psychiatrist selected to interview and analyze Jack Ruby in the Dallas County jail after Ruby shot and killed Lee Harvey Oswald following Kennedy's assassination. Robert Storey was also among those who visited Ruby there, at least once, along with Chief Justice Earl Warren, by the official record. It was a close circle that had access. It was hardly likely that it included a part-time teenaged ambulance driver, as Wright has written.

While it might be tempting to question whether Lawrence Wright was subjected to psychological manipulation on his journey to becoming an influential American journalist, I found no evidence of that. He has his own well-publicized interests in hypnosis and, in particular, in the psychology of "recovered memory" which, along with religious beliefs, is another particular interest he shares with the CIA.

Rather, Wright sprang to national prominence from within a privileged and secretive circle of influential and powerful individuals who were able to create their own psychological warfare, affecting not only foreign policy around the world, but domestic events. This network most disturbingly sought to color the foundational cultural perspectives within what – at least ideally – was intended to be a free society, unencumbered by the existence of such plutocracies.

What seems clear now is that Wright consciously sought to hide that history and his associations with it. The evidence suggests he mischaracterized his conflicts with his father over avoidance of military service during the Vietnam War, and how he came to become a conscientious objector. His account of his matriculation to American University in Cairo is marred by facts omitted and contradictions. He created a cover story to explain how he came to Helen Venn's little publishing course, and then to AUC, which had become an active participant in U.S. foreign policy interests in the region, and a milieu of intelligence activities designed to give America an advantage in wresting from communist influence control of the oil-rich and politically unsettled Middle East.

Throughout his work – from his memoir, to his accounts of Al Qaeda to his "investigative" accounts concerning the Church of Scientology – he distorted facts, created stories from whole cloth, and hid vital information from his readers about his origins in journalism and the influences over his career path. His career influences behind this curtain of intrigue have never been mentioned elsewhere – outside the speculations of Mamadou Chinyelu.

Memoirists who have distorted their own history for the sake of making a compelling story have often been held to harsh scrutiny when discovered. Greg Mortenson, who wrote the compelling and widely popular memoir *Three Cups of Tea* saw his reputation as a writer trashed by revelations that he had presented events as factual that were instead fiction. *A Million Little Pieces*, a memoir by James Frey, was not withdrawn after it was revealed that his story of drug addiction contained fictional accounts, but it was remarketed by its publisher as "semi-fiction." Bob Woodward – who was the editor for fabulist Janet Cooke, who won and lost in disgrace the Pulitzer and with it her journalistic career – avoided responsibility for the paper's failure to do its due diligence, though he himself has been repeatedly called to question but never to account for his use of anonymous sources and undocumented assertions in his writing. His past intelligence ties are treated by the press as either unacknowledged, or unimportant, or invisible.[218]

Popular and respected writers in this country have also run afoul of accusations of plagiarism and other unacknowledged and inappropriate use of the works of others. Stephen Ambrose, who wrote so believably and credibly about events of World War II, was among them, and the list of others is uncomfortably long. Writers make mistakes, they may make innocent errors of omission in crediting sources of materials. No matter how careful, errors will occur. When they are acknowledged and corrected, the damage is mitigated.

But a writer who deliberately sets about to deceive has no cachet of credibility with which to cover his own misconduct. And when others – editors, publishers and fact checkers – allow such deception to occur on their watch, the cancers of propaganda and media manipulation now infecting this country's faith in itself are allowed to grow unchecked, undermining the very foundations of this democratic union. There is little doubt that what was justified by ideological threat – the compromising of a free press – was preface to the present – and that such manipulations and insider relationships continue today.

The Church of Scientology's efforts to convince *The New Yorker* of Wright's errors in the work he was preparing to publish about film director Paul Haggis' defection, and the Church's own history, were routinely dismissed by the magazine's editor, David Remnick, and by the magazines vaunted fact-checkers. Perhaps those decisions were justified by assumptions drawn from the long history of distorted and "tabloid" reporting about the Church. Instead of taking Church officials seriously and examining their complaints and arguments fairly, as Wright would himself describe later, and I would continue to remind myself, Remnick suggested privately to Wright – in the men's room – that the Church had essentially, and *unwisely*, handed over to Wright enough material for a book.

Editors are supposed to believe in their writers, and support them. But that is only half the job, and Remnick, who has his own history with the intelligence communities through the Council on Foreign Relations and his work as a journalist and student of Soviet relations, could have shown some skepticism, like Woodward with Cooke, but apparently did not. What Remnick thought goes unrecorded here, since he did not respond to a letter requesting comment.

The perpetuation of religious intolerance and creation of a public license to discriminate against – to even hate – practitioners of a particular set of religious beliefs, even to the point of stimulating violence against its members, is more than a moral or ethical failure. It feeds the roots of decay that undermine all of the principles of inclusion and tolerance on which the American democracy was founded. It is no small matter.

***

In the course of my investigation into Lawrence Wright I noted that he sought and achieved a broader cultural impact than he could have as a journalist alone. He wrote fiction as well as non-fiction. He staged plays and one man shows. He wrote screen plays and authored films.

He published a novel about Manuel Noriega, the military dictator of Panama who had risen to power with the help of the CIA despite his deep involvement in drug trafficking that ultimately destroyed American lives by the tens of thousands. Wright's novel, curiously, seemed to contain as much factual detail as fictional detail, but by being set in a fictional pose still attempted – albeit clumsily it appeared to me, though the *New York Times* remarked that it "worked closely from the historical account" – to create a distorted picture of the American intelligence community's own involvement in that sordid Latin American history.

How much of his novel, I wondered, had also been drawn from intelligence files to which most writers might not be privy? There was no way to know, given Wright's reticence to talk about that, but, as most any experienced journalist will likely concede, sources are everything.

His Noriega novel – a curious pick of subject matter – was not the only time that Wright has walked the line between fiction and fact and I came to see the shadows of fiction coloring his accounts of Scientology – some of his own creation and some simply adopted, unexamined, untested and unverified from the prior work of others.[219]

He has, the record shows, repeatedly discussed publicly his use of factual research to underpin his fictional work and give it legitimacy. It reflects what credible writers of fiction do, where the record is available. But in Wright's case – pointedly in his screenplay for *The Siege* about terrorist violence in New York, which preceded the real event by two years, and more recently his novel about a pandemic – the prescient reporting with which he is publicly credited is as eerie as it is uncomfortable, and unexplained.

What writers don't do – if they are honest with themselves and their readers – is the reverse: introducing elements of fiction into supposedly factual work. And while many memoirists leave some things out that may be pertinent to their story at some point, when they seek to deceive by factual misrepresentation, the web they weave is more than tangled.

In pulling that web apart, the context and past associations could not be more important. It is the source, finally, of understanding where Wright had come from in his complicated journey from the quiet and hidden places of political power, to a powerful voice within American letters. Nowhere did I find any discussion of Wright's past or the points at which his life and that of his family touched the electric current of these powerful influences.

* * *

The late Charles P. Storey, Robert Storey's son, was a very close friend of Wright's father and when Donald Wright died Charles Storey was quoted extensively in the *Dallas Morning News*, praising the senior Wright's civic contributions, his work with the city's parks department, his leadership in a bond issue that brought air conditioning to Dallas' public schools, and other social achievements. Storey's remark noted earlier that Donald Wright "could have been mayor" of Dallas was not casual. Other former protegés of Wright's father told me his more pointed disappointment was not being granted the presidency of Republic National Bank of

Dallas – the CIA's powerful banking partner in its clandestine domestic intelligence network.

Charles Storey didn't mention that the bank that his father owned, and that Donald Wright ran, was peopled with personalities who were very powerful in Dallas and Texas politics, and other intrigue. He didn't note that the FBI had checked the little Lakewood Bank and Trust for savings accounts by Lee Harvey Oswald after the Kennedy assassination. Nor did Lawrence Wright mention it, nor other interesting asides about the bank that Robert Storey founded: Jack Evans, who *would* become mayor of Dallas, was employed by Wright's father's bank. Robert Gemberling, the senior resident agent in charge of the FBI field office in Dallas at the time of the Kennedy assassination – and who became something of an official historian about it – was later hired by Wright's father as an officer at the bank. Never mentioned.[220]

Charles Storey, who was a guest at Wright's home, who sat around the dinner table for conversation, was a close friend and intelligence protegé of Charles Cabell, the brother of former Dallas Mayor Earle Cabell, and who, as a top operative of the CIA, was most famously fired by Kennedy, along with Cabell's boss, CIA director Allen Dulles, for their reckless conduct in the attempted Bay of Pigs invasion in Cuba – yet another CIA attempt to conduct foreign policy that put the nation at risk of nuclear war.

Dulles, with Storey's endorsement and encouragement, would be appointed to the Warren Commission that later investigated Kennedy's murder. So, would John McCloy.

Wright never thought to mention that either. All of that might have seemed at odds with his descriptions of his father in his memoir. Perhaps the story Wright created about his magical grant of conscientious objector status by a tough and no-nonsense Dallas draft board – on the strength of a single essay – was sufficient to withstand mild scrutiny, but not the scrutiny of serious journalists. That leaves open the question, where have those serious journalists been? Too often, perhaps, they've been among the friends and cronies from whom Wright has enjoyed unwavering and uncritical support and acceptance, for more than 30 years.

This account will be faulted for its own failures, but it remains to be seen if any of those who do or do not cast fault care to pick up where it leaves off and where questions are unanswered. Wright himself has refused to answer questions, while repeatedly and publicly, and erroneously, characterizing me as a "private investigator" masquerading as a legitimate journalist. I found some irony in that.

There is yet much more to be discovered. Any good detective of history will tell you that there is always more to be known and that what is learned is evolutionary and creates more building blocks for truly understanding history, with always more clues and facts to discover. All of the sciences teach us that. And perhaps there are writers out there who might care enough about the importance of the historical record to take this story further than I have taken it.

* * *

When Dexter Filkins, the *New York Times* writer and author, chided Wright in print in a review of *Looming Tower* for putting "quotes" around English words supposedly spoken more than a decade earlier by others, recounted second or third or fourth hand, uttered most likely in the eastern Arabic language of Pashto, he touched a small nerve that should have reverberated with Wright. But it obviously did not. Wright has never varied his pattern of putting other people's words – that he had not himself heard, could not verify, or perhaps even imagined – into quotes. It is a flaw that should not be ignored and that I could not reconcile.

Wright's secret history, and the specter of disinformation in his personal account of his life are also flaws that should not be ignored. Those issues raise questions about Wright's honesty, and integrity and responsibility of the editorial directorate of the once-great magazine *The New Yorker*, I believe, should dictate then that each and every piece of writing contributed by Wright on the War on Terror, and the attacks of 9/11, their roots and origins, should be carefully examined – and if improperly influenced stricken from the record.

Wright's Pulitzer Prize, on which he has traded so heavily, should also be examined with the same skeptical eye that the journalistic community to date has failed to exercise where his work – amid his undisclosed connections to the wider intelligence community – has confused fact with fiction, strayed into propaganda, or betrayed the code that all journalists should adhere to about fair and honest reporting.

And the national reporter's organization, Investigative Reporters and Editors, which awarded Wright a national award in 2014 for 'Best Investigative Journalism' for his book *Going Clear,* should be asking similar questions of themselves.

Whether or not that happens may be a litmus test for the survival of journalism itself. Or at least for its righteous reform.

CHAPTER 11

THE JOURNEYMAN'S NOTEBOOK

I drew my first paycheck as a reporter at 17, ran a small local weekly at 18 and was hooked hard into street journalism after landing a night cops beat on a gritty morning daily while a sophomore in college. I was still too young to take a legal drink but was up in the excitement of deadline reporting night after night. I chased shots with city detectives at the end of the shift when I dropped off stacks of the paper's last edition at 2 A.M.

In the process of learning journalism on the streets, I found opportunities for colorful, descriptive stories. I worked on storytelling. The deadlines were addictive. Police stories evolved into column writing, telling human stories where no one else was reporting. That led to uncommon sources. That led to investigative work.

In 1969, the year of Wright's Radcliffe experience, I was a novice police reporter learning to work *the traps* – the places where cops and firemen kept incident reports before they turned them in downtown, and the locations where they hung out. I was shy, a church kid, but I found friends. Roy Griffith, a shift sergeant, took me under his wing and one night directed me to a nearby house where shots had just been fired. I arrived as the cops did and followed them through the front door of the house. The shooter, an elderly woman, was holding a .22 long-barrel in her lap and had just put an end to decades of abuse. Down a half-darkened hallway, beneath a swaying bulb, her husband lay face up, dead on the floor. It was my first glimpse of a violent world.

Chuck Sanders, a Black fire dispatcher – I discovered the first night on the beat – had worked at the busy Texaco station my father owned in the early 1950s, an era in my heavily segregated, Klan-friendly hometown when Blacks were not paid living wages, if they were hired at all. My father had taught him mechanics, paid full wages, hired his brothers. The experience helped Chuck get into business college, and onto the fire department. He repaid that legacy 20 years later by calling me whenever he heard newsworthy things developing while the police scanner was quiet. In these ways I learned lessons in trust, and the importance of well-meaning sources.

As a feature columnist, I worked the human stories in parts of town that were never covered. But there seemed to be more urgent things to write about and when I was offered a job as an investigative reporter at the *Indianapolis Star,* I moved into complex project work. The paper was owned by the Pulliam family, and it made something of a name for itself doing the kind of investigative reporting that came into vogue in the 1970s. *The Star* and its sister paper, the *Arizona Republic,* had been at ground zero in the formation of Investigative Reporters and Editors, the now-international group built around the multi-newspaper investigation into the murder of Arizona reporter Don Bolles. The *Indianapolis Star* had already developed a standalone investigative team that, under Dick Cady, won a Pulitzer for exposing police corruption. [221]When Cady left for *Newsday,* I filled the vacancy.

Before and after that I wrote extensively about statewide prison conditions; stories on sexual abuse at the state women's prison led to lawsuits, and reforms. I wrote about conditions of confinement, gangs and drugs behind prison walls, went undercover to investigate traffickers among prison guards. I wrote about a hostage-taker who'd been acquitted, yet went to prison anyway. And I investigated a klavern of the Ku Klux Klan among guards at the state prison. I came to know elements of the criminal underworld on many levels.[222]

In the course of that coverage, often in conflict with prison and state officials, I built a source network that touched almost every segment of the prison system: inmates, trustees, guards, administrators, secretaries, medical workers, union leaders, former employees. It was that coverage that in 1986 – as Wright was making his book tours with his memoir – resulted in a call one afternoon from a state prison official. There had been an uprising on death row. Hostages taken. They were trying to negotiate their release, but the inmate leaders were demanding to talk with me. A state police car picked me up at the paper and two hours later, under lights and sirens, I was walking down the long corridor to the death house door.

I would tell the story of that night time and again in journalism classes at universities where I taught reporting and newswriting part-time, and at writing and reporting seminars. I told it as a story not about the excitement or the deadlines, or the anxieties of the moment, but about the true nature of impartiality in reporting. The detachment required. The need to cling to that impartiality when the emotion of the moment and the temptation toward judgmentalism work hard to erode the underlying principles of neutrality. I told them because I had failed that test.

That night on death row, across the chipped and aging bars, the hostages were periodically brought to the second-tier rail above us, prison knives to their throats, to show they were still alive. Throughout, I negotiated with Ray Wallace who had led the uprising. He was facing execution for killing a family of four when they returned home during a burglary. While prison officials waited through the night nearby, Ray and I talked face to face with only the bars between, about living conditions and the indignities of death row. At one point, standing in the dim light, in a quiet moment, I asked Ray how he had ended up there. What had happened in the house he burglarized that night. He told me, in cold, clinical detail. Within the surreal gray walls and bars around us, I saw the picture of his crime as starkly as shadows on the floor beneath the bare-bulbs overhead, and witnessed the scene of the murders through his eyes.

I remember feeling that the cool objectivity to all things that I'd developed as a reporter strained by his descriptions. Finally, I asked him the question that laid bare my empathy for his victims, and hinted at the threat to the impartiality I held so dear. Why, Ray, I asked him, did you kill the two kids?

"Because," he told me, peering thru the bars, his long hair, sharp features and fierce eyes framing a portrait of anger and bitterness. "I didn't want them to grow up without parents." [223]

I had made a promise to Wallace and the others that night in our peaceful settlement, a promise that I would come back to write more about the conditions that death row inmates were living under. But after the wild ride of that incident, the banner story the next morning splashed across the front page, and long hours thinking about Ray's description of his own crime, I felt an estrangement. I let the imagery of the murders pierce my impartial intentions. I was bothered by it. Bothered by the line between evil and simple injustice, by my thoughts as a father, over the inhumanity of his crime, and what his victims had faced.

I left for Paris a week later and carried with me the front page of the paper with the banner story, my picture next to it on page one. I thought throughout the trip about that night and the moments within it. When I returned, I put off going back to death row; I didn't write to Ray to talk about future discussions, or human dignity among the condemned. I went back to work on other things. It weighed on me, but I did nothing. Then one afternoon, a guard at the state school for boys – a juvenile reformatory – called to say he had just quit his job and taken with him

150 case reports demonstrating rampant child abuse at the facility. A whistleblower.

With the help of inside sources among lower-level prison administrators, I obtained a key to a room in the department's forgotten storage offices where boxes of records from the reform school had been placed. I labored there for days on end, into the nights, laying bare what had been covered up for years. One evening, as I lifted a box onto the table and pulled loose the lid, I saw a file with Ray Wallace's name on it. He'd been an inmate at the school.

I saw Ray's record. He had repeatedly been in trouble with the law – the product of a broken home, absent parents – before being sent to the Indiana Boy's School where he had, case reports showed, been the victim of abuse.[224]

Then I came across a startling notation– his assignment of a roommate and notes about their placement. The roommate was Charles Manson.

Ray would teach me about impartiality in the days that followed, and thereafter I would consider more closely how impartiality is the key that unlocks the truth, that brings confession, that lets you inside. The lesson came in Ray's handwritten response to my letter asking to talk with him about Manson. He had written it on a plain folded manila card in an envelope that had been opened and taped closed again at the prison. His note didn't speak to the neglect of the promise made too many months before. His response was just two-words long. And we never spoke again.

I had broken my promise and let emotion, and revulsion and the horror of the vision of Ray's coldhearted rage, prevent me from returning to investigate conditions on death row. My own reaction had surprised me, because by then I was no stranger to violence, its perpetrators, and those harmed by it.

The lesson was a reminder that the loss of innocence cuts more than one way and more deeply than we can know. Things are not as simple as good and evil. There is always more to the story. What I could relate about the life that Ray Wallace had lived, and what led to his execution years later, became a story untold. What it taught me was that as a journalist I should never judge, or let emotion get in the way. I should stick to the facts, detail my observations and even conclusions, but let the story tell itself.

That is how the truth, in its literal incarnations, is finally recognized.

Lawrence Wright's twitter and website posting, during my inquiries, warning friends that I was not a reporter but a private investigator hired to stalk him, had resulted – some three years later – in a related posting by Alex Gibney.

Though I didn't see Gibney's follow-up, it would prompt reflection on how the style of journalism that he and Wright practiced was marred by half-truths and missing context – most especially their failure to tell both sides of a story. Here was one more example.

The posting occurred about the time that I had figured out the relationship between Gibney's father, Frank Gibney, and Wright's advocate, Helen Venn, and had asked Venn's daughter, Tamsin, to speak with me. Gibney tweeted that, as an investigative reporter at the *Indianapolis Star*, a story I had written resulted in the "biggest front-page retraction in the paper's history."

I had two reactions. I wondered what had prompted Gibney to make that assertion some three years after Wright's original, and fictitious, post. And I noted that Gibney's representations were made without any inquiry – for, if he knew the real story, he'd not disclosed it.

Gibney was right, in part. *The Indianapolis Star* had published what it called a "clarification," on the front page, after some three years of my front-page stories investigating a national political scandal involving illegal campaign contributions by a national vocational school that funded campaigns with money bilked from federal guaranteed student loan programs.

To protect its government-subsidized cash cow, the company used high level political connections – former White House fund raiser under Ronald Reagan, Mitch Daniels, and a high-profile Democratic attorney, and provided favors and services to office holders, particularly to members of the U.S. Senate Education Committee, which had oversight of guaranteed student loans. The company's corporate jet became nick-named the "Senate Shuttle."

The newspaper supported my investigations. I crisscrossed the country documenting fraudulent practices, political fixes, and uncovered unreported travel and gifts from the company to elected leaders – including senators Ted Kennedy, Bob Dole, Dan Quayle and others.

My stories were picked up nationally and re-reported by ABC's 20/20 news program. The exposure ramped up pressure on federal investigators and eventually the U.S. Department of Education, through the Justice Department, sued the company for $366 million in fraudulently-obtained loan funds. The company closed in bankruptcy.

The stories drew praise from mid-level editors and won a series of awards. But the paper's support took a drastic turn after I discovered that a state-court judge, during the company's rising prominence, had presided over the company CEO's divorce case, had vastly undervalued the company's assets in order to minimize what the CEO would have to share with his wife. And, he'd taken trips on the corporate jet – while the case was before him.

Then something curious happened.

As I worked alone in the windowless office of the *Star's* investigative team late one night, the phone rang. It was Ed DeLaney, a prominent figure in the state's democrat political circles. His wife would later run for governor of the state, unsuccessfully, and he would later be elected to the state legislature. He was also the newspaper's principal attorney.

I wondered how DeLaney knew I would be there that night – we had seldom talked – or why he hadn't called during the day when he was more likely to reach me, or even contacted an editor first. But my curiosity turned to concern when he told me what he wanted.

DeLaney said he'd learned I was "looking into" the state court judge and wanted to know if this was true. I hesitated. While I wouldn't have confirmed that to an outsider, he was the paper's attorney. I told him it was and asked him why he wanted to know? He told me he wanted me to know that the judge was "a good guy," that he was a respected judge and attorney and was likely on his way to being named to the state Supreme Court. He wanted to "make sure" that I talked to the judge before I wrote anything about him. [225]

I didn't realize it immediately, but I was about to receive a full immersion baptism in the the dark side of a corrupted press, and its power to influence public perceptions.

DeLaney had ample reason to recognize that his phone call alone had crossed a line. I'd not asked him for advice, had no issue on the table for him to review. No editor to my knowledge had requested that I speak with an attorney prior to my inquiries into the judge. In fact, no editor at that moment knew where I was headed with the judge. I didn't know myself.

But DeLaney should have seen the implications behind his call – and the ethical questions they posed. After all, he had been directly involved in the creation of the most visible organization for investigative reporters in the county – Investigative Reporters and Editors (IRE). He was their founding attorney, and would be the now-international organization's secretary for years afterward. [226]

The state circuit court judge had been on the circuit bench for most of a decade in a rural county, adjacent to the Indianapolis metroplex. His court I found was a particularly popular venue for cases transferred out of the metropolitan courts, by a particular segment of Democrat lawyers within the Indianapolis bar. The divorce of the company CEO was one such case, and as I studied other cases in the judge's court, I saw that those attorneys had been particularly successful there. I also noticed the judge was using his office phone to make personal long-distance calls to some of those attorneys, and billing charges to the county. I reported it, and the judge was indicted for theft by a state grand jury. But months later, in a series of politically-inspired maneuvers, a special judge appointed to hear the charges dismissed enough of them on a technicality that a special prosecutor folded his casebook and walked out of the courtroom without a word. Charges were dropped.

I persisted and obtained financial records showing the judge had income not included in his judicial disclosures. He'd received a gift of a Rolex watch. There had been other gifts. Then a source told me that the paper itself had been a defendant in a multi-million-dollar suit by a trust that owned the property where the *Star* was published. The judge hired an attorney to act as gatekeeper with me over attempts to get answers to my questions. That attorney was Ann DeLaney, wife of the *Star's* attorney.

My life at the *Indianapolis Star* began changing. I was moved out of the investigative office and given other assignments. But I continued to work on the related stories. And then the managing editor, and the papers attorneys with DeLaney's firm said they were considering giving the judge the opportunity to respond in print to my stories – to offer a "clarification" on behalf of the judge.

And that was the "retraction" Gibney tweeted about.

A couple of weeks after the "clarification" – which I had opposed and over which I had no input – the judge sued for libel, naming me and the paper as defendants. He'd gotten new attorneys for the action. It was at best a long-shot for the judge. He was a public figure, the stories had been well-documented, there was no malice, and even his explanations in what the paper published over my objections didn't remove the fact that his conduct was questionable – and was now under investigation by the disciplinary commission of the Indiana Supreme Court.

Because of DeLaney's conflict, I refused representation from the paper's attorneys, and denied them access to my confidential investigative files. They finally agreed to "outside" counsel, but would only hire a politically-active friend of the Pulliam family, the campaign manager for then-Senator and later vice president Dan Quayle, nephew of the publisher, who was one of those who accepted funds and favors from the largesse of the corrupt vocational school's looting of guaranteed student loan funds.

Reporting on the story was picked up by other *Star* reporters, but not much was written. One afternoon in the midst of the conflict I got a call from an editor of the *Rocky Mountain News* in Denver. They were looking for an investigative reporter to lead projects. A week later, the chief justice of the state Supreme Court sent a message to my office, inviting me come in and talk. He told me that afternoon that he knew what was going on at the paper, and said he hoped I would "hang in there." He couldn't talk about the pending judicial investigation, he said, but wanted me to know "the cavalry is coming."

It was too late. I had accepted the job in Denver.

A year later, as the chief justice predicted, the Supreme Court's disciplinary commission acted. The judge was found to have violated the ethics canons. The gifts, the ex-parté contact with attorneys in his court, and favors, had caught up with him. He became the only sitting circuit court judge in state history to be removed from the bench for cause.[227]

The lawsuit disappeared.

That was the rest of the story – the other side that Gibney's tweet did not address. The real message was he hadn't bothered to go beyond his assumptions, to check his facts. He had done the same thing with Scientology. He hadn't investigated any of the stories told in his documentary. He took Wright's word for it. He said so. Just as he had relied on a half-told story about a newspaper "retraction" long ago, to create a false impression. Among the lessons of journalism, that is one Gibney's followers should learn.

* * *

The newsroom saying about reporters being only as good as their sources is as common as it is true. I saw many occasions when the ability of a reporter to tap sources on a frantic deadline made clear the value of developing source networks. Early warning signs of journalism's impending demise began to flash when major metropolitan papers lost institutional knowledge and failed to maintain institutional beat structures where solid source relationships were built. Journalism found its path to a troubled future within its own newsrooms.

At the *Rocky Mountain News* in Denver, I had gotten caught up in a disagreement with editors over a national story that had become compromised by the actions of one of the editors. I had led the project, but refused to put my byline on what had required months of difficult and expensive investigation. Nothing was published and the editor in question was forced out. But his replacement reassigned me to cover the state legislature. It was a plum job to many journalists, but not what I wanted and I considered it a punishment detail.

I was covering the general assembly session when the biggest story in the state's modern history – the Columbine High School massacre – suddenly hit the news.

Reporters from every beat across the city were called into the newsroom and reassigned to the shootings, but as legislators walked the hallways of the statehouse in tearful silence, postponing committee hearings, cramming themselves into caucus rooms, I sat in the bureau office waiting for a phone call that never came. A second day went by with the front pages of the *Rocky* and *Denver Post* consumed in Columbine coverage, but no call. On the third day, the phone rang. It was the Rocky's city editor, Steve Meyers. And I recall his first words.

"We have a problem," he said. "We need some help."

The paper – as others would do in the shrinking world of daily newspapers – had diverted resources from its traditional police beat to other things. It was a big paper covering a large metropolitan area and doing national reporting. But it had, under a new youthful editor with little reporting experience lost track of the basics. The *Rocky* had let the beat slide. Now the fruits of that decision were being harvested.

"We can't get through to anyone at the Jefferson County Sheriff's office," the city editor told me. "They are not answering their phones or returning calls. We can't even find out who is running the police investigation."

"So, what is it you want me to do?" I asked.

"Can you just find out who is running the investigation?"

I remember those quotes because I wrote them down in a notebook on my desk. In truth, I had some residual bitterness about being moved away from investigative – what I had been hired to do. But there was no refusing this request.

"Call you back in an hour," I told him.

Several years earlier I investigated an attempt to take over operations of Yellow Cab, the major cab company in Denver, by Jesse Gaddis, the mob-linked Broward County, Florida taxi king. I'd exposed the secretive deal, and the fact that cab drivers for multiple companies were using taxis for illegal trafficking in firearms and drugs. [228] I had explored the gun running to the point of threats by those involved and a confrontation in a bar I'd linked to gun running. I had developed a number of good sources along the way.

The teenage Columbine killers had obtained firearms illegally, and that was a focal point of the police investigation. But how had they done that? I began calling old sources in the underground gun trade. Within the hour I reached one who had been a confidential police informant. I asked him what he was hearing about the Columbine weapons, and he said he couldn't tell me directly, but reminded me of the murder four years earlier of a county sheriff's deputy who had been ambushed with a .50 caliber rifle.

"I think you'll find the Columbine guns came from the same place that the .50 caliber came from," he said.

I called the paper's library and asked for clips on the murder case, found the name of the detective who had investigated and rang his phone. Like every other line into the sheriff's investigators, I got only the detective's voice mail. I identified myself and left a message.

"Can you tell me," I asked, "where the gun came from that was used to kill officer Mossbrucker?" That was all. I left my number.

Fifteen minutes later the phone rang. It was Lt. John Kiekbusch from the sheriff's department. [229]

"You called one of my detectives and asked a question about the gun used to kill one of our deputies, he said. His voice was stern, brusque. "I want to know why you asked that question?"

"Meet me for coffee," I told him. "And I'll tell you."

An hour later across a white Formica table, I learned that my source had been right. And from that moment on, I was on the inside of the police investigation into Columbine, with nearly full access, meeting with officers nearly every day behind closed doors.

The next day I was back in the newsroom, full-time on Columbine. I would see everything, hear everything, and most of it I would never forget. It would also be my last major investigative story in daily journalism.

The lessons in journalism are learned by doing. What Wright has learned on the streets of his own world I cannot say for sure. But I know those lessons were different. I would come to believe that they were different for a reason.

CONCLUSION

JOURNALISM AND THE AMERICAN EXPERIENCE

L awrence Wright's journey into the world of journalism was far different than the vast majority of reporters who learned their trade in American newsrooms. He spent no time working newsroom deadlines nor did he work his way up from the break-in beats that were once the training ground for young print reporters, covering police beat or city hall or working the mundane and routine coverage of local events that lead a reporter to being informed of the world where common people live. He took a different, uncommon path.

Though he described in his 1986 memoir his apparent humble beginnings, his coming of age was a path of privilege and insider assistance that he has never acknowledged. From the beginning of his career as a writer for small magazines and later his elevation into the world of literary non-fiction through *Texas Monthly, Rolling Stone* and ultimately *The New Yorker,* he characterized himself as an outsider whose curiosity, talent and intuitive understandings produced his extraordinary experience in American letters. In fact, he closeted his true history and his access of elite channels involving a clandestine intelligence network, creating a certain fiction about his own life. Instead of covering stories for the commonweal, Wright built a cover story.

Unlike the majority of journalists who come to this craft from a desire to write about our lives and times, from an objective or at least a fair and inclusive point of view, Lawrence Wright came to the world of journalism with an agenda, and one that I believe was not his own alone. His perspectives were shaped and formed by a cadre of elite insiders who both seized power and used the institutions of authority to create the ability to persuade, and who were never fully visible to the American public they sought to influence. They were akin to the backroom bareknuckle politics of America's middle class, but instead of local councils, city halls and state legislatures, these insiders built an American empire and the stage across which they walked was international.

They not only could populate the news columns of major newspapers and television and radio networks with their influence and views, as William Randolph Hearst and Joseph Pulitzer had done in a different era, but they did so under a cloak of invisibility while commanding the ability to shape world events and our own domestic political history. Through the powerful civilian intelligence agency that was developed by people like John McCloy and Robert G. Storey, through their American minions and protégés like the CIA's Allen Dulles and the FBI's J. Edgar Hoover, through their power and influence over figures within the U.S. Supreme Court, Congress and the Presidency, and most importantly by their influence over the American media, they even influenced the record of history that we teach our children and accept as true.

Within that world, Lawrence Wright was only a product of that system, a cog in the wheel of influence, but one who I believe secretly used the mechanisms of those quiet institutions to rise to prominence in the journalistic milieu. And perhaps the biggest and most damning fault of that event and others like it is the betrayal of the institution of journalism, which has worn the mantle of a warrior for freedom and liberty and justice for all. For all the corruption within journalism's seamier side, for the unseen hands of influence that have helped shape it, and for all the public disgust and distrust that has developed around it, American journalism is perhaps the most powerful ideal within the world of the common good, capable of preventing tyranny by its exposure and delivering what is needed most to secure the ideals of individual liberty – if it clings tenaciously to its anchor, which is truth.

But if those ideals are to be preserved, then the masque of agenda and manipulation within that journalistic community must be exposed to show what is true – just as the Fourth Estate, conceived as a watchdog and defender of freedom, must be independent to achieve its loftier goals. Lawrence Wright is not the problem, but the exposure of his undisclosed history and intelligence connections serve as evidence of a larger problem: The powerful political organization to which he was understudy and with whom it seems he shared a secret agenda has infected the institutions of journalism, using fear of communism and then of terrorism to favor and preserve a system fueled by political plutocracy and oligarchy.

That this evidence should surface in the arena of religious intolerance and the persecution of individuals over their right to practice their religion as they see fit harkens to the very reasons that the American ideals were created, to replace such privileged minority rule with a democratically-run and open society where freedom of expression is a right and not an entitlement.

Over the nearly five years of my explorations into Wright and into the target of his "investigative reporting" on the Church of Scientology, I found a commonality with what I had done my whole life – explore the stories of people's lives and what they believed, how they lived, what had shaped them, and then to tell those stories in ways that gave insight to the world around us.

I had made a habit of transforming myself from a stranger to a confidante, much, I often imagined, as an explorer in earlier times might have walked into an unknown tribal community and been allowed to sit with the chiefs of that tribe, to become not a member but a scribe of sufficient integrity to be trusted to tell the stories of that tribe to others.

That happened repeatedly in the 1980s and 1990s as I explored, through inside contacts, worlds foreign to me but in which, over time, those who had access to facts and evidence came to trust me. It included the prison culture, law enforcement and the world of Chicago's organized crime where individuals who were powerful within that syndicate brought me within their circle. And in an even greater sense, it happened within the culture of the Church of Scientology.

With the former, I found a deep sense of distrust of journalism and journalists and a cynicism about the media's deepest culture, a perspective that came from hard men who understood political power and influence in ways that belie common beliefs about the nature of our culture.

Within the latter, I found something different, a sort of innocence that, in spite of all evidence that journalists had mis-described the Church, or used attacks against its culture to promote themselves, still believed that journalism might do them justice and tell their story fairly and without bias or agenda.

It was that innocence – or lack of cynicism – that both surprised and attracted me, because the Church, it became clear, had seen so little fairness and balance in the reporting about it. That balance was so rare, I would discover, that when reporters did describe the Church's work without apparent bias, it stood out as unusual because it ran against the grain of the mainstream media. Yet, even its most devoted members continued to believe that fair coverage was possible – and perhaps that is why they opened their doors, and sometimes their hearts, to this stranger.

I've worn the mantle of "investigative reporter" and of being a "Pulitzer winner" to open doors, and I have done that not to gain attention or notoriety but to help find stories to tell. Stories and the telling of them are the way we understand our lives and our place within the world. That is an ancient thing that runs like a thread through the DNA of humanity. If I have learned anything from the culture within journalism and the journalism within our culture, it is that when it is done honestly and fairly and without guile, it is honorable. There is much honor and honesty within the ranks of those who still practice within its boundaries. And I have met more journalists who believe in that ideal than those who don't – though I have met both.

But those who claim the title of "investigative reporter" and don't do honor to that ideal, are corrupters. And there is much corruption within journalism's yellowed history.

Lawrence Wright has throughout his very public career, occasionally claimed the mantle of "investigative reporter" and a fawning and credulous press has itself conveyed that characterization upon his work in widespread ways. *The New Yorker's* editor, David Remnick, has bestowed the term upon Wright's work concerning the history and nature of terrorism, and it is only one of the dissembling contributions Remnick has made to what we can only guess is his true knowledge of Wright's personal history, since he failed to respond to questions.

The press, in its reviews of Wright's work, has also described him as "prescient" and even respected reporters who have made a career on their skepticism of posers, have appeared on such national programs as MSNBC's *Morning Joe,* quick to praise Wright lavishly and repeatedly with these epithets, despite the opprobrium underlying them.

But it is also true that the term "investigative reporting" no longer means what it once did, and little of the reporting described as investigative is actually that. Television reporting often claims to be "investigative," but there is little of that – except for Public Broadcasting's Frontline, CBS's *60 Minutes* and the occasional local reporter who truly digs below

the surface and rejects the assumption-driven journalism that characterizes so much reporting today. And therein lies the problem. Investigative
reporting requires fact-finding beyond the obvious, requires skepticism
about what is already known, and rejects assumption – even the assumption that the reporting of others is accurate.

A former compadre in the business, Gary Massaro, one of the great
reporters I encountered in my career, came on occasion to speak to a
journalism class when I was teaching and always told those young report-
ers-to-be that when you "assume" something "...you make an 'ass' of 'u'
and 'me.'" They may have laughed at the humor, but understood the seri-
ousness of that advice.

Lawrence Wright – who has repeatedly bragged about his lack of "journalism training" – could have benefited from Massaro's lesson in the long
term. His assumptions may fit neatly into the acceptable perspectives, but
they do nothing for the art of journalism itself. And indeed, as I was first
told by Ernie Williams, editor of a modest-sized Indiana newspaper, who
understood the business as well as any editor anywhere, journalism was
always "art not science." Ernie was one of those who thought preserving
the legacy of an honorable profession was a calling that rose above ambition.

Clearly ambition was larger than the craft for Lawrence Wright. He
graduated to big league journalism directly from small, obscure magazines, supported by the same foundation network that served the CIA's
domestic intelligence work and involved the banking community of
Wright's father, and the legal communities created by Robert Storey, his
father's mentor and confidante. And for all those who blindly assume,
without knowing the facts, that Wright's rise to prominence was deftly
made on the strength of his writing ability, his insights into human nature
and of the realities of our culture, should themselves take an investigative
look at what his history has shown was an achievement driven by something other than talent alone.

Wright – like E.B. White, whose admonitions of the duties and responsibilities of writers were noted at the outset of this book – was interested
in literature, in becoming a literary "writer." His ethos was schooled by
writers like Norman Mailer and Joan Didion who brought the kind of literary skill that White possessed to bear on the non-fiction narrative, probably more honestly and accurately than maybe Truman Capote and some

others who mingled fact and supposition into their narrative descriptions – yet combined journalistic reporting with the accurate and colorful observation of detail that brought those facts to life.

But those who helped create this non-fiction narrative culture also knew that it was the reporting – the ability to move inside the culture of others and to describe it fairly and accurately – that brought a writer to the position of speaking with moral authority. Literature gets you to a more creative place, but the foundations of truth and accuracy can't waiver if narrative non-fiction is to be truthful.

For Lawrence Wright – as he has said publicly himself – truth has been a "relative" thing.[230]

As I followed Wright's undisclosed path to these conclusions about his work – including conclusions on his reporting about the Church of Scientology and the War on Terror – what I came to understand was that the arc of his untold story was about more than his experience as a writer or a journalist; it was also about more than his undisclosed intelligence connections or his failure to be candid with his readership over the roots of his rise to a position of power and influence within the media.

It was about the nature of the world of American journalism itself, and its true impact on this country. Moreover, it was about things left unsaid, the secret side of a public career, and how those matters, kept in the shadows, could color – and have colored – what we think we know about the world around us.

As I began my investigation into the question of Wright's journalistic practices, I had not considered anything but the idea that he had earned his place in American letters by virtue of hard work and a talent for literature and story-telling. Indeed, who would imagine that a writer of his notoriety and popularity would have come to that position by anything other than hard work and an uncommon facility with "the word."

Like so many of us who labored in journalism amid dreams of one day creating something literary and lasting, I had looked at the writers who published in *The New Yorker* and in places like *Rolling Stone*, or *Harpers* or *The Atlantic* as icons of a tradition and could only imagine what it must take to create stories so well done, so truthful, and so insightful as to win such an audience.

Even when I began to learn in the course of a long career that newspapers and magazines were not always upholders of the bright lights of liberty and democracy – and that often those vaunted writers themselves had feet of clay, straying into the swamps of journalistic prejudice – I was still something of a true-believer. At least I wanted to believe in the righteous cause of the journalistic community.

In some ways, as I've explored the anatomy of Lawrence Wright's fealty to that community, I must admit that he reinforced for me a lesson I believed I'd already learned long ago – if it was only the truth of the old cliché about not believing anything you read and only half of what you see.

He may have then also been responsible for showing me the real importance of the Fourth Estate and those who faithfully represent what it should be – by what I see as his failure to uphold that somewhat sacred trust.

When newspapers were still locally owned, before the big corporate buy-ups of the 1980s, they may have not always carried the lantern of truth. As I saw happen, newspapers sometimes failed to publish stories that might offend advertisers or prominent citizens, at times diverting reporters away from sensitive stories that might offend the owners' friends or cronies, or the political establishment. They may have done an inadequate job of exposing institutional racism, police misconduct, and public corruption. But in the larger frame, they served an important and honorable purpose, often holding up the proverbial mirror to society. As the demise of those papers has gripped communities all over this country, we are perhaps beginning to understand that we've lost even that – a change unfathomable.

The value of truth and transparency is becoming ever-more apparent with its loss. And that is what we can see in what Lawrence Wright has kept hidden from his considerable public. The exposure of those secrets, I hope, will serve a purpose, if the present press, even as a shadow of its former self, will take its lesson from what is disclosed here.

This is not the definitive story of the Central Intelligence Agency's influence over the American media and its practitioners, or of its propagandistic influence over what we believe is true, and how we believe the world works. There is much more to know and the work of journalists who believe in pursuing the whole story – who are strong enough to convince those who publish their work to have the courage to do so – can help put the shattered ideals of a Fourth Estate back together again.

But that must start with the lessons we learn from what Wright's true history lays bare. The truth is out there. Waiting.

PHOTOGRAPHS

Lawrence Wright, Pulitzer Prize-winning author of The Looming Tower, in an appearance on May, 9, 2013 at the LBJ Presidential Library in Austin, Texas, with Mark Updegrove, CEO of the LBJ Foundation, discussing his then-new book on the Church of Scientology, Going Clear. (Photo by Lauren Gerson, U.S. National Archives.)

Documentary filmmaker Alex Gibney, in Manhattan at the 67th Annual Peabody Awards, June 16, 2008, prior to the release of his film Client 9, on former New York Governor Eliot Spitzer.

Robert G. Storey, immediately at President John F. Kennedy's right, is pictured with other members of the U.S. Civil Rights Commission; Storey was chairman of the State Department's Board of Foreign Scholarships, president of the American and International Bar associations, and founder and owner of the bank where Lawrence Wright's father was president.

Robert G Storey, executive trial prosecutor at the Nuremberg War Crimes trials, presents evidence of plundering of art and cultural artifacts during the procedings in December, 1945.

John McCloy (center), high commissioner for the occupation of Germany, is pictured with President Truman and Secretary of War Henry Stimpson. A central figure in the creation of the CIA and its private-sector intelligence operations, McCloy was characterized by The New York Times at his death as the Chairman of the Establishment. He led Chase Manhattan Bank, The World Bank, the Ford and Rockefeller foundations, the Council on Foreign Relations, served as Assistant Secretary of War and supervised the internment of Japanese Americans in WWII.

John McCloy (right), with President Johnson and McGeorge Bundy, national security advisor to Presidents Kennedy and Johnson. He was closely tied to the CIA, and advised on secret CIA-led-and-funded anti-communist activities in Europe under undisclosed strategies linked to the Marshall Plan. He headed the Council on Foreign Relations, the Ford Foundation, and played strategic Cold War roles throughout.

Republic National Bank of Dallas, Texas, was closely involved with aspects of the American intelligence community. Its chairman emeritus, Karl Hoblitzelle, used his foundation to support clandestine CIA propaganda programs. Renelibrary, Creative Commons.

The American University in Cairo, Tahrir Square, downtown Cairo, Egypt, 2008 (Public Domain/WikiCommons)

AUC's president during Wright's graduate school tenure was Christopher Thoron, who was acknowledged as an operative of the Central Intelligence Agency.

Karl Hoblitzelle, who made a fortune in the movie theatre and Texas oil industry, funded CIA anti-communist propaganda programs through his foundation. He helped found the Southwestern Legal Foundation with Robert G. Storey and was a University of Texas trustee who sought to censor texts and remove faculty over ideological issues.

Shepard Stone was a key figure in the funding of CIA-related propaganda and cultural programs through the Ford Foundation and other foundations and front organizations. He was the director beginning in 1967 of the Congress for Cultural Freedom. Pictured here at the Aspen Institute in Berlin in 1988. (Creative Commons)

Cass Canfield, the powerful and influential American publisher at Harper and Row, was a close friend and tennis partner of John McCloy, and close friend of the CIA's Allen Dulles; he served as a trustee of Farfield Foundation, a front organization that laundered CIA money for its propaganda activities. Canfield served as an important link between the intelligence community and the publishing world. He solicited through a mutual friend a publishing relationship with Lawrence Wright's sister.

Helen Venn, director of the Radcliffe Publishing Procedures Course for four decades, pictured with Richard Bernstein, president of Random House and a powerful influence in the American publishing industry. Bernstein, a co-founder of Human Rights Watch, was among a litany of influential voices in publishing with whom Venn had close relationships. (Photo courtesy of: Schlesinger Library, Harvard Radcliffe Institute, Cambridge, Mass.)

Frank Church holds CIA poison dart gun at committee hearing with vice chairman John Tower on September 17, 1975 (Source: U.S. Capital, photo by Henry Griffin)

Helen Venn, a prominent recruiter for the CIA's cultural Cold War propaganda programs, is pictured with *Texas Monthly* magazine founder Michael Levy, (kneeling), and associate publishers at *Rolling Stone* magazine D. Claeys Bahrenburg, left, and Donald Welsh, right. The previously unpublished photo was taken during the Radcliffe Publishing Procedures summer course in Cambridge in 1978. At the time, Bahrenburg and Welsh had just co-founded *Outside Magazine* with Jann Wenner, publisher and founder of *Rolling Stone*. Bahrenburg and Welsh would go on to influential roles in publishing with major U.S. magazines. Levy would hire Venn-associate Lawrence Wright at *Texas Monthly* in 1981 for his first major magazine job, before he went on to *Rolling Stone* and the *New Yorker*. Levy and *Texas Monthly*'s first editor, William Broyles, along with now-famous writer Daniel Okrent, created a clone of Venn's Radcliffe summer course at Rice University in 1978, which aided in recruiting individuals to journalism and publishing for 20 years. (Photo courtesy of: Schlesinger Library, Harvard Radcliffe Institute, Cambridge, Mass.) .

The author, with David Miscavige, Chairman of the Board Religious Technology Center and ecclesiastical leader of the Scientology religion, at an International Association of Scientologists annual event at Saint Hill in 2015, near East Grinstead in Sussex, England. (Author's personal photo)

The author, with Norman Starkey, trustee and executor of the L. Ron Hubbard Estate, in California in 2018. (Author's personal photo).

199

BIBLIOGRAPHY

BOOKS, MONOGRAPHS, MANUSCRIPTS

Albarelli, H.P. *Coup in Dallas: The Decisive Investigation into Who Killed JFK*. New York: Skyhorse Publishing, 2021.

Albarelli H. P. *A Terrible Mistake: The Murder of Frank Olson and the Cia's Secret Cold War Experiments*. Walterville OR, Chicago IL: Trine Day, 2009.

Agee, Philip. *Inside the Company: CIA Diary*. New York: Stonehill Publishing Company, 1975.

Atack Jon. *A Piece of Blue Sky: Scientology Dianetics and L. Ron Hubbard Exposed*. New York: Carol Publishing Group, 1990.

Bagdikian, Ben. *The Media Monopoly*. Boston, MA: Beacon Press, 1987.

Barnhisel, Greg, and Turner, Catherine. *Pressing the Fight: Print, Propaganda, and the Cold War*. Amherst, MA: University of Massachusetts Press, 2012.

Berghahn Volker Rolf. *America and the Intellectual Cold Wars in Europe: Shepard Stone between Philanthropy, Academy, and Diplomacy*. Princeton N.J: Princeton University Press, 2001.

Berman, Edward H. *The Ideology of Philanthropy: Influence of the Carnegie, Ford and Rockefeller Foundations on American Foreign Policy*. New York: State University of New York Press, 1983.

Bird, Kai. *The Chairman: John J McCloy & The Making of the American Establishment*. New York: Simon & Schuster, 1992.

Bradlee, Ben. *A Good Life: Newspapering and Other Adventures*. New York, Simon and Schuster, 1995.

Brewton, Peter. *The Mafia, CIA & George Bush: The Untold Story of America's Greatest Financial Debacle*. New York: S.P.I. Books Division, Shapolsky Publishers, 1992.

Burke, Jason. *The Road to Kandahar: Travels Through Conflict in the Islamic World*. Toronto: Bond Street Books, 2006.

Burke, Jason. *The New Threat: The Past, Present, and Future of Islamic Militancy*. New York: The New Press, 2015.

Davis, Caroline. *African Literature and the CIA: Networks and Authorship of Publishing*. Cambridge, UK: Cambridge University Press, 2021.

Chaneles, Sol. *CIA and the Books*. Fragmented, unpublished manuscript on the Central Intelligence Agency funding of book publishing and cultural exportation. Washington, DC: National Security Archives, George Washington University, 1989.

Chenyelu, Mamadou. *Motive, Means and Opportunity: Probable Cause for Indicting George W. Bush, his Sponsors and Aides for the Attack of September 11, 2001.* New York: Mustard Seed Press, 2004.

Chinyelu, Mamadou. *Harlem Ain't Nothin' but a Third World Country: The Global Economy, Empowerment Zones and the Colonial Status of Africans in America.* New York: Mustard Seed Press, 1999.

Cooley John K. *Unholy Wars: Afghanistan America and International Terrorism.* London: Pluto Press. 2000.

Coll, Steve. *Ghost Wars: The Secret History of the CIA, Afghanistan, and Bin Laden, from the Soviet Invasion to September 10, 2001.* New York: Penguin Books.

Colodny, Len, and Gettlin, Robert. *Silent Coup. The Removal of a President.* New York: St. Martin's Press, 1991.

Colodny, Len, and Shachtman, Tom. *The Forty-Years War: The Rise and Fall of the Neocons, from Nixon to Obama.* New York: HarperCollins, 2009.

Condon, Richard. *The Manchurian Candidate.* New York: McGraw Hill, 1959.

Fallows, James M. *Breaking the News: How the Media Undermine American Democracy.* United States: Vintage Books, 1997.

Haldeman, Harry R. *The Haldeman Diaries: Inside the Nixon Whitehouse.* New York: G.P. Putnam, 1994.

Heller Kevin Jon. *The Nuremberg Military Tribunals and the Origins of International Criminal Law.* Kettering, UK: Oxford University Press, 2011.

Hench, John B. *Books as Weapons: Propaganda, Publishing, and the Battle for Global Markets in the Era of World War II.* Ithaca, NY: Cornell University Press, 2010.

Herman, Edward S., and Noam Chomsky. *Manufacturing Consent: The Political Economy of the Mass Media.* London, UK: Vintage Digital, 2010.

Hubbard L. Ron. Dianetics: *The Modern Science of Mental Health: A Handbook of Dianetic Therapy.* New York: Hermitage House, 1950.

Kinzer, Stephen. *The Brothers: John Foster Dulles, Allen Dulles, and Their Secret World War.* New York: St. Martin's Griffins, 2014.

Krell, Mary. *Taking Down Backpage: Fighting the World's Largest Sex Trafficker.* New York: New York University Press, 2022.

Laugesen Amanda. *Taking Books to the World: American Publishers and the Cultural Cold War.* Boston, MA: University of Massachusetts Press, 2017.

Marchetti, Victor, and Marks, John. *The CIA and the Cult of Intelligence.* New York: Alfred Knopf, New York, 1974.

Maasri, Zeina. *The Hot Third World in the Cultural Cold War: Modernism, Arabic Literary Journals and U.S. Counterinsurgency.* Cambridge, England: Cambridge University Press, 2020.

Menard, Louis. *The Free World: Art and Thought in the Cold War, New York:* Farrar, Straus and Giroux, 2021.

Mellen, Joan. *A Farewell to Justice: Jim Garrison, JFK's Assassination, and the Case that Should Have Changed History.* Sterling, Va: Potomac Books, 2005.

Mellen, Joan. *Our Man in Haiti: George de Mohrenschidt and the CIA in the Nightmare Republic.* Walterville, Or: Trine Day, 2012.

Mellen, Joan. *Faustian Bargins: Lyndon Johnson and Mac Wallace in the Robber Baron Culture of Texas*. New York: Bloomsbury USA, 2016.

Miller, Russell. *Bare-faced Messiah*. New York: Henry Holt & Company, 1987.

Mills, Charles Wright. 1956. *The Power Elite*. New York: Oxford University Press, 1956.

Murphy, Lawrence R. *The American University in Cairo 1919-1987*. Cairo, Egypt: American University in Cairo Press, 2005.

O'Neill, Tom and Piepenbring, Dan. *Chaos: Charles Manson, the CIA, and the Secret History of the Sixties*. New York: Little Brown, 2019.

Paget, Karen. *Patriotic Betrayal: The Inside Story of the CIA's Secret Campaign to Enroll American Students in the Crusade Against Communism*. New Haven, CT: Yale University Press, 2015.

Plimpton, George. *Writers at Work: The Paris Review Interviews Second Series*. New York: Penguin Books, 1963.

Price, David H. *Cold War Anthropology: The CIA, the Pentagon and the Growth of Dual Use Anthropology*. Chapel Hill, NC: Duke University Press, 2016.

Price, David H. *Threatening Anthropology: McCarthyism, and the FBI's Surveillance of Activist Anthropologists*. Chapel Hill, NC: Duke University Press, 2004.

Price, David H. *Weaponizing Anthropology: Social Science in Service of the Militarized State*. Chico, CA: AK Press, 2016.

Prouty, L. Fletcher. *JFK: The CIA, Vietnam and the Plot to Assassinate John F. Kennedy*. New York: Birch Lane Press, 1992.

Prouty, L. Fletcher. *The Secret Team: The CIA and Its Allies in Control of the United States and the World*. Upper Saddle River, NJ: Prentice Hall, 1973.

Reitman, Janet. *Inside Scientology: The Story of America's Most Secretive Religion*. New York: Houghton Mifflin Harcourt, New York, 2011.

Rich, Paul. *Cinema and Unconventional Warfare in the Twentieth Century*. New York: Bloomsbury Academic, 2018.

Rubin, Andrew. *Archives of Authority: Empire, Culture, and the Cold War*. Princeton, N.J.: Princeton University Press, 2012.

Saunders, Francis Stonor. *The Cultural Cold War: The CIA and the World of Arts and Letters*. New York: The New Press, 2000.

Scott, Peter Dale. *The American Deep State: Big Money, Big Oil and the Struggle for U.S. Democracy*. Washington, D.C.: Rowman and Littlefield Publishers, 2014.

Scott, Peter Dale. *Dallas 63: The first Deep State Revolt against the White House*. Open Road Media, 2015.

Scott, Peter Dale. *The War Conspiracy: JFK, 911 and the Deep Politics of War*. New York: Skyhorse Publishing, 2013.

Storey, Robert G. *The Final Judgment: Pearl Harbor to Nuremberg*. San Antonio, TX: The Naylor Company, 1968.

Storey, Robert G. *Our Unalienable Rights*. Springfield, IL: Charles C. Thomas, Publisher, 1965.

Storey, Robert G. *The Current Peril of the Legal Profession*. Monograph, 1955. Washington and Lee Law Review, pp. 159-181.

Schwartz, Larry. *The Ford Foundation, Little Magazines and The CIA in the Early Cold War*. Monograph: Cultural Logic: Marxist Theory & Practice, 2014, Vol. 21, pp. 76-96.

Talbot, David. *The Devil's Chessboard: Allen Dulles, The CIA and the Rise of America's Secret Government*. New York: HarperCollins, 2015.

Taylor, Telford. *The Anatomy of the Nuremberg Trials*. New York: Alfred Knopf, 1992.

Tolley, Howard B. Jr. *The International Commission of Jurists: Global Advocates for Human Rights*. Philadelphia, PA: University of Pennsylvania Press, 1994.

Weiner, Tim. *Legacy of Ashes: The History of the CIA*. New York: Doubleday, 2007.

Whitney, Joel. *Finks: How the CIA Tricked the World's Best Writers*. Berkley, CA: Counterpoint Press, 2016.

Wilford, Hugh. *The Mighty Wurlitzer: How the CIA Played America*. Cambridge, MA: Harvard University Press, 2009.

Wright Rosalind. *Rocking*. New York: Harper & Row, 1975.

Wright, Lawrence. *City Children, Country Summer: A Story of Ghetto Children Among the Amish*: New York: Scribner, 1979.

Wright, Lawrence. *In the New World: Growing up with America from the Sixties to the Eighties*. New York: Knopf, 1987.

Wright, Lawrence. *Saints and Sinners*. New York: Knopf Doubleday, 1993.

Wright, Lawrence. *Remembering Satan: A Case of Recovered Memory and the Shattering of an American Family*. New York: Knopf, 1994.

Wright, Lawrence. *God's Favorite*. New York: Simon & Schuster, 2000.

Wright, Lawrence. *The Looming Tower: Al Qaeda and the Road to 9/11*. New York: Knopf Publishing Group, 2006.

Wright, Lawrence. *Going Clear: Scientology, Hollywood and the Prison of Belief*. New York: Alfred A. Knopf, 2013.

Wright, Lawrence. *Thirteen Days in September: Carter, Begin and Sadat at Camp David*. New York: Knopf, 2014.

Wright, Lawrence. *The Terror Years: From al-Qaeda to the Islamic State*. New York: Knopf Publishing Group, 2016.

Wright, Lawrence. *God Save Texas: A Journey into the Soul of the Lone Star State*. New York: Knopf Publishing Group, 2018.

Wright, Lawrence. *The End of October*. New York: Alfred A. Knopf, 2020.

Wright, Lawrence. *The Plague Year: America in the Time of Covid*. New York: Knopf Publishing Group, 2021.

Zinn, Howard. *A People's History of the United States*. New York: Harper & Row, 1980.

Zinn, Howard. *You Can't be Neutral on a Moving Train*. Boston, MA: Beacon Press, 1994.

Maasri, Zeina. *The Hot Third World in the Cultural Cold War: Modernism, Arabic Literary Journals and U.S. Counterinsurgency*. 63–100. Cambridge, England: Cambridge University Press, 2020.

END NOTES

Prologue

1 St. Petersburg Times editorials in 2009 urged the Internal Revenue Service to reexamine and deny the Church its non-profit, tax-exempt status, following a series of stories that highlighted allegations by expelled or former Church members. The reporters, in consultation with editors, at the last minute canceled a scheduled interview offered by the Church with the religion's leader David Miscavige about those allegations and published an extensive profile without interviewing him. A police investigation followed but charges brought were dropped after a coroner ruled – as a medical autopsy had already shown - that the death was instead the result of a pulmonary embolism stemming from a deep bruise sustained in a minor traffic accident. Source: Coroner's report, affidavits, news reports, Church legal pleadings, internal Church records.

2 Source: Poynter Institute for Media Studies 5013c records, annual reports; real estate records, public record on transition of ownership of *St. Petersburg Times* to Poynter Institute for Media Studies.

3 See www.freedommag.org/special-reports/sptimes/the_critical_omission.html

4 1980 Pulitzer Prize for National Reporting, Charles Stafford, Bettie Orsini. https://www.pulitzer.org/prize-winners-by-year/1980

5 Freedom magazine reporters documented land transfers involving the Poynter Institute that were not reported by the local press at the time nor received public notice, but that positioned the Institute to obtain valuable land adjacent to the University of South Florida. The *St. Petersburg Times* owner, Times Publishing Company, and the Poynter Institute for Media Studies, were owners and operators of Congressional Quarterly; they were accused in an anti-trust complaint by owners of Federal News Service, a competitor of *Congressional Quarterly*, of cybertheft and corporate espionage in the alleged theft of FNS confidential material in an effort to drive FNS out of business. See https://www.courthousenews.com/congressional-quarterly-accused-of-anti-trust-violations-by-rival-news-service-in-capital/

6 Interview, Lawrence Wright, Institute of International Studies, U/C Berkley, 2007. See http://globetrotter.berkeley.edu/people6/Wright/wright-con2.html

7 Wright, Lawrence, Saints and Sinners. (New York: Knopf Doubleday, 1993), 185-189.

Introduction

8 While many journalists may not have journalism degrees, Wright's education as a writer included elements of an American literary network that was heavily influenced and shaped by CIA Cold War intelligence programs carried out and funded through private interests; that network involved CIA-funded programs using money laundered through private foundations and loans through CIA-linked banks. Cass Canfield president of Harper & Brothers, later Harper & Row, was closely tied to the CIA propaganda network of Allen Dulles and directly involved in war propaganda programs through the Committee on Books Abroad, a wartime intelligence and propaganda program. Canfield mentored and heavily influenced others in the publishing industry, most particularly Simon Michael Bessie, who worked with major literary figures at Harper and later at Alfred Knopf, and who was also active in the psychological warfare, of the Cold War, including those same programs were created in league with the State Department for foreign policy reasons and that informed Wright's literary and journalistic interests. This elite influence has been noted in academic studies describing its anti-democratic impact. See: https://www.cambridge.org/core/journals/perspectives-on-politics/article/testing-theories-of-american-politics-elites-interest-groups-and-av-

erage-citizens/62327F513959D0A304D4893B382B992B See Simon Michael Bessie's obituary for an outline of some of his connections: https://www.nytimes.com/2008/04/08/books/08bessie. html See Bird, *The Chairman*, 1992, 457-458.

9   See Church Committee hearings, 1976 https://www.senate.gov/about/powers-pro-cedures/investigations/church-committee.htm; Iran Contra hearings https://www.brown.edu/ Research/Understanding_the_Iran_Contra_Affair/h-themajorityreport.php. See coverage of Terry Anderson hearing, July, 1996: https://forgottenbooks.com/it/download/CiasUseofJournalistsand-ClergyinIntelligenceOperations_10573005.pdf

10   C.D. Jackson, w an influential member of the Time-Life organization of Henry Luce, and a liaison to the CIA propaganda programs under CIA director Allen Dulles, was a member of the Psychological Strategy Board, which was a central operation in the creation of wartime, and later Cold War propaganda programs. For a thorough analysis See both Whitney, Joel, Finks: How the CIA Tricked the World's Best Writers. (Berkley, CA: Counterpoint Press, 2016) and Wilford, Hugh, The Mighty Wurlitzer: How the CIA Played America. (Cambridge, MA: Harvard University Press, 2009. For additional background on C.D. Jackson's role in intelligence and journalism, his papers are archived at the Eisenhower Presidential Library. See https://www.eisenhowerlibrary.gov/sites/default/files/ finding-aids/pdf/jackson-cd-papers.pdf. See Scott Lucas, Campaigns of Truth: The Psychological Strategy Board and American Ideology, 1951–1953, The International History Review, 1996, Vol. 18 No. 2, 279-302. See https://www.nytimes.com/1977/12/26/archives/worldwide-propaganda-net-work-built-by-the-cia-a-worldwide-network.html

11   In fact, the original cartoon character (1904) in the *Indianapolis Star was* called Joe Crow until the name was changed in 1948 to Jim, and then discontinued in 1985. https://www. indystar. com/story/life/2014/08/22/indianapolis-star-looks-back-years-n-pennsylvania-street/14472977/

12   Operation Mockingbird, Psychological Strategy Board, and numerous other OSS and CIA-designed programs designed for ideological control, and for thought control under programs like MK Ultra, were part of the tools of the CIA that involved propagandizing the American public and foreign citizens. See: https://www.intelligence.senate.gov/sites/default/files/hearings/95m-kultra.pdf

13   Saunders, Francis Stonor, *The Cultural Cold War: The CIA and the World of Arts and Let-ters.* (New York: The New Press, 2000). Saunders book names individuals, writers, intellectuals and publications co-opted by the CIA, and demonstrates that many authors, writers, journalists and artists knew who was paying for their cultural influence. See Tom Braden, *The Saturday Evening Post,* May 20 ,1967, 10–14 https://www.cambridgeclarion.org/press_cuttings/braden_20may1967. html. See James Petras, Monthly Review, November 1, 1999, Vol. 51, No. 6. https://monthlyreview. org/1999/11/01/the-cia-and-the-cultural-cold-war-revisited/

14   Fredrick Praeger of Praeger Press, and Edward Booher, chairman of McGraw Hill, were major figures in American publishing while deeply involved in the CIA's Cold War propaganda programs. Both were frequent speakers at the Radcliffe Publishing Procedures Course and close associates of its director, Helen Venn; Booher and Praeger were major links between American and foreign publishing, the State Department's USAID and CIA programs through which Venn worked around the world to bring western perspectives to foreign countries, and foreign publishers into the U.S. networks. Booher was also a member of the State Department's Board of Foreign Schol-arships where Robert Storey was chairman. See Booher's testimony before the Senate Committee on Labor and Public Welfare, Subcommittee on Education, August-September 1966. See Eighth Semi-annual Report on Educational Exchange Activities, January 3, 1953, 83rd Congress, House Document 45. See Laugesen, Amanda, *Taking Books to the World: American Publishers and the Cul-tural Cold War.* (Boston, MA: University of Massachusetts Press, 2017). Additional sources: Interview with professor of Arabic studies, Levi Thompson, University of Colorado, Boulder, 10/2020. See https://www.nytimes.com/1990/09/25/obituaries/edward-e-booher-79-an-executive-in-publish-ing.html. See The Cultural Cold War and the Circulation of World Literature *Insights from Franklin Book Programs in Tehran, by Esmaeil Haddadian-Moghaddam,* University of Leuven. See https://brill. com/view/journals/jwl/1/3/article-p371_6.xml?language=en

15   See https://www.courier-journal.com/story/news/2018/11/20/courier-journal-report-er-who-couldnt-type-cia-spy/1123581002/

16   See https://www.carlbernstein.com/the-cia-and-the-media-rolling-stone-10-20-1977. Operation Chaos, another domestic spying operation conducted by the CIA, was directed at sub-verting alternative publications; it was exposed in a *New York Times* story by Seymour Hersch in

1977. See https://www.documentcloud.org/documents/238963-huge-c-i-a-operation-reported-in-u-s-against.html

17   Colodny, Len, and Shachtman, Tom. *The Forty-Years War: The Rise and Fall of the Neo-cons, from Nixon to Obama*. (New York: Harper Collis, 2009). Texas A&M University has archived documents from Len Colodny's investigations related to Washington Post Watergate reporter Bob Woodward's involvement with the intelligence community. https://www.watergate.com/colod-ny-collection/texas-a-m-university.

18   Burke, Jason, *The Road to Kandahar: Travels Through Conflict in the Islamic World*. (Toron-to: Bond Street Books, 2006) 135-138.

Chapter 1

19   Plimpton, George and Van Wyck Brooks. *Writers at Work: The Paris Review Interviews Second Series*. (New York: Penguin Books, 1985).

20   Wright, Lawrence, "Why Do They Hate Us So Much," *Texas Monthly*, November, 1983. https://www.texasmonthly.com/news-politics/why-do-they-hate-us-so-much/

21   John Donald Wright military service records, National Archives. See Wright, In the New World, 1986.

22   Personal Interviews, May 5, 2017, Dallas Texas, Larry Foster, former director of Lake-wood Bank & Trust, and Al Goode, former senior vice president, Lakewood Bank.

23   See https://www.nytimes.com/1988/01/14/books/books-of-the-times-343688.html

24   Sources: Ford Foundation annual reports, Ford Foundation archives and reports and cor-respondence related to funding of Race Relations Reporter, and Race Relations Information Center; See digital archives of minutes of AUC trustee meetings for background of AUC relationships and funding from the Ford Foundation. http://digitalcollections.aucegypt.edu/cdm/search/collection/p15795coll3/searchterm/board%20of%20trustees%20minutes%201971/order/nosort See https://www.nytimes.com/1997/02/02/us/carlton-goodlett-82-doctor-and-a-campaigning-publisher.html. See https://www.cia.gov/readingroom/docs/CIA-RDP70B00338R000300030009-3.pdf

25   Jess Kornblum, "Judith Miller Carried Water for the USA's Worst Debacle Since Vietnam," *The New York Observer*, April 8, 2018. See https://observer.com/2015/04/judith-miller-carried-wa-ter-for-the-usas-worst-debacle-since-vietnam/

26   Gardner Cowles, publisher and founder of *Look* magazine, closed the publication in 1971 over losses; Wright's article on astronauts was during a revival of the magazine that lasted one year, in 1979. Gardner Cowles was, along with Cass Canfield, a director of the Farfield Foundation, the CIA front organization that helped fund CIA-related publications and western cultural propaganda programs. See: https://www.cia.gov/readingroom/docs/CIA-RDP80R01731R000400230011-5.pdf

27   Lawrence Wright, *Going Clear: Scientology, Hollywood and the Prison of Belief*, New York: Alfred Knopf, 2013.

28   Disclosures by Freedom concerning CIA experiments on the civilian public, and many other matters, were covered in the 1960s and 70s by *The Washington Post, The New York Times*, and others as the magazine's (and the Church's) use of the Freedom of Information Act began producing evidence of those experiments. See https://www.washingtonpost.com/archive/pol-itics/1979/12/17/report-suggests-cia-involvement-in-fla-illnesses/5b10205e-170b-4e38-b64e-2e9bca8f50df/

29   Personal interview, December 2014. Multiple requests to Wright for interviews about issues raised here was consistently refused, including just prior to this book's completion.

30   FOIA documents obtained by the Church show interagency communication about the Church—FBI, CIA IRS – in in which intelligence and law enforcement agencies passed along ru-mor and innuendo about the organization and encouraged agencies to conduct surveillance and generate intelligence reports. The agencies files are littered with evidence of backchannel efforts to undermine the development of the Church. False reports about the Church began circulating within the CIA as early as 1951 after the Church worked to expose the CIA drug-related mind con-trol experiments; document show CIA and State Department contact with the government of Aus-tralian ahead of repressive measures there in 1963. The CIA used its network of journalists to place stories about the Church in foreign journals, documents note, including a Washington Post report from its correspondent in Portugal describing Hubbard's ship Apollo as a "CIA communication ves-sel;" documents from Spain also described the Apollo as a spy ship. A State Department "airframe,"

document, dated November 21, 1963 - the day before John F. Kennedy was assassinated - from the American Counsel in Melbourne, seeking information on the Church to forward to the legislative council of Parliament of Victoria, where legislation was later enacted restricting the activities of Scientologists.

31   Mark Rathbun's review was posted online. See https://markrathbun.blog/2013/01/20/going-clear-muddies-the-water/

32   Wright claimed during the show he was hypnotized to try to recall if he laughed when Kennedy was killed, as other Dallas school children, he said, were rumored to have done. Rogan asked how old he was at the time of the shooting and Wright said 13. In fact, he was a junior in high school. See https://podtail.com/en/podcast/the-joe-rogan-experience/-1588-lawrence-wright/

33   Ben Zeller, professor of new religions, Lake Forest College, Lake Forest, Illinois, review of *Going Clear* documentary; and, personal interview. See https://www.academia.edu/40339380/The_Going_Clear_Documentary_A_Matter_of_Framing

34   *Amy Kauffman, HBO's "'Going Clear' documentary on Scientology sparks debate," Los Angeles Times,* March 30, 2015. See https://www.latimes.com/entertainment/tv/la-et-st-hbo-going-clear-scientology-20150328-story.html

35   Tony Maglio, "Going Clear Director Demands IRS Repeal Scientology's Tax-Exempt Status," *The Wrap,* April 11, 2015. See https://www.thewrap.com/going-clear-director-demands-irs-repeal-scientologys-tax-exempt-status/

36   See www.scientologyreligion.org/landmark-decisions/

Chapter 2

37   Ivan Matsitsky remains in pre-trial detention. He was originally detained on June 6, 2017. He was in custody from June 8, 2017 until November 14, 2019. He was released but prohibited from doing certain actions from November 15, 2019 until March 16, 2021. He was in custody again from March 16, 2021 until April 8, 2022. He was under house arrest from April 8, 2022 until May 25, 2022. He was remanded back into custody in a pre-trial detention center on May 25, 2022 where he remains. That detention order was in force until August 2022.In total: 1 334 days in custody (as of July 15, 2022); 46 days of house arrest; 487 days of a prohibition on certain actions. Source: Church legal documents and communications. See: https://www.uscirf.gov/religious-prisoners-conscience/current-rpocs/ivan-matsitsky.

38   The Church has noted in legal documents that L. Ron Hubbard wrote the Snow White Program in 1973 as a result of harms suffered by the Church due to the maintenance and dissemination of false reports about the Church in government files. Its aim was to have "all false and secret files of the nations of operating areas brought to view and legally expunged." On January 23, 1985, Ontario, Canada Supreme Court Justice John Harty Osler remonstrated Crown lawyers for filing an affidavit by an Ontario Provincial Police officer that omitted the word "legally" from the above phrase to falsely suggest that the program called for actions outside the law. Justice Osler called the affidavit "incomplete and misleading," noting that all actions called for in the program "must also be interpreted in the light of the phrase 'legally expunge.'" (Reasons for Judgment, January 23, 1985, Osler, J.)

39   See Society of Professional Journalists Code of Ethics https://www.spj.org/pdf/spj-code-of-ethics.pdf

40   In 1993 William Horne, a reporter for the *American Lawyer*, revealed to Church counsel, and published in an article, that Judge Swearingen had discussed his belief in the cause of the dog's death with the reporter. (Swearinger admitted that the family's veterinarian had surmised that the old dog had died of a heart attack and fallen into the pool. But this did not influence Swearinger's conviction that the Church had killed the dog.) The Church was denied an opportunity to challenge the Wollersheim verdict on the basis of prejudice, which the judge himself later acknowledged. See *Church of Scientology of California v. Wollersheim,* 42 Cal.App.4th 628, 49 Cal. Rptr.2d 620. See https://law.justia.com/cases/california/court-of-appeal/4th/42/628.html

41   The Church has detailed the Graham Berry issues that Wright failed to mention: See https://www.lawrencewrightgoingclear.com/wright/chapter-9/graham-berry.html

42   Judith Herman, *Presuming to Know the Truth,* Niemen Reports, Vol. 48, Issue 1, Spring, 1994, 43-45. See https://www.proquest.com/docview/216760781

43   Susan Ross, PhD., a professor of English and media studies at Washington State Univer-

sity. who has authored texts and taught extensively about media law, ethics and journalistic practices, said that because the book was promoted "as the work of a premier investigative reporter," it should be held to those standards. While she said some "gray areas" exist currently in the debate over what constitutes plagiarism - and she described examples of text in the book as clearly questionable - the Society of Professional Journalists in its code of ethics says: "Never plagiarize, always attribute." https://www.spj.org/ethicscode.asp

44   Wright, *Going Clear*, 372. Fact-checkers: Axel Gerdau was a freelance videographer and producer at the time, working with the Austin, Texas National Public Radio affiliate; he later worked for Alex Gibney's Jigsaw Productions; Lauren Wolfe was then a recent journalism graduate at the University of Texas.

45   The appellate court left open New Era's claim for damages for Miller's unauthorized use of 41 passages from L. Ron Hubbard's copyrighted unpublished works. See *New Era Publications International v. Henry Holt and Company*, 873 F.2d 576, United States Court of Appeals, Second Circuit (April 19, 1989).

46   On October 1, 1993, following a two-year examination, the Internal Revenue Service recognized Church of Scientology International – the Mother Church of the Scientology religion – and more than 150 affiliated Churches, missions and social-reform organizations as fully tax-exempt religious organizations. See www.scientologyreligion.org/landmark-decisions/church-of-scientology-irs-tax-exemption.html

47   Janet Reitman, "Inside Scientology," *Rolling Stone,* March 6, 2006, 55. Jon Atack, who wrote the anti-Scientology book *A Piece of Blue Sky*, in an interview posted online, accused Reitman of plagiarizing his work. He made a similar claim against Russell Miller, author of *Bare Faced Messiah,* with whom he had shared his unpublished manuscript. See https://vimeo.com/57494206

Chapter 3

48   Lawrence Wright, Lawrence Wright, actor and Alex Gibney, director. *My Trip to Al-Qaeda* Cinedigm, 2010. See https://www.youtube.com/watch?v=l2tFyEqhYRc

49   John McCloy, who was chairman of the CRF from 1953 to 1970, was replaced by David Rockefeller, who served as chairman until 1985. CIA Director Allen Dulles served as president from 1946 to 1950; McGeorge Bundy, former national security advisor to President Kennedy and former head of the Ford Foundation, his brother William Bundy, a former CIA officer, and Walt Rostow, national security advisor under President Johnson, were among its lengthy list of distinguished members. Rostow, through the LBJ Presidential Library and other connections, maintained ties to Lawrence Wright. All were principal proponents, creators or and participants of the CIA's privately-supported extraneous intelligence network.

50   Wright's memoir came more than six years after the U.S. Senate Select Commission on the Assassination reported that evidence indicated a conspiracy and more than one gunman involved in the murder: See https://www.archives.gov/research/jfk/select-committee-report

51   The term 'deep state" was conceived as a group of powerful individuals well-connected to what President Eisenhower termed the military industrial complex, able to influence elected government officials behind the scenes and capable of altering political events; the term has been applied more recently to actions involving political activism within the government's administrative bureaucracy that allegedly coordinated efforts to undermine the Donald Trump presidency, very similar to fears of communist influences within the federal government during the McCarthy era communist witch hunts. In this context, the term refers to the former.

52   Carl Bernstein, "The CIA and the Media," *Rolling Stone*, October 20, 1977 was among the first to write in depth about Operation Mockingbird, the CIA's media infiltration and propaganda program. See https://www.carlbernstein.com/the-cia-and-the-media-rolling-stone-10-20-1977. See Hugh Wilford, *The Mighty Wurlitzer* (Cambridge, MA: Harvard University Press, 2009). See CIA declassified document "The Family Jewels" https://www.cia.gov/readingroom/docs/DOC_0001451843.pdf

53   A review of Oklahoma Bar Association records contained scant information about Don Wright's law degree, but officials confirmed he was listed as admitted to practice on September 12, 1939, with an office in the First National Bank building. Al Goode, former senior vice president at Lakewood Bank & Trust, told me he discussed with Don Wright his work in law before he became a banker.

54   Larry Foster and Al Goode, personal interview, 2019; The significance of non-official cover would take on more importance upon the discovery of Republic National Bank's close ties to the CIA, and its cooperative working relationships with Lakewood Bank & Trust. Those ties would be publicly identified by author and Temple University professor Joan Mellen, with whom I spoke early in the investigation. Goode said Don Wright expected to become president of Republic National Bank, but said it never came to fruition.

55   Personal interview with Joe Palmer, former professor at AUC, just prior to his death; he had earlier posted online a brief description of AUC's coterie of students who had won conscientious objector status during the Vietnam War. Palmer said he helped Wright's fellow-student and C.O. Robert Van Camp of Michigan, obtain a fellowship position at AUC. Van Camp, whose documents for his Selective Service requirements were intact at the university, according to a review of archived files there, later became a teacher in Michigan and formed a non-profit foundation to support Asian-American student exchange programs in Michigan. Van Camp was later honored in Congress for contributions to education. He said in a personal interview (2017) that he did not come to know Wright at AUC; he said he had heard 'rumors' of CIA involvement at the university, but said he had no personal knowledge of it.

56   British war correspondent for *The Guardian* newspaper and author, Jason Burke, and British documentary filmmaker Adam Curtis, while seeing some value in his reporting, have questioned representations in Wright's book on Al Qaeda. See Andy Beckett, *The Making of the Terror Myth,* The Guardian, October 15, 2004. https://www.theguardian.com/media/2004/oct/15/broadcasting.bbc. See Jason Burke, "The Road that Led to 911," *The Guardian,* September 10, 2006, a review of *Looming Tower* https://www.theguardian.com/books/2006/sep/10/shopping.politics1

57   Robert Storey was appointed on the day of Kennedy's assassination as special counsel for the state investigation for the Texas Supplemental Report on Kennedy's murder. While there was a report prepared, no investigation beyond the Warren Commission 's work was done in Texas. The successor organization to the Southwestern Legal Foundation (founded by Storey and Karl Hoblitzelle), The Center for American and International Law (CAIL) still observes Storey's appointment annually. https://twitter.com/CAIL_LAW/status/1462918913642180615

58   In the Forward to the Warren Commission Report, in review of the powers of the commission, Storey, and Leon Jaworski, were acknowledged by the Commission for their service and assistance in the investigation into the Kennedy assassination. The passage notes that the Texas attorney general, Waggoner Carr and both attorneys were kept informed of the Commission's progress throughout the investigation. See https://www.archives.gov/research/jfk/warren-commission-report/foreword.html

59   Southwestern Legal Foundation, *Southwestern Legal Center News, Vol. 1, No. 6" (1948).* Southwestern Legal Center News, 1948-1957. https://scholar.smu.edu/swlegalcenternews/9. The Southwestern Legal Foundation, through its supporters, trustees and affiliated organizations, played multiple and prominent roles in American foreign policy, national and international political circles, and within the intelligence network created among the CIA's private support communities. In 1948, less than two years after the Nuremberg trials, figures central to the prosecution with Robert Storey became closely involved with Southern Methodist University's law school, with the Southwestern Legal Foundation, and with Republic National Bank of Dallas. The Foundation was headquartered in offices at Republic National Bank, and its membership included Fred Florence, who would succeed Foundation co-founder Karl Hoblitzelle as president of Republic National Bank. Its trustees included Charles E. Dunbar Jr., of New Orleans, La., who taught at Tulane University law school, designed the civil service system for the state of Louisiana, and was on the executive board of the American Bar Association while Storey was president.

60   Karl Hoblitzelle was a significant financial supporter of the University of Texas; a residence hall there is named after him. He also served on the executive committee of Southern Methodist University in Dallas, where Storey was dean of the law school; Hoblitzelle was also a trustee of Texas A&M University and of Texas Tech University. However, controversy surrounded his anti-communist activities after they led him to support censorship of 'liberalism' at the University of Texas in the 1940s. He supported efforts to remove professors and the president of the University, Homer Rainey, through an attorney and lobbyist who worked for him, D. Frank Strickland, a member of the university's board of regents. For a succinct account see Katherine E. Bynum, *Weeding Out the Undesirables: The Red Scare in Texas Higher Education, 1936-1958,* master's degree thesis, University of North Texas, August, 2014. https://digital.library.unt.edu/ark:/67531/metadc699918/m2/1/

high_res_d/thesis.pdf

61   Southwest Legal Foundation named Don Wright to its investment committee according to records of the not-for-profit foundation. As such, he would have had a fiduciary responsibility to review spending for scholarships and other activities of the foundation that were used for intelligence networking. Source: Southwest Legal Foundation documents.

62   See https://vimeo.com/22032352

63   John Le Carre' *The Secret Pilgrim*, (New York: Alfred Knopf, 1991). The author describes in his novel an agent in Berlin using a group of index cards to create a crib sheet of contacts, which are then lost, destroying a secret intelligence network. David Cornwall, for whom John Le Carre' is a pseudonym, was a British intelligence agent prior to his literary career.

64   See *New York Times* obituary of John McCloy. https://www.nytimes.com/1989/03/12/obituaries/john-j-mccloy-lawyer-and-diplomat-is-dead-at-93.html

Chapter 4

65   Wright, *In the New World,* 1986.

66   Wright, *In the New World,* 1986. Wright often compresses time, in this case making it sound like he left for Radcliffe immediately after graduation. Instead, he returned to Dallas, his last semester at Tulane ending in the last week of May, according to university records; the Radcliffe Course did not begin until the third week of June and ended in mid-July. It was indicative of a skewed timeline in his descriptions of his two-year expatriation from the U.S. According to a letter from Helen Venn regarding two additional scholarships for the 1969 Radcliffe Course that he attended, the deadline for accepted students had passed well before April of that year. An application for Wright to determine when he applied was inaccessible because of Radcliffe College archives privacy restrictions.

67   Dutch Hurst Motors 309 High Street, Muncie, Indiana, 1963.

68   Katheryn, McNamara, "*A Conversation with Cornelia and Michael Bessie,*" *The Archipelago*, Vol. 1, No. 4 Winter 1997/98. McNamara's interview offers insights on

publishing recruitment, including through the Radcliffe summer course and an increasing number of similar courses elsewhere. Simon Michael Bessie became a major figure in American publishing and was first mentored in the publishing business by Cass Canfield at Harper & Brothers (later Harper & Row) where he worked for several years. Bessie later joined Alfred Knopf. See http://www.archipelago.org/vol1-4/bessie.htm and http://www.archipelago.org/vol2-1/bessie-2.htm

69   One of the surviving documents from Wright's Selective Service record is a ledger of draft status reports on individuals under the Dallas draft board authority, and their ultimate classification record. Wright's notations indicate he was declared I-A on June 17, 1969, before he left for Radcliffe Publishing Procedures Course. His conscientious objector status approval date was listed as August 19, 1969, while he was living in Boston. The next box on the ledger line reads: "I-W 10/21/69" which is when Wright's status was approved by the draft board as a C.O. It is followed by an entry that's says "I-W Rel" on August 17, 1971, indicating his release from his two-year alternative service commitment; the final entry reads "4W" on May 24, 1972, which designates a conscientious objector who has "completed alternate service contributing to the maintenance of the national health, safety, or interest in lieu of induction into the Armed Forces of the United States." These timelines do not match with Wright's descriptions in his memoir. The six-week Radcliffe course began the third week of June - and ended of July. His notice of approval was dated August 19; if he didn't get the notice personally until mailed, which made it the week of August 25th, he then had only until September 8 - Monday- to find his work and notify the board. Records of any notification to the draft board were absent from his American University in Cairo student file, as released by university archivists. His official application at AUC was not dated until after the deadline for his draft board approvals. Source: University records, available records of the Dallas draft board.

70   Wright, *In the New World,* 1986.

71   For AUC trustee minutes, see https://digitalcollections.aucegypt.edu/digital/collection/p15795coll3/search/searchterm/board%20of%20trustees%20minutes%201971/order/nosort

72   While Wright described in his memoir living in a dorm room with a roommate from Kentucky, and later in a dorm with then-future wife Roberta, and hiding their dog, city directories show that at the time of Wright departure from Boston, they lived at an address in Old Town, near the Paul Revere historic trail, in a small apartment there. The address was listed on his post-dated AUC

fellowship application. While a class list of the 1969 Radcliffe course that Wright attended includes two students from Kentucky, both were female.

73   Student records at American University in Cairo, including communications between the university and the Selective Service Administration and draft boards relating to graduate students from the late 1960s through mid-1970s, were among of a group of records requested and provided by university archivists as part of this inquiry. Wright's records were included. The records of other conscientious objectors who had graduate fellowships and alternative service authorization at AUC, contained communications regarding their draft board authorizations and verifications. Records of verification of alternative service and other communications with the Dallas draft board or Selective Service were not present among Wright's records.

74   Archived records of the Radcliffe class contain extensive letters and memorandums to and from Helen Venn and publishing executives, their assistants, and others, concerning recruiting efforts through English programs and various publishers' regional representatives. Applicants were frequently offered scholarships, though student privacy rules restricted access to individual scholarship information; Interviews with former students indicated many students paid fees which were augmented by financial grants from individuals or entities, primarily publishers. In the year Wright attended, 1969, two last-minute scholarships were added in April to accommodate two additional students, but records did not identify the awardees. The scholarships were from Beacon Press in Boston and the R.R. Bowker Company in New York. Former assistant to Venn, Charlotte Robinson, in an interview in Boston in 2020, noted the elegant literary events hosted by Venn, and her husband, Richard 'Diggory' Venn, and the extent of her friendships within the upper echelons of the American literary community. (Radcliffe Publishing Procedures Course Archives, Schlesinger Library, Harvard Radcliffe Institute.

75   Cass Canfield, Harper & Brothers president, a close friend of Allen Dulles, was active with Venn and his hand-picked successor Michael Bessie would reflect on the importance of the "prestigious" Radcliffe summer course, and some others at universities in the Northeast. Columbia University took over the Radcliffe Publishing Course under the auspice of its journalism department in 2000. Canfield, a powerful influence in selecting who and what works reached American readers, was a director in a CIA front organization to finance propaganda activities, the Farfield Foundation, identified as such in Congressional reports. See https://monthlyreview.org/1999/11/01/the-cia-and-the-cultural-cold-war-revisited/ In addition, as noted by biographer Kai Bird (Kai Bird, The Chairman, 1992), Canfield was a close personal friend, and weekly tennis partner, of John McCloy.

76   Source: Radcliffe Publishing Procedures Course Archives, Schlesinger Library, Harvard Radcliffe Institute.

77   Wright does not identify Thoron as the AUC executive in New York who offered him a scholarship on the spot, but Thorn occupied that post at the time of Wright's account, according to university records. Wright does in his memoir identify Thoron as a former CIA operative, attributing his outing to a prior public disclosure by agent Philip Agee (Philip Agee, Inside the Company: CIA Diary, 1975. He mentions that Soviet 'spies' in Cairo at the time, courted him, but and declenched from the idea of CIA influence at AUC. Thoron, in his early 30s at the time of his appointment, would leave his post died after contracting cancer of the big toe, which was amputated but not in time to save his life (Murphy, American University in Cairo, 2005). See https://www.nytimes.com/1974/01/10/archives/christopher-thoron-dies-headed-university-in-cairo.html

78   Companies like ARAMCO had representatives on the board of trustees at AUC after World War II, and American interests were thoroughly represented by law firms representing those interests which also had ties to Allen and Foster Dulles's firm, Cromwell and Sullivan, and McCloy's law firm, and through McCloy's son, who became a long-term AUC trustee. See: https://digitalcol-lections.aucegypt.edu/digital/collection/p15795coll3/search/searchterm/board%20of%20trust-ees%20minutes%201971/order/nosort

79   The General Accounting Office's Office of Inspector General in 1982 filed a report to Congress complaining about a failure by the USAID to allow access to information, and personnel, to conduct reliable audits of the agency's use of Congressional funding. It noted efforts make to frustrate GAO auditors and described unsuccessful "attempts" to obtain audit cooperation. The US-AID according to Marchetti and Marks (The CIA and the Cult of Intelligence) and Philip Agee (Agee, Inside the CIA, 1975) funded clandestine activities around the world. Their presence and funding at American University in Cairo was ubiquitous. See: https://www.gao.gov/assets/id-82-9.pdf

80   Office of Inspector General, Central Intelligence Agency, Report analyzing the efficacy

of agency training programs at the American University in Cairo. 1972.

81   Helen Venn's maiden name was Doyle; the frequent reference to "Doylie" was apparently a derivation of her maiden name, and used as companion to her husband's nickname, "Diggory," as in: "Diggory and Doiley Venn." Source: Personal correspondence, Radcliff Publishing Course
Archives, Schlesinger Library, Harvard Radcliffe Institute See https://hollisarchives.lib.harvard.edu/
repositories/8/archival_objects/2385467

82   A biographical sketch of Helen Venn is attached to the course description in the Radcliffe Publishing Course Archives at Schlesinger Library, Harvard Radcliffe Institute: "Venn was active in the publishing world: she taught the Franklin Book Program Seminar for publishers from
developing countries (1965); led the Radcliffe seminar "Communications for the Volunteer (1965-
1968) in which volunteers learned how to conduct meetings, plan publicity and promotion, speak
in public, and fund raise; and organized the Brazilian Seminar sponsored by the United States
Agency for International Development (1967-1969). Venn was honored for her contributions to
publishing: she received the Dwiggins Award from Bookbuilders of Boston (1978) was chosen one
of Boston's 100 New Female Leaders by Boston Magazine (1980), inducted into the Publishing Hall
of Fame (1984), and received a Women's National Book Association Book Women Award (1987). See
https://hollisarchives.lib.harvard.edu/repositories/8/archival_objects/2385467

83   Former CIA operative Victor Marchetti and John Marks detailed in the government-cen-
sored *The CIA and the Cult of Intelligence* how the State Department's U.S. Agency for International
Development was used for clandestine funding and cover for the CIA's spy work. They wrote: "Nine
years later Laurence Stern of the Washington Post finally exposed the CIA's massive clandestine effort
in the I974 Chilean election. He quoted a strategically placed U.S. intelligence official as saying, "U.S.
government intervention in Chile was blatant and almost obscene." Stern reported that both the
State Department and the Agency for International Development cooperated with the CIA in funnel-
ing up to $52 million into the country, and that one conduit for the funds was an ostensibly private
organization called the International Development Foundation." Former CIA operative Philip Agee
also listed USAID as cover and facilitator for clandestine CIA espionage and propaganda programs in
his book. (Agee, *Inside the Company*, 1975) See https://www.cia.gov/readingroom/docs/CIA-RDP88-
01315R000200010022-1.pdf   See   https://www.google.com/books/edition/Refugee_and_Human-
itarian_Problems_in_Chi/GjMrAQAAIAAJ?hl=en&gbpv=1&dq=BY+lawrence+stern,+WASHING-
TON+POST,+Aid+for+INTERNATIONAL+DEVELOPMENT&pg=PA36&printsec=frontcover.   See
https://www.cia.gov/readingroom/docs/CIA-RDP88-01350R000200320010-8.pdf

84   See https://www.nytimes.com/1977/12/25/archives/the-cias-3decade-effort-to-mold-
the-worlds-views-agency-network.html

85   Kai Bird, *The Chairman,*1992 483-484.

86   Andy Antippas, New Orleans, telephone interviews, 2022.

87   Charles Stewart Kennedy, The Association for Diplomatic Studies and Training Foreign
Affairs Oral History Project, interview with Andrew F. Antippas, July 19, 1994. See https://adst.org/
OH%20TOCs/Antippas,%20Andrew%20F.toc.pdf

88   Heller Kevin Jon, *The Nuremberg Military Tribunals and the Origins of International Criminal Law*. Kettering, UK: Oxford University Press, 2011. The National Archives collection on John Mc-
Cloy reflects a full record of McCloy's federal government appointments. See https://www.archives.
gov/research/guide-fed-records/groups/260.html

89   The Independence Foundation in Boston and the Kentfield Foundation in Texas were
two examples of shell-foundations used as fronts for the laundering of CIA funds through its intelligence work. Those like the Hoblitzelle Foundation, the Farfield Fund, the Hobby Foundation,
the MD Anderson Foundation, were legitimate non-profit foundations that funded legitimate
programs - but also laundered money for clandestine propaganda programs for the CIA. Source:
Church Committee Report, 1976. See https://www.senate.gov/about/powers-procedures/investi-
gations/church-committee.htm

90   Gordon MacDonald, a renowned scientist, studied plate tectonics and environmental
issues, but also designed the so-called "McNamara Fence" in South Vietnam, a network of surveil-
lance-coordinated minefields. He later designed data-gathering surveillance satellites and coordinated their use for environmental surveys. He served on the CIA's JASON Committee for almost
four decades. http://www.nasonline.org/publications/biographical-memoirs/memoir-pdfs/mac-
donald-gordon.pdf

91   See http://www.archives.nd.edu/Observer/v12/1978-02-02_v12_074.pdf

92   See Neil Sheehan's *New York Times* story of February 19, 1967: "Dean's Fund got Conduit Money." https://www.nytimes.com/1967/02/20/archives/harvard-deans-fund-aided-deans-fund-got-conduits-money.html

Additional documentation can be found in CIA declassified memorandums available online in their FOIA reading room, and in the Church Committee Report.

93   See https://www.cia.gov/readingroom/docs/CIA-RDP73-00475R000402460001-1.pdf

94   Karen Paget, Patriotic Betrayal: The Inside Story of the CIA's Secret Campaign to Enroll American Students in the Crusade Against Communism, New Haven, CT: Yale University Press, 2015.

Chapter 5

95   Wright's characterization of 'chance' events dictating his direction is undermined by his direct ties to those who developed this network. AUC's cultural contributions included intelligence outreach, CIA training programs, extensive State Department support - to the tune of 70% of its needs according to one State Department analysis. See https://www.gao.gov/products/id-78-20. Ford Foundation support for programs also involved directly those who created these propaganda programs. See Volker Rolf Berghahn, *America and the Intellectual Cold Wars in Europe: Shepard Stone between Philanthropy, Academy, and Diplomacy*. Princeton, N.J: Princeton University Press, 2001. See Telford Taylor, *The Anatomy of the Nuremberg Trials*. New York: Alfred Knopf, 1992.

Taylor was a member of the prosecution team, and identified the extensive influence of a small group of lawyers, including John McCloy and Supreme Court Justice Robert Jackson. Jackson recruited Robert Storey to the Nuremberg trial team as executive trial prosecutor.

96   The story of Hiwar's CIA ties was first mentioned by the New York Times deep in a story about CIA satellite spy gadgets in April, 1966 and reported two months later in the London Observer. See Elizabeth Holt, *Bread of Freedom: The Congress for Cultural Freedom, the CIA, and the Arabic Literary Journal Hiwar (1962-67)*, Brill Academic Publishers, January, 2013. See https://brill.com/view/journals/jal/44//1/article-p83_4.xml?language=en

97   The Eisenhower Presidential Library has an extensive collection of materials related to the Psychological Strategy Board and those media figures who were directly involved in its implementations from the beginning of the Cold War. See a compilation of holdings by David J. Haight, 2008: https://www.eisenhowerlibrary.gov/sites/default/files/research/subject-guides/pdf/propaganda-psychological-warfare.pdf

98   Edmund Andrews, "I.G. Farben: A Lingering Relic of the Nazi Years," *New York Times*, May 2, 1999. See https://www.nytimes.com/1999/05/02/business/the-business-world-ig-farben-a-lingering-relic-of-the-nazi-years.html

99   David Price, *Cold War Anthropology*, 2016. For details on U.S. government funding for AUC, see https://www.gao.gov/products/id-78-20

100   Richard Crabbs would also serve on the Board of Foreign Scholarships with Robert Storey. A former professor at Indiana University, Crabbs was instrumental in the creation of the Ford Foundation-funded English Language Institute. For a guide to Richard Crabbs' archived records at AUC, see https://lib.aucegypt.edu/showxmlattach/b1450652:0

101   The English Language Institute (ELI) has operated for decades and is a fundamental vehicle for cultural contact, bringing programs to foreign students, encouraging western cultural exploration. In the process it helped the CIA develop ties to political and socially prominent families using scholarship opportunities in Egypt, and the U.S. TEFL (Teaching English as a Foreign Language) was an affiliated State Department initiative around the world for the purpose of cultural exportation, exchange, and development of intelligence ties. See https://files.eric.ed.gov/fulltext/ED101591.pdf . A Ford Foundation study of the ELI program in 1970 by J. Donald Bowen of UCLA found difficulties in the AUC ELI program related to graduate students who were not adequately prepared to teach English to non-English speakers. He cited lack of supervision of graduate fellows who, he observed, frequently had limited teaching experience.

102   Murphy, *The American University in Cairo 1919-1987*, 2005.

103   Bird, *The Chairman*, 1992.

104   Robert G. Storey, *Our Unalienable Rights*. Springfield, IL: Charles C. Thomas, Publisher, 1965.

105   Francis Stonor Saunders, *The Cultural Cold War: The CIA and the World of Arts and Letters.* New York: The New Press, 2000.

106   Prominent American author Dwight MacDonald, in a series of stories in *The New Yorker*, detailed cultural efforts of the Ford Foundation, and would become an editor of the CIA-funded Encounter magazine. https://www.newyorker.com/magazine/1955/11/26/part-i-foundation-the-french-just-dont-believe-it. He was a guest speaker at the Radcliffe Course in 1963.

107   Stratfor, based in Austin where Wright resides, offered copies of Wright's book *Looming Tower*, gratis, to new subscribers, and Wright appeared at events with Stratfor executives to sign his book and greet security clients, according to copies of Stratfor emails that were released by WikiLeaks. See https://wikileaks.org/WikiLeaks-Impact-is-Stratfor-s.html. According to a confidential source with close ties to Stratfor, who spoke with Hank Albarelli on a non-attribution basis, Wright both provided and received information through his contacts with the private security firm, which has retained close ties to the Central Intelligence Agency.

108   Bird, *The Chairman*, 1992.

109   Zeina Maasri, *The Hot Third World in the Cultural Cold War: Modernism, Arabic Literary Journals and U.S. Counterinsurgency.* Cambridge, England: Cambridge University Press, 2020, 63–100. https://www.cambridge.org/core/books/abs/cosmopolitan-radicalism/hot-third-world-in-the-cultural-cold-war/284373C3061601131ECBFC0E0ABDFEF0

110   Louis Menard, *The Free World: Art and Thought in the Cold War, New York:* Farrar, Straus and Giroux, 2021. Menard's careful analysis of the involvement of the New York Museum of Modern Art, and the influence of anti-communists and the CIA as part of its propaganda-linked funding, was first detailed in a story *for The New Yorker.* see Louis Menard, *Unpopular Front: American Art and the Cold War*, The New Yorker, October 9, 2005. It describes intelligence-related support for the arts, and the attitudes of MOMA trustees. He notes that publisher and former CIA operative Tom Braden was, early in the Cold War, MOMA's executive director. Various trustees were also involved with the CIA-front Farfield Foundation. Menard, however, suggests distance between the spy agency and individual artists whose work was promoted. https://www.newyorker.com/magazine/2005/10/17/unpopular-front. The author's book expanded on those themes in 2021.

111   Howard Zinn, *What the Classroom Didn't Teach Me About the American Empire,* TomDispatch.com, 2008 See https://www.salon.com/2015/10/17/what_the_classroom_didnt_teach_me_about_the_american_empire_partner/

112   A letter, April, 1969, by Helen Venn, concerning scholarship opportunities for the Class of '69, noted that the course was scheduled to begin June 18 and end July 29. Radcliffe Publishing Course Archives, Schlesinger Library, Harvard Radcliffe Institute.

113   Files released by AUC archivists include a memorandum from AUC President Christopher Thoron to Roberta Wright in 1971, regarding her early return to the U.S., and grants permissions for completing her degree; a memo to Lawrence Wright from Thoron addresses payment of her airfare by the University.

114   The majority of Wright's draft records were destroyed in the National Archives fire in 1973, according to responses to FOIA requests, but some exist. His draft registration card, showing he'd filed his registration eight days late, and a classification ledger recording dates of his draft status changes, survived. The absence of documents in his AUC file reflecting confirmation of his alternative service was only one of the peculiarities of his draft exemption. According to Bill Gavin, a conscientious objector during the Vietnam War and later counseling director for the Center on Conscience and War, said in an interview that Wright's experience, as described, was highly unusual. Wright, according to his own described timelines, had no hearing before the Dallas draft board on his conscientious objector application and offered no witnesses; Gavin said failing to present evidence in support at a hearing was a ticket to having a C.O. application rejected. He noted that as the war intensified, and after the U.S. Supreme Court redefined religious belief criteria for C.O.s, the number of applicants rose steadily, along with rejections.

115   Wright, *In New World,* 1987. In fact, what for Wright sounds like a casual observance, bombings in Helwan were also drawing the interest of CIA operatives in Egypt. Declassified documents released under FOIA show that in the winter of 1969, numerous previously classified human intelligence reports had been filed by the agency on bombings in the industrial sector; high-altitude surveillance reports described structures and damage, and assessed impact on the areas continued industrial capacities. See https://www.cia.gov/readingroom/docs/CIA-RDP-

Chapter 6

116   Ford Foundation report on status of scholarships and other funding for American University in Cairo programs and on graduate programs at AUC, 1969-70.

117   In an interview on National Public Radio in 2010, concerning his research on *Looming Tower*, Wright noted the problems for journalists who are perceived as CIA-affiliated, and hw denied any personal affiliation on his part: "One of the worst problems that a foreign correspondent has, especially in that part of the world, is that people are constantly accusing you of being in the CIA, which is, you know, almost like a fatwa on your head and that always was following me around. And, you know, I was not in the CIA and yet there was that common idea that if you wanted to know this kind of information you must have an affiliation with the intelligence community." See https://www.npr.org/transcripts/129697986

118   Price, *Cold War Anthropology, 2016*. Personal interviews: Prof. David Price, St. Martin's University, (2021); Prof. Joan Mellen, Temple University, (2017); Prof. Peter Dale Scott, University of California, Berkley, (2016-2021).

119   Bird, *The Chairman*, 1992. Extensive and detailed records of McCloy's history of public service and his government appointments are contained in his archived papers at Amherst, University, records of the Ford and Rockefeller Foundations, the Congressional Record, U.S. State Department, Library of Congress, and the presidential libraries of presidents Franklin Roosevelt through Ronald Reagan.

120   Bird, *The Chairman*, 1992.

121   Saunders, *The Cultural Cold War, 2000*.

122   Sen. William Fulbright, a democrat from Arkansas who service with Robert Storey, his political opposite, on the Board of Foreign Scholarships, publicly opposed the CIA's propaganda programs, though scholarships though the U.S. State Department, both at home and abroad, were routinely used to develop intelligence-related relationships, witting and unwitting. A story in March, 1967 by *United Press International* and *New York Times* reporter Henry Raymont, collected in CIA now-declassified files, recorded Fulbright's threat to defund any financing for book publishing programs used to "propagandize" U.S. foreign policy under the Johnson administration. See https://www.cia.gov/readingroom/docs/CIA-RDP88-01350R000200320010-8.pdf

123   Editorial, *New York Times*, September 4, 1964. See https://www.nytimes.com/1964/09/04/archives/misusing-cia-money.html

124   The *Saturday Evening Post* was purchased and moved to Indianapolis, Indiana by former OSS member Burt Servvas, and his wife, Cory, served as publisher; Braden's status in the CIA was not as well-known as his roles in journalism and the entertainment media; he was close to Stuart Alsop and his brother Joseph, both political journalist with witting ties to the Central Intelligence Agency, disclosed in press reports on Operation Mockingbird. See https://www.nytimes.com/1977/12/26/archives/worldwide-propaganda-network-built-by-the-cia-a-worldwide-network.html?smid=url-share

125   Congressional testimony in the Church Committee hearings in 1975 revealed widely-reported CIA excesses that included domestic propaganda; Some 20 years later, congressional testimony by journalist and then recently-released hostage Terry Anderson, and leading journalists like Ted Koppel, again raised concerns about journalists used as agents or intelligence sources by the CIA. Those are matters that argue against widely-held beliefs that CIA influence over American journalism was dismantled following disclosures of foundation-funded influences and cold war infiltration, corrupting journalism. Evidence - most particularly Lawrence Wright's Pulitzer-winning testimonial on terrorism - suggests that those ideas, ideologies or intents, despite public pronouncements and presidential orders, were never really abandoned.

126   Freedom of Information Act requests to the Federal Bureau of Investigation regarding Race Relations Reporter related to ColntelPro surveillance and pertinent issues, yielded more than 800 pages of documents, many of which were unreacted and disclosed the depth of contact that FBI field offices engaged in through the illegal political and ideological surveillance that the now-discontinued program conducted. No appeal for redactions portions or omitted documents

was filed.

127   Among research that explored some of those reasons is the remaining parts of the un-published and now missing manuscript on these issues by sociologist Sol Chaneles, referenced above. The surviving portions, essentially end notes, are housed at the National Archives. Copies were obtained courtesy of anthropologist David Price.

128   Joe Simnacher, staff writer, *Don Wright, banker, dies at 85. Dallas Morning News*, April 13, 2001. Charles Storey died July 14, 2008, at age 85. See https://www.legacy.com/us/obituaries/dallasmorningnews/name/charles-storey-obituary?n=charles-storey&pid=113546044

129   Eli Whitney Debevoise was also a founder of the International Commission of Jurists, who, along with John McCloy, and in coordination with Robert Storey, representative of the American Bar Association at ICJ meetings internationally, helped create the organization in post-war Berlin to oppose communism internationally (Originally named the International Congress of Jurists). Storey was an influential promoter of the ICJ and its usefulness in intelligence development in foreign countries. Storey, later became president of the Inter-American Bar Association, and was honored for his work in international law and service with the International Commission. Philip Agee, former CIA operative – in his book *Inside the Company: CIA Diary* – identified the ICJ as a CIA-funded anti-communist organization at its inception, through the American Fund for Free Jurists. The organization, Agee noted, later said publicly it had cut ties with the agency. The organization today is a body promoting international justice and human rights. See: https://www.icj.org/wp-content/uploads/1959/01/Rule-of-law-in-a-free-society-conference-report-1959-eng.pdf See: Center for American and International Law (formerly Southwestern Legal Foundation) https://cailaw75.org/cailaw-history/about-dean-storey/

130   Howard B. Tolley Jr., *The International Commission of Jurists: Global Advocates for Human Rights* (Philadelphia, PA: University of Pennsylvania Press, 1994). According to Tolley, the CIA funding was unknown to most jurists who participated and after disclosure of such funding in 1967, the ICJ severed ties with the agency, but not with the individuals who were responsible for those relationships. See Bird, *The Chairman*, 1992, 437-439. Additional detail on funding can be found in Ford Foundation annual reports.

131   Congressional Quarterly, Special Report on CIA Disclosures, February 24, 1967; See http://jfk.hood.edu/Collection/Weisberg%20Subject%20Index%20Files/C%20Disk/CIA%20Foundations/Item%20041.pdf

132   See *The Rule of Law in a Free Society,* Conference Report, New Delhi, India, January 1959. https://www.icj.org/wp-content/uploads/1959/01/Rule-of-law-in-a-free-society-conference-report-1959-eng.pdf

133   See Minutes of Trustees, American University in Cairo. https://digitalcollections.aucegypt.edu/digital/collection/p15795coll3/search/searchterm/board%20of%20trustees%20minutes%201971/order/nosort

134   Race Relations Reporter Archival Collection, Amistad Center, Tulane University, New Orleans. Ford Foundation, annual reports. See https://amistad-finding-aids.tulane.edu/repositories/2/resources/554

135   *New York Times*, "Magazine on Race forced to quit," April 16, 1972, 17. https://www.nytimes.com/1972/04/16/archives/magazine-on-race-is-forced-to-quit-foundation-aid-is-halted-for.html

136   The Manhattan Institute. See https://www.manhattan-institute.org/expert/judith-miller

137   William Broyles Jr., archived collection, biography, Texas State University; Texas Monthly, Rice University alumni newsletter, Rice Publishing Procedures Course. See https://www.thewittliffcollections.txst.edu/research/a-z/broylesjr.html

138   See https://twitter.com/lawrence_wright/status/1465760198170136581

139   See http://www.denverpi.com/investigators/ The author volunteered his time to encourage pro bono investigation into matters of public interest.

140   The New Yorker "In the Mail" section, November 8, 1994.

141   See Neiman Reports, 1994, *Presuming to Know the Truth*, Judith Herman, MD, Professor of Clinical Psychology, Harvard School of Medicine. See:http://niemanreports.org/wp-content/uploads/2014/04/Spring-1994_150.pdf

142   Polk City Directory, Dallas, Texas, 1965; Entry: Donald B. Wright, 2610 Knight Street, Knight Aire Apartments #101; Employer: O'Neal Funeral Home. He was no longer listed at a Dallas address in 1966; Jack Ruby died January 7, 1967 of a pulmonary embolism, fewer than 30 days after his diagnosis of lung cancer.

143   Wright, *In the New World,* 1987.

144   Wright could have heard a more interesting story than that of his cousin, stemming from his father's close connection to Robert Storey. Their relationship, according to Al Goode, former senior vice president with Lakewood Bank and Trust, was "close." Storey was in a position to relate stories of his own visit at the Dallas County Jail with Ruby, alongside Supreme Court Justice Earl Warren, during the Warren Commission inquiries, and of Ruby's communications with CIA-funded psychiatrist Louis Jolyon West, who examined Ruby there.

145   Dexter Filkins, *The Plot Against America,* book review, *The Looming Tower,* by Lawrence Wright, *New York Times,* August 6, 2006. See https://www.nytimes.com/2006/08/06/books/review/06filkins.html

146   Wright, in a 2007 interview with UK magazine *Stop Smiling* said: "I was in London the week that Adam Curtis's *The Power of Nightmares* documentary appeared on the BBC. He and I had dinner and he went so far as to deny the existence of Al-Qaeda. I said, "Adam, I've got the foundation documents for Al-Qaeda in my briefcase." And he didn't ask to see them. For me, that was a very telling moment." See https://www.prospectmagazine.co.uk/magazine/arealnightmare. See https://www.bbc.co.uk/iplayer/episodes/p088s5k4/the-power-of-nightmares.

147   Jason Burke, "The Road that Led to 911," review of *The Looming Tower,* *The Guardian,* September 10, 2006. See https://www.theguardian.com/books/2006/sep/10/shopping.politics1.

148   Burke, "The Road that Led to 911."

149   Wikileaks, Public Library of U.S. Diplomacy, State Department Cable, May 1, 2009. https://wikileaks.org/plusd/cables/09RIYADH651_a.html

Chapter 8

150   *See The Church of the New Faith v. Commissioner of Pay-Roll Tax (Victoria)* 154 CLR 120, 57 ALJR 785, 14 ATR 769, 49 ALR 65, 83 ATC 4652 http://uniset.ca/other/cs6/154CLR120.html

151   The Psychological Practices Act in the state of Victoria in 1965 banned the practice of Scientology. The Australian High Court's 1983 decision found that the Act "discriminated expressly" against the Church of Scientology. The court's ruling created a seminal definition of religion that has resonated around the world, the Church has noted. The court found: "Whenever the legislature prescribes what religion is, or permits or requires the executive or the judiciary to determine what religion is, this poses a threat to religious freedom. Religious discrimination by officials or by courts is unacceptable in a free society. The truth or falsity of religions is not the business of officials or the courts. If each purported religion had to show that its doctrines were true, then all might fail. Administrators and judges must resist the temptation to hold that groups or institutions are not religious because claimed religious beliefs or practices seem absurd, fraudulent, evil or novel; or because the group or institution is new, the number of adherents small, the leaders hypocrites, or because they seek to obtain the financial and other privileges which come with religious status. In the eyes of the law, religions are equal. There is no religious club with a monopoly of State privileges for its members. The policy of the law is "one in, all in." http://uniset.ca/other/cs6/154CLR120.html

152   In the 1970s, through an investigation conducted with Simon Wiesenthal, *Freedom* documented Interpol's roots in Nazi intelligence services from WW II. [Letter from Simon Wiesenthal to Church of Scientology, March 14, 1975. The Church's *Freedom* magazine investigated and published media accounts that exposed Interpol's Nazi roots. "Church of Scientology to Warn of Interpol Dangers," *Rocky Mountain News,* September 13, 1975; "Interpol's Nazi Problem," *San Francisco Examiner,* October 4, 1975; "FBI's Nazi Ties Uncovered," *Freedom* magazine, December 1977-January 1978.

153   See: https://www.theguardian.com/society/2012/oct/04/thomas-szasz.

154   A collection of video statements concerning the Church of Scientology and its history in the human rights arena can be found at www.scientologyreligion.org.

155   See statement from Church of Scientology International at www.leahreminiaftermath.com

156   New York church members who knew Remini as a teenager when her family attended there told me during a rally in New York City that her behavior then and now had changed little. They recalled her as a teenager obsessed with calling attention to herself. Remini, a sit-com actress, was "not qualified" to act as a senior advisor within the Church hierarchy, I was told. Later, officials denied receiving any formal request and noted that "no such advisory position existed." Remini sued the Church for defamation in 2023, though a majority of her claims were dismissed by the court in the Church's favor over First Amendment issues. The suit was pending at publication. The church had previously noted its position on the Remini matters online. See www.leahreminithe-facts.org.

157   On August 12, 1991, Church of Scientology International filed a $120 million lawsuit against 17 IRS agents accusing the IRS of waging a 33-year war against the Church and individual members. Illegal tactics of the IRS included: "the use of mail covers, paid informants, summonses to dozens of financial institutions and church members, and infiltration of Scientology's ecclesiastical hierarchy." Complaint, Church of Scientology International v C. Phillip Xanthos, et al. United States District Court for the Central District of California, Case No. 91-4301 SVW(Tx); "Scientologists Sue 17 IRS Officials," *Los Angeles Times*, August 13, 1991. https://www.latimes.com/archives/la-xpm-1991-08-13-mn-861-story.html

158   On November 20, 1988, Scientologists from around the world gathered in Madrid, Spain, for a convocation of the International Association of Scientologists. In attendance were the President of the Church of Scientology International and executives from Scientology Churches in many countries. During that religious gathering, Guardia Civil, armed with machine guns, raided what was a peaceful assembly and arrested all foreigners in attendance. They handcuffed 72 Scientologists in all and paraded them in front of the media before carting them off to a prison in Spain that was notorious for violence and inhumane condition. Fourteen years after the initial raid and 17 years after the investigation was opened, the charges were finally brought to trial and all defendants unequivocally exonerated of all charges. The court stated: "acquitted without reservation." [Judgment No. 335/2001, Provincial Court of Madrid, November 28, 2001]; Following those exonerations the Spanish Church achieved official religious recognition. On October 31, 2007, the National Court in Madrid issued a unanimous landmark decision recognizing that the National Church of Scientology of Spain is a religious organization entitled to the full religious rights that flow from entry in the government's Registry of Religious Entities. [National Court of Spain, Decision of October 31, 2007; Official Registration of Church of Scientology, December 13, 2007] Church leaders said the recognition marked the end of an era in which Spanish Scientologists were forced to fight for their rights to religious freedom, vindicated the Church in Spain and signaled a new era for the practice of Scientologists there.

159   The civil case alleging rape was adjudicated in New York and was went to trial in late October 2022. Haggis was found responsible for rape and sexual assault and ordered by the judge to pay $10 million in damages. Haggis' arrest in Italy on June 19, 2022 on suspicion of sexual assault led to temporary house arrest, but he was released subsequently by a judge who found insufficient evidence to hold him. Meanwhile, prosecutors considered an appeal of his release in late summer 2022, but no criminal charges were brought..

160   Marty Rathbun posted a series of videos about his reactions to false claims by Wright and Gibney. www.youtube.com/sthtexlensman/videos. In particular, for Wright's distortions about the IRS, see Going Clear, Part 13 IRS – Actual Malice on Wright's Behalf, Mark Rathbun, June 15, 2017 https://youtube.com/watch?v=2OOw9FahGks. Rathbun also details what he terms lies and hypocrisy in the *Anti-Scientology Cult*. See www.youtube.com/watch?v=ZFJdOhV29WM

161   On April 28, 1991, *Time* magazine published an eight-page negative cover story on the Church of Scientology. The Church's PR firm, Hill & Knowlton, immediately terminated its relationship with the Church. The Church fought back with series of full-page ads in *USA Today*, which ran all summer. These included a 28-page insert entitled "The Story Time Couldn't Tell," in which the Church disclosed that drug giant Eli Lilly was the source of the *Time* article and the resignation of Hill & Knowlton. Objecting to the Church's disclosures about the dangers of Its drug Prozac, Eli Lilly had influenced the publication of the *Time* article in exchange for purchasing 250,000 reprints to send across the country. At the same time, for a year leading up to the *Time* article, Eli Lilly had pressured the owner of Hill & Knowlton, WPP Group, to sever the Church's account or lose Lilly's account with WPP Group subsidiary, J. Walter Thompson PR firm. In 1992, Church of Scientology International sued Eli Lilly, WPP and the PR firms for their interference in the Church's relationship

with Hill & Knowlton. Discovery in the case supported all the claims that the Church had made in "The Story Time Couldn't Tell." After the Church defeated the defendants' attempt to have the suit dismissed (CSI v. Lilly, 848 F.Supp.1018 (1994)), the defendants settled the case on the eve of trial for a confidential amount, as reported in the *Wall Street Journal*. See "WPP/Lilly Suit Settled," *Wall Street Journal*, July 6, 199. https://www.nytimes.com/1996/11/01/business/magazine-settles-libel-suit-by-scientologist.html

162   When CNN criticized Backpage.com Ortega came to its defense attempting to brush off the harms done by its personal ads. Ortega used "junk science" from vested interest groups to argue that sex trafficking of underage girls is something less than the national epidemic it is. CNN reporter Amber Lynn felt the wrath of Ortega after her expose of child prostitution and Backpage.com, entitled *Uncovering America's Dirty Little Secret*.

Ortega wrote: "CNN leads the media's mass paranoia." He attacked the broadcast as a "sensationalistic piece," that he labeled "manipulative" as well as Lynn's "involvement in a semireligious crusade." See Tony Ortega column *CNN's* "Amber Lyon Ambushed Craigslist – But She Won't Talk to the Village Voice," *Village Voice*, July 6, 2011. https://www.villagevoice.com/2011/07/06/cnns-amber-lyon-ambushed-craigslist-but-she-wont-talk-to-the-village-voice/

163   Wayne Barrett, a legend in New York investigative journalism, in a September 2, 2016 interview with L.A. Rivera, described Ortega as a "twisted human being." Barrett described Ortega's editorial relationships as fraught and said he'd suspended an award-winning writer for not responding to an email while away on vacation. Barrett said in one incident he was working to meet a cover-story deadline when his wife was injured in a fall and hospitalized. Barrett said Ortega told him he needed to make deadline anyway, but after finishing the story, it didn't appear. Ortega, he said, forced Barrett had to get outside help for his wife, though he had already decided to hold the story. He said Ortega's disrespect to accomplished staff did not sit well. Ortega later fired Barrett, he said, but never told him why. Barrett, one of the *Voice's* investigative legends, told Rivera that, as an editor, Ortega was over his head. "I didn't like the guy at all," he said.

164   In November, 2023, A federal jury in Phoenix, Arizona convicted Michael Lacey and two other former owners of Backpage.com, of promoting prostitution enterprises and multiple counts of money laundering and conspiracy. James Larkin committed suicide before the trial began. See Office of Public Affairs, U.S. Department of Justice, prss release: https://www.justice.gov/opa/pr/backpage-principals-convicted-500m-prostitution-promotion-scheme

165   Krell, Mary, *Taking Down Backpage: Fighting the World's Largest Sex Trafficker*, New York: University Press, 2022. See https://www.washingtonpost.com/outlook/2022/04/08/prosecutors-fight-against-sex-trafficking-backpagecom.

166   Kara Bloomgarden Smoke, "Runnin' Scared: Was Tony Ortega pushed out at the *Village Voice?" New York Observer*, September 14, 2012. See Tom McGeveran and Joe Pompeo, "Village Voice' editor-in-chief (and chief Scientology antagonist) Tony Ortega leaves the paper, amid downsizing and turmoil," *Capital New York*, September 14, 2012. The Church published its own response to Ortega's anti-Scientology writings at www.whoistonyortega.org.

167   At least three members of the Sea Organization working with Freedom told me over time of incidents in which Rinder, enraged, engaged in physical violence against other staff members.

168   The Church's online response to Lawrence Wright's book and the film adaptation by Alex Gibney contains white papers, which document their arguments on principal sources for *Going Clear*, including Rathbun and Rinder. https://www.freedommag.org/going-clear/white-papers/documentary-sources.html

169   The Church has summarized allegations of malfeasance and lying that resulted in the removal of Rathbun and Rinder from ecclesiastical positions. See https://www.freedommag.org/special-reports/sptimes/what_really_happened.html

170   The Church has posted a set of detailed reports on the coverage by the St. Petersburg Times. https://www.freedommag.org/special-reports/sptimes/the_critical_omission.html

171   Emma Bubola and Sarah Bahr, "Paul Haggis Arrested on Sexual Assault Charges in Italy," *New York Times*, June 19, 2022. See https://www.nytimes.com/2022/06/19/arts/paul-haggis-arrested-sexual-assault-italy.html

172   Church officials note that Paulette Cooper's problems were with the same individuals associated with the former Guardian's Office. In March of 1985, following the disbanding of that

rogue unit, records show that the Church of Scientology settled all outstanding lawsuits with Pau-lette Cooper.

173   Joshua Fechter, "Police: Texas woman crashed car into Scientology church because it is 'evil,'" *San Antonio Express-News*, December 16, 2015. See https://www.mysanantonio.com/news/local/crime/article/Police-Texas-woman-crashed-car-into-Scientology-6702730.php

174   Karen Paget, Patriotic Betrayal, 2015. Paget notes that William Sloane Coffin, former chaplain at Yale, Alex Gibney's stepfather, an advisor to the National Student Association, was affil-iated with the Central Intelligence Agency. Paget discloses a student's recollection of Coffin's tacit admission that he knew of the intelligence agency's infiltration, control and funding of the Nation-al Student Association before its public disclosure in 1967.

175   The Church notes that the Citizens Commission on Human Rights (CCHR) is a men-tal health watchdog established in 1969 by the Church of Scientology, co-founded with noted psychiatrist Thomas Szasz. According to its public positions, its goals are eradicating psychiatric abuses and ensuring patient protections, The organization has supported enactment of more than 200 laws protecting individuals from abusive psychiatric practices, including ensuring informed consent for psychiatric treatment, ending enforced drugging and electroshocking of children, and mandating severe penalties for sexual abuse of patients by psychiatrists and psychologists. See: https://www.cchr.org

176   Abrutyn wrote: "[T]here is no requirement, legal or otherwise that they [documenta-ries] treat all points of view equally…. [T]he Church will in no way be impeded from using its re-sources and access to other channels of communication to share its point of view with the public." Stephanie S. Abrutyn, Counsel for HBO, December 5, 2014 "I trust that going forward, you will focus your efforts on providing any pertinent factual materials in a timely fashion that you wish Mr. Gib-ney to consider, and that the Church will use its resources and experience to share its point of view, along with any information it wishes to provide with the public." Stephanie S. Abrutyn, Counsel for HBO, December 19, 2014. Despite appearing to offer this opportunity to share pertinent factual in-formation, Alex Gibney refused to speak with or meet with anyone from the Church, going so far as to refuse to respond to letters, emails or phone calls, the Church notes. A January 23, 2015 commu-nication from Church spokesperson Karin Pouw to Alex Gibney is posted at: www. Freedommag.org/going-clear/

177   Interview, Eric C. Rodenberg, former investigative reporter, *Indianapolis Star*, 2021.

178   Ken Ringle, Army Sprayed Bacteria on Unsuspecting Travelers, *Washington Post*, Decem-ber 5, 1984. See https://www.cia.gov/readingroom/docs/CIA-RDP90-00806R000201000006-2.pdf

179   *Deseret News*, Paul Newman Liked to Joke about his Baby Blues, September 30, 2009. The story, from Associated Press, quoted Newman's daughter, Nell, who said he was "delighted to learn he was on Richard Nixon's enemies list."

180   Reports about an alleged punishment facility originated in 2009 with excommunicat-ed Sea Organization executive Marty Rathbun, then embittered but who later renounced fellow apostates, and who was three years later a principal source for Wright – long after the Church had roundly refuted those allegations and offered access to media – including CNN's Anderson Cooper. Cooper interviewed Rathbun in 2010. When denied opportunity to disprove the allegations a vid-eo and transcript were posted concerning Anderson's refusal to tour the facility in question, or air the Church's side of the story: https://www.freedommag.org/special-reports/cnn/anderson-coo-per-marty-rathbun-video.html. Church officials have said Wright could have easily found those responses, and his failure to include them reflects bias.

181   In a letter to Wright from then-spokesperson Tommy Davis the Church offered to make facilities and individuals available to Wright if he wanted to profile the Church, and offered inter-views, but objected to Wright's characterization of Haggis as defecting from the Church because it would not take a political stand on a California ballot measure banning same sex marriage. The Church had noted that as a 5013C corporation, a religious entity, it could not engage in political activities. It also noted that Haggis had not been active in the Church in more than two decades at the time of his supposed resignation from Scientology.

182   See https://markrathbun.blog/2013/01/20/going-clear-muddies-the-water/

183   In reality, when this apocryphal conversation took place, the program for the then-up-coming Frankfurt Book Fair already contained a listing by Wright's agent, selling a book by Law-rence Wright about Scientology based on his research for the *New Yorker* article. Letter from Antho-

ny M. Glassman to Lynn Oberlander, November 16, 2010.

184   Letter from Monique E. Yingling to Jay Awrd Brown, February 27, 2015. See http://www.
alexgibneypropaganda.com/letters/march-18-alex-gibney-late-night-appearance.html

185   Church officials note that there have been minor civil suits in which the Church has
been plaintiff, regarding property loss; the Church has also responded to suits initiated against
it, largely by apostates. However, the Church has initiated no litigation against others, including
journalists, since its 10-year defamation lawsuit against *Time* magazine that began in 1991, over a
series of articles by Richard Behar. The case was settled by *Time* magazine after the Church's appeal
of a ruling that no defamation occurred was rejected by the courts.

186   See *Paul Haggis Invented False Narrative on Aftermath, Mark Rathbun Says.* https://www.
leahreminiaftermath.com/videos/mark-rathbun-on-aftermath-paul-haggis-false-narrative.html

187   A police report, photos and doctor's statements from Rinder's former wife addressed
one incident of domestic violence in which she suffered permanent nerve damage; details were
posted by the Church in response to Arts and Entertainment Networks promotion of Leah Remini's *Aftermath* programming with Rinder: https://www.leahreminiaftermath.com/articles/when-
it-comes-to-domestic-abuse-aes-buccieri-shuns-zero-tolerance.html#att-lr-mike-rinder-abuse.
Similarly, Wright, who appeared in Remini and other apostate programming with Rinder, never
addressed that issue.

Chapter 9

188   David H. Price, *Cold War Anthropology: The CIA, The Pentagon and Dual Use Anthropology,*
Chapel Hill, NC: Duke University Press, 2016. For background on the infiltration of academic communities by intelligence interests, also see David H. Price, *Threatening Anthropology: McCarthyism,
and the FBI's Surveillance of Activist Anthropologists,* Chapel Hill, NC: Duke University Press, 2004.

189   For a closer understanding of the mechanisms by which the CIA's broader intelligence
networks cooperated, Tim Weiner's *Legacy of Ashes* (Tim Weiner, Legacy of Ashes, Weiner, Tim. *Legacy of Ashes: The History of the CIA.* New York: Doubleday, 2007.) documents attitudes that enabled
political manipulation abroad, and at home; Fletcher Prouty's accounts of his experience in WWII
as a U.S. Air Force Colonel, confidant of military figures and eventually as liaison between the CIA
and the Joint Chiefs of Staff as JCS chief of special operations, during the Kennedy administration,
offers unique perspectives on the power elite (Fletcher Prouty, *JFK: The CIA, Vietnam and the Plot
to Assassinate John F. Kennedy*, New York: Birch Lane Press, 1992.) See Karen Paget, *Patriot Betrayal,
2015,* for a well-documented analysis of how intelligence goals were served by manipulation of
the National Student Association, and, see David Talbot, *The Devil's Chessboard: Allen Dulles, The CIA
and the Rise of America's Secret Government*, New York: HarperCollins, 2015 for an understanding of
the roles that the Dulles brothers played in press manipulation and how their coterie of legal and
business relationships influenced post-war cultural and social attitudes.

190   The Fourth Estate is defined generally as the public press, derived from the concept of a
politically motivated public speech, and eventually as journalism and the news media specifically.
Part of that concept is that the free press is a pillar in the structure of any democratic union. See
Delbert Tran, *The Fourth Estate as the Final Check,* The Media Freedom and Information Access Clin-
ic, Yale Law School, November 22, 2016. https://law.yale.edu/mfia/case-disclosed/fourth-estate-fi-
nal-check

191   Peter Dale Scott, *The American Deep State: Big Money, Big Oil and the Attack on U.S. Democracy,* Washington, D.C.: Rowman and Littlefield Publishers, 2014.

192   Clayton Koppes, and Gregory Black, "What to Show the World: The Office of War Information and Hollywood, 1942-1945," *Journal of American History*, Vol. 64, Issue 1, June 1977. https://
doi.org/10.2307/1888275

193   The film *Mission to Moscow* (May, 1943) reflected early support for Russian cooperation, and Mellette and Poynter played key roles in those perspectives and the transition later to
anti-communist suspicions and Cold War attitudes. Both shared a strong connection to Indiana
University, a powerhouse of journalistic theory and practice and itself a participant in intelligence
intrigue through its Chancellor Herman B. Welles, who was named an honorary members of the
board of trustees of American University in Cairo.

194   Nelson Poynter's fingerprints are to be found throughout American journalism's intelligence affiliations. Poynter Institute, in an obituary for their founder, made note of his many

connections, but failed to identify the depth of his relationship - and that of journalism - with the American intelligence community. See https://www.poynter.org/newsletters/2018/nelson-poynters-1978-obit-ill-haunt-you-like-the-devil-if-my-wishes-arent-carried-out/

195   Colodny, Len, and Gettlin, Robert. *Silent Coup. The Removal of a President.* New York: St. Martin's Press, 1991. Colodny and Gettlin offer a well-documented and detailed account of Bob Woodward's intelligence connections.

196   Interviews with Len Colodny, December, 2019 and January, 2020.

197   Cass Canfield, president of Harper & Brothers (later Harper & Row) was a close personal friend of Allen Dulles and a director of the CIA front Farfield Foundation (See Church Committee Report https://www.senate.gov/about/powers-procedures/investigations/church-committee.htm) which provided clandestine funding for the Congress for Cultural Freedom and other CIA propaganda programs. He later employed Michael Josselson, who oversaw *Encounter Magazine* and the *Paris Review*, among many others, through the Congress for Cultural Freedom for the CIA. Canfield, who also had direct ties to Lawrence Wright's family, published several CIA-promoted books (See Francis Stonor Saunders' *The Cultural Cold War*) and allowed the CIA to review a Alfred McCoy's The Politics of Heroin in 1972; Canfield was also a protege of Tom Braden, journalist, publisher, a propaganda program coordinator for CIA. Canfield was a close friend of John McCloy, and his regular tennis Partner (Bird, *The Chairman*, 1992.)

198   Bird, *The Chairman,* 1992, 303-4, 353-354. Bird notes that John McCloy endorsed and encouraged the distribution of millions of dollars in clandestine funding used to influence elections in foreign countries, and other clandestine operations to subvert or promote political interests. Bird also notes that McCloy was an early advocate of anti-communist, pro-western propaganda programs, and was deeply involved in the recruiting of Nazi Eastern Bloc spies into the German and American intelligence networks.

199   Hank Albarelli, *Coup In Dallas,* New York: Skyhorse Publishing, 2021. See Albarelli's analysis of Robert Storey's intelligence background, particularly his involvement in recovering Russian intelligence files that led to the discovery of crates of Nazi documents used in the Nuremberg war crimes prosecutions.

200   According to the descriptions of operations by former Lakewood senior vice president Al Goode, (a well-known Dallas banker who was a close friend of Roy Evans, son of Lakewood Bank director and later mayor of Dallas, Jack Evans), the bank had the characteristics of "non-official cover" for intelligence activities. He described the hiring of loan officers, all with military background, whose positions exceeded the available loan work. He also noted that Donald Wright, Lakewood president, would make loans based on criteria other than ability to repay. Don Wright, he said, seldom talked about his military experience but his military background was widely known. Goode said that when Wright's son Lawrence became a conscientious objector, "employees refrained from discussing it because they feared it would embarrass his father." (Personal interview, 2019).

201   The CIA's involvement in regime change – including, allegedly, in the U.S.- has been the subject of endless discussion, research and documentation by reputable journalists and also by those involved in conspiracy theorems. But factual material showing the U.S. involvement in Latin America, in Nicaragua and Panama especially, in Iran in the deposing of a democratically-elected government, in the attempted assassination by the CIA of France's Charles de' Gaulle, and in the lack of unexpurgated answers to questions surrounding the Kennedy assassination, the Warren Commission's investigation and conclusion, the Watergate events, and the war on terror, resistance to detente' and disarmament, to tolerance of other political ideologies, has been largely written out of the American history and textbooks and left primarily to those outside the mainstream to record. See Howard Zinn, *A People's History of the United States,* Harper & Row, 1980.

202   The term Deep State, used by Peter Dale Scott in his book *American Deep State* to describe forces outside the elected leadership, has come in the wake of the MAGA political movement to take on different connotations. The term as used here indicates levels of elite and influential individuals and groups who made the CIA's domestic intelligence network part of the cultural and social fabric of America.

203   John M. Crewdson and Joseph B. Treaster, World Wide Propaganda Network Built by the CIA, *The New York Times*, December 26, 1977. See https://www.nytimes.com/1977/12/26/archives/worldwide-propaganda-network-built-by-the-cia-a-worldwide-network.html?smid=url-share See also https://www.nytimes.com/1977/12/25/archives/the-cias-3decade-effort-to-mold-the-

worlds-views-agency-network.html. See https://www.cia.gov/readingroom/docs/CIA-RDP88-01350R000200320010-8.pdf

204   Connections to the publishing industry and its intelligence links through Helen Venn and her publishing procedures class touched many levels of influence. C.R. Devine, Vice President of Reader's Digest's international operation - they had an Arabic language edition that circulated through the Middle East, and editions in Latin America and elsewhere – was a close contact of Venn's, and he became a trustee of the American University in Cairo. Edward Booher of McGraw Hill, and Fredrick Praeger, were both involved with the CIA's Franklin Books programs; Praeger was and a member of the Board of Foreign Scholarships with Robert Storey. Those connections, and others, speak to the depth of this 'railway."

205   Carl Bernstein, *Rolling Stone*, October 20, 1977. https://www.carlbernstein.com/the-cia-and-the-media-rolling-stone-10-20-1977

206   Rabbi Michael Shevack, author and public figure, is one prime example of such relationships in the U.S. Shevack, a periodic liaison between the Patton Foundation and the Vatican on matters of peace and politics, has participated in interfaith ventures with the Church and has spoken positively and publicly about the value of Scientology, and its place in the spiritual environment.

207   The late Hank Albarelli, who worked on this project, and who mined his contacts within the security and intelligence community, said he had received multiple indications that Wright enjoyed a "special" relationship with the CIA, but no definitive answers. Contacts included a former defense intelligence operative who acknowledged Wright's close relationship to the Stratfor intelligence firm of Austin. As noted elsewhere, Peter Dale Scott contended that the possibility of uncovering a classified relationship was virtually impossible. Wright was also a guest and speaker with the Esalen Society at Big Sur, which had long been a subject of FBI surveillance in part due to its Soviet-American Exchange Program, through which it has claimed some credit for an end to the Cold War. See: https://archive.org/details/EsalenInstitutesSoviet-AmericanExchangePro-gram/6-13-16_MR22279_RES_ID1339530-000/page/n1/mode/2up And, https://www.atlasobscu-ra.com/articles/how-a-famed-new-age-retreat-center-helped-end-the-cold-war.

208   The Volunteer Ministers is a well-regarded organization funded by the International Association of Scientologists through its membership, that provides disaster relief and assistance, at their own expense. Within the Church they are known best by the bright yellow shirts they wear at disaster sites. See: https://www.volunteerministers.org.

209   Reitman's book, *Inside Scientology*, was published in July 2011, five months after Wright's New Yorker story on Haggis. The Church has said, as did Haggis' family and individuals I talked with who knew him (one a Sea Org member shared an apartment with Haggis early in his involvement with the Church), that Haggis had not been active in Scientology for more than two decades before his "celebrity defection," which the Church, and apostate Marty Rathbun assisted. Rathbun now describes Haggis'"exit' as carefully stage-crafted. See: www.youtube.com/sthtexlens-man/videos.

210   While never an employee of the Church, I served as executive editor of Freedom magazine as an independent freelance writer, during a limited transitional period in the magazine's editorial reorganization; otherwise, I was a freelance contributor to the magazine for investigative project reporting, which facilitated my access to Church archives and documents, scientologists throughout the U.S. and around the world, executives and clergy, former members and friends of the Church.

211   Peter Dale Scott, personal interview, 2021.

212   Ben Bagdikian, *The Media Monopoly*. Boston, MA: Beacon Press, 1987.

213   See Society of Professional Journalists, code of ethics, https://www.spj.org/ethicscode.asp.

Chapter 10

214   Hugh Wilford, *The Mighty Wurlitzer*, (Cambridge, MA: Harvard University Press, 2009).

215   Joel Whitney, *Finks: How the CIA Tricked the World's Best Writers*, (Berkley, CA: Counterpoint Press, 2016) See Mary Von Aue, *How the CIA Infiltrated the World's Literature*, review of Finks by Joe Whitney, January 4, 2017. https://www.vice.com/en/article/pgp53z/how-the-cia-infiltrated-the-worlds-literature.

216   David Miscavige, personal interview and observation, by author, October, 2016.

217   O'Neill, Tom and Piepenbring, Dan. *Chaos: Charles Manson, the CIA, and the Secret History of the Sixties.* New York: Little Brown, 2019. See excerpt, O'Neill, Piepenbring, Inside the Archive of an LSD Researcher with Ties to the CIA's MKULTRA Mind Control Project, *The Intercept*, November 24, 2019. https://theintercept.com/2019/11/24/cia-mkultra-louis-jolyon-west/.

218   In appearances on national television and in the media, the myth of the Watergate scenarios as described by Len Colodny in my conversations with him, are never raised, and Woodward's own intelligence ties are never discussed or questioned, at least within the mainstream press. They were raised in broadcast reports at one time, in interviews with Colodny and co-author Gettlin, but have been largely forgotten. A scathing review of Colodny's book by Stephen Ambrose was later called into question over conflicts of interest by Ambrose and it was defended in *The Nation* magazine. See: https://www.nytimes.com/1991/07/07/nyregion/editors-note-354291.html See: https://www.youtube.com/watch?v=iDJNf8dRbKs

219   The intelligence network of which Robert G. Storey was a co-creator had a particular interest in Panama. Four years before Wright started his journey through CIA affiliated organizations, Storey was appointed by President Lyndon Johnson as chairman of the Atlantic-Pacific Interoceanic Canal Study Commission. Storey, along with his close associate Leon Jaworski, were appointed that same year to the President's Commission on Law Enforcement and Administration of Justice. Law enforcement and its administration would be the subject of studies by the Southwestern Legal Foundation, continued under its successor, The Center for American and International Law.

220   *Texas Banking Red Book.*

Chapter 11

221   https://www.pulitzer.org/winners/staff-12

222   See: https://apnews.com/article/7e961a8c22e9ee7ad8ee4b8fe37334c7

223   Personal conversation with inmate Ray Wallace during death row hostage crisis, 1986.

224   Dan Luzadder, Susan Headden, Bruce Smith, "Indiana Boys School: Campus in Crisis." *Indianapolis Star*, October 15, 1989. See https://www.newspapers.com/newspage/106113871/

225   Personal conversation with Ed DeLaney, attorney for Indianapolis Newspapers Inc.

226   See https://indianahousedemocrats.org/members/ed-delaney/media

227   See Indiana Supreme Court disciplinary record: https://law.justia.com/cases/indiana/supreme-court/1992/06s00-9005-jd-358-4.html

228   Dan Luzadder, "Denver's Taxi Mess", *The Rocky Mountain News*, 1994.

229   Lt. Kiekbusch was in charge of the Jefferson County police investigation into Columbine High School attack, and provided me with access to officers and information throughout the investigation. He, like other officers involved in the investigation, suffered the brunt not only of criticism for police response to the killings, but from the stress of the investigation in 13 deaths and numerous injuries. The criticism, however emotionally charged, I concluded, failed to recognize the difficulties police faced in investigating the tragedy and in making responsible decisions on releasing information in the case to the public. Lt. Kiekbush, who had a long history of investigative success, provided strong leadership throughout; his retirement from police work after Columbine, was a loss to the department and to law enforcement in general. See https://dartcenter.org/content/columbine

230   Wright, *Going Clear*, 2013

ACKNOWLEDGMENTS

In the course of investigation, the list of those who deserve thanks is long. Most particularly, three stand out: Joe Taglieri, L.A. Rivera, and the late Hank Albarelli were of singular importance to this work. Joe's dedication to the project, his inspired research and due diligence helped light the way.

I benefited from insights shared by Jon Sinton, John Sugg, Peter Gallagher, Mike Brennan, and Ajay Singh. Eric C. Rodenberg, one of the best investigative reporters I ever worked with, helped me test theories and discoveries in late night phone calls to his haunted house in Indiana's backwoods. Thanks to Leslie Sharp, co-author with Hank Albarelli of *A Coup in Dallas*, for her observations and suggestions; my discussions with the late Len Colodny, to whom Hank made introduction, were invaluable to understanding the less visible world of the press and its political purposes. I hope he and Hank are sharing reunion.

Within the Church I met many defenders of religious freedom, and some who were also pioneers of investigative journalism: Tom Whittle, Richard Weiland, Linda Weiland, Linda Hight, Gail Armstrong, Linda Sarkovich, Karin Pouw, and Lynn Farny – a living archive of Church history – and most especially David Bloomberg, who endured, challenged, argued, supported transparency, and told me stories of his boyhood in New Zealand. Importantly, my thanks to David Miscavige, who opened the door and left it ajar; and, to the late Norman Starkey, who carried me through it into history with the eloquence and artistry of an oracle.

Special thanks to Rabbi Michael Shevack and Harlan Boll for their encouragement and to Steven Brill, Peter Dale Scott, Joan Mellen and David Cullen for offering to read the advance manuscript; also to Jeff Marck in Egypt and UK journalist Jason Burke, for assistance and advice. To Brooke Harris, thanks for helping unpack the junk from the trunk; to Isaias, Luis, Art, Gary, Jason, Raul, Tamara, Bruce and Danny in Hollywood, thank you for listening to stories and telling your own.

If journalists transcend to a higher plane, Ernie Williams, the editor who taught me that journalism is art not science, will know my gratitude, as will David Iliff, who taught me to hurry.

Finally, there is no word but love to describe my family's endless support through this and years of other stories: Nancy, Aaron, Hannah, Michael, Robert, and my sister Ann Long, poet, writer, publisher and fire-fighter. You are all the light in my life.

Index